In Service to Love

Book 1: Love Remembered

A Dynamic Experience of Consciousness, Transformation and Enlightenment

DARLENE GREEN

Emissary of Love

Waterside Publishing

Printed in the United States of America

First Printing, 2019

ISBN-13: 978-1-949003-95-6 print edition
ISBN-13: 978-1-949003-94-9 eBook edition

 Waterside Publishing

2055 Oxford Ave
Cardiff, CA 92007
www.waterside.com

IN SERVICE TO LOVE

To Love.

TABLE OF CONTENTS

BOOK 1: LOVE REMEMBERED

WELCOME

Today, I stand 9 months after the completion of one year and one day of writing with the Council of Light. *In Service to Love* began as a journal for my own spiritual process on 12-26-17. The experience Day 1 through Day 366 has been sacred and profoundly personal. I have been guided through the limitations of my human nature to living the reality of my divine nature. I am happier and more peaceful, than I have ever been. I live the experience of divine beauty. I have a feeling of finally being "home" in my body and in my life. My daily experience is multidimensional and is aligned with the vast perspective of Love. What I first thought was an exalted gift for those exploring their spirituality, now, through the expansive lens of Love, I see as the invitation for all humanity to live up to our potential in a way that makes a difference in how we live life.

I began sharing the daily writings with a close group of friends and family as it became clear this work was more than a journal. The work touched each person in a way that was personal to them. I have many years of study and practice in vibrational healing and energetic work. I recognized the body of work as an expanding energetic field. *In Service to Love* is an evolving matrix of Love and light. The reader has the benefit of interaction with the Masters of the Council of Light and is met personally, participating step by step as they choose to do so.

You will find this is not a linear process. It can't be. Each day's writing holds a different frequency. Some days the frequency will draw you inward, others will draw your attention to the edges of your awareness. There are many exercises and meditations as well as light infusions, consciousness downloads and activations. Each day's writing is a golden thread contributing to the realization of the fabric of Love.

This body of work of 366 Days is divided into 3 books. You may want to go to the end of Book 3 and get it all. That's not how this works. I have been on my consciousness path for over 30 years and would consider myself as advanced. And I began on Day 1. I don't believe the years put in so far are relevant anymore. Whether new to your spiritual path or a leader holding the light of Love for a long time, what we each have in common is our humanity. Consider the constraints of our human nature cloud living the reality of our divine nature. Even if you already hold the ability to move through the vast realms of light, Book 1 takes you through a process of releasing layers of who you are not so that who you are may be fully integrated in a new way in your life and lived as a reality. Your enlightenment is not something that is earned. You already ARE. *In Service to Love* provides a rich environment where your frequency will increase, your perspective will broaden, and your next steps become illuminated. As you choose consciously you live a life led by the voice of your soul.

If you have a resonance with this work, my recommendation is to begin on Day 1. Be present as if you are the one receiving the writing and each day is a message just for you. The writings are full, meaning you may only be able to digest a few Day's writings at a sitting. Pay attention to your own inner knowing. Allow the frequency of each day to work.

I have not met you, but I know you. I see you. Thank you for your courage to be All of you. Thank you for answering the call of your heart's mission. Thank you for the contribution you are to your friends, family, global consciousness and the expression of Love's light. Thank you for everything that has brought you to Now. I am honored to be in your company.

Take care of yourself and Love the people around you.

Darlene Green
September 29, 2019

"In Service to Love addresses an imbalance in life experience. The collective consciousness that is pervasive is one that represents old ways of being. Much of the pain within the physical experience reflects the separation that exists in consciousness between who you are, your perceptions, and how you live. You are on the precipice of a new world. One that is in alignment with who you are as a divine expression of God.

The purpose of our divine collaboration is to offer a new way of being that is in alignment with your innate divine expression and allows you to be in the physical experience in a way that is seamless. Meaning that you access all of you, beyond limitations, and live a life that is heart centered, and soul centered. From the stance of your divine nature, you hold the light and Love that is you and bring your gifts and light to the world to be the unique expression of Love that you are.

The consciousness that drives many of the world's most visible imbalances at this time is grounded in division and separation. This applies to all areas of concern; the environment, politics, and humanitarian crises. In order to transform these issues, you are invited to move to a place where your best resides. Your best resides beyond your perceived limitations and the consciousness of past eras to a new space that is inhabited only in the Now moment, where you have available the vision to create from your highest expression. You are already the answer. When you align with your highest expression, your frequency is naturally at a level that is authentic for you, you hold the light of Love, and your presence transforms. When you align with your divine truth, you hold space for collaboration of the highest form, which brings heaven to earth and opens new avenues of possibility and ways of being. You hold open the space of possibility that is divinely created. When you align with the limited frequency and consciousness that is the reflection of the problem, there can be nothing else possible, beyond more of the same. As you choose the "more" that resides beyond what you already know, you access the vast expanse of your being and the light of possibility. The vibrating field of potential that is guided by the sacredness of being is catalyzed.

What can be possible as you align with your divine nature? Equally, what is no longer possible within the framework and pervasive presence of Love?

The challenge is to BE the courage that is willing to see beyond what is taken for granted, and then, through your inspired moments, to move into action and BE all that is for you to BE.

YOU are the light of the world. Now what?"

We remain,
In Service to Love
The Council of Light

About the Author

An innate empath, teacher, and healer, Darlene was aware of her Council as early as four years of age. Profound events and sensitivities revealed an ability to reach beyond the reality seen by most. Darlene found a home for her sensitivities as she began studying vibrational healing in 1992. She has written and led programs on living consciously, beginning in 1998 in Seattle, Washington. As a practitioner of Natural Force Healing and a Reiki master, she has utilized her intuitive gifts as a massage therapist practicing in clinical settings in Seattle from 1992 to 2012, when she left to answer a deeper calling. At sacred sites in Southern France, Darlene connected powerfully with her Council of Light and returned to her ancient heritage as Scribe. In 2015 Darlene was invited to create and host a radio program in Phoenix, Arizona, through VoiceAmerica's 7th Wave Channel, titled *The Inner Frontier*. All external work ended as of a severe auto accident early in 2017 when focus turned deeply inward for healing.

On December 26, 2017, Darlene awoke to exalted spiritual events and an invitation by the Council of Light for divine collaboration in a body of work titled *In Service to Love*.

Darlene resides in Seattle with her husband, Ed Green, and their sweet golden retriever, Hailey Grace.

About the Council of Light

Composed of Masters, the Council of Light includes the voices of: Jesus, Mary Magdalene, Archangel Michael, Archangel Gabriel, Melchizadek, Infinite Oneness, Isis, the Elohim, Buddha, Sanat

Kumara, Metatron, the Hathors, Gaia, the Grandmothers, the Grandfathers, St. Germain, Legions of Light, and many more. The Council's presence is vast. The configuration shifts depending on the topic. Thoth, as "Patron of the Scribe" is the facilitator of frequency in light. The experience of the Council of Light is one of Love itself. Throughout the year of writing that is *In Service to Love*, the Council of Light evolves, from identification of individual masters to the singular voice of Love.

"My experience is one of divine collaboration. I am challenged daily to elevate my awareness and fine-tune my senses. I am a student, Scribe, and member of the Council of Light." – Darlene Green

"You are invited to engage with your own divine process. The invitation rests upon the altar of your sacred space. As you choose a new perspective, to see what's possible, to see what you have not seen before, we are here. Love beckons. When you choose to accept the invitation upon your altar, we begin." – The Council of Light

APPRECIATION

With *In Service to Love,* my closely held work reaches a global audience. I appreciate every step of this sacred expression. Each person, each event, each conversation of my life has brought me to this Now moment. Each meeting is a gift beyond compare.

Thank you to my parents, whose love and wisdom supports me still. To my grandparents, thank you for your courageous journey to new frontiers.

Thank you to my sisters, Debbie and Bonnie, for your unwavering Love and support. I hold as a sacred gift the path we walk with each other in this life. Your Love has fueled my courage to be seen.

I Love my family. I am blessed with each precious relationship. Thank you, Shelley, Mark B., Rob, Mark S., Kenny, Deb, Hannah, Colby, Michelle, Braedon, Mason, Sean, Cara, Brandon, Bailey, Parker. Thank you for the beautiful contribution you have been and continue to be in my life.

Jeanne Kreider, your powerful, loving, healing gifts and presence have supported me for decades. Thank you, Bellevue Wellness Center for your vision, mastery, and support. Kenneth Y. Davis, DC and Lisa Davis, thank you for introducing me to Natural Force Healing and the possibility of divine collaboration that brings forth work that contributes to well-being and expanded consciousness for All.

George Bullied, thank you for introducing me to my Essene roots. There have been sisterhoods formed and we have walked for a while, side by side in our exploration of truth. Thank you, Debbie D., JoBeth E., Diana C., MaSanda G., and Bethany F., for the friendship and rich contribution you so generously offered. Lynn H. and Kristin W., our sisterhood is a balm for my soul. In our connection I find voice for the sacred unspoken.

Thank you, Maureen St. Germain. When I met you, I felt a deep resonance, and an important connection to "home," that existed beyond my comprehension at the time. Thank you for your kindness and wisdom. Thank you, Esther Hicks and Abraham. I will never forget the moment I really got it, and the floodgates opened.

Danielle Rama Hoffman, thank you. Ours is a destined reunion. You are a brilliant master teacher. Your invitation reconnected me with my Scribe heritage and soul's mission. With you in Southern France I was reunited with treasured soul friendships in light and in form. Thank you, Mary M., Terri G., Mary Elizabeth A., SandraAlyse W., and Laima Z. The magnitude of your light's mission of Love emanates throughout creation. Mary M. and Terri G., Danielle H., thank you for our sisterhood, a divine alliance of Love and light. Mary Elizabeth A., thank you for your friendship, sisterhood and vision. This started with your question.

Thank you, Heather Clarke, Director of the Arizona Enlightenment Center. Your clarity of vision has served the divine remembering for so many. Thank you to the members and contributors of the Arizona Enlightenment Center. Emil and Susan Faithe, I recognized the brilliance of your mission when I met you. Thank you for your generosity. KahMaRea, thank you for your love, wisdom, support, and alliance. We are soul sisters reunited. You are a treasured gift and divine cohort. Thank you, Maria Radloff, for your expertise as I foray into a new expression.

I first started sharing the daily writings of *In Service to Love* with a small group of friends. Thank you for the gift of your feedback and for being willing to participate in this magical journey. Thank you, Ed G., Debbie B., Bonnie H., Katannya C., Michelle W., Mary M., Terri G., Mary Elizabeth A., KahMaRea M., Bethany F., Lynn H., Kristin W., Lynn L., Jeff S., Tresje S., Marcia P.

Thank you, Randall Libero, Senior Executive Producer of VoiceAmerica Talk Radio and TV. Through your compassionate guidance and support I found my voice and a global reach. Thank you, Sheila Gillette, Marcus Gillette, and Theo. Our meeting represented a pivotal moment of clarity for me. Thank you for your generosity.

Thank you, Bill Gladstone, of Waterside Productions, for saying "Yes!" to *In Service to Love.* You too are a stand for Love's light. Our journey begins.

Thank you, Frank Ferrante; it's all about divine timing. Thank you, Kenneth Kale and Emily Votruba, for your editing expertise that polishes the diamond of *In Service to Love.* Thank you, Ken Fraser, for your graphic design. Thank you, Joanne, of Joanne West Photography, you have the gift of capturing light.

To all the divine Masters of light in light, at the top of Sainte Baume in Southern France, your words, through Danielle Rama Hoffman, rang with clarity and Love: "My voice, your voice, our voice, one voice." Our divine collaboration is a sacred treasure of my soul. New in each immaculate Now moment, with a deep reverence and appreciation, I say thank you God. Thank you, Thoth, for the gift of our divine partnership. Thank you, Jeshua, Archangel Michael, Archangel Gabriel, Mary Magdalene, Mother Mary, Isis, Metatron, Melchizadek, the Hathors, Infinite Oneness, the Grandmothers, the Grandfathers, Gaia, Sanat Kumara, Legions of Light, Council of the Golden Heart, Abraham, Theo, St. Germain, the Council of Nine, the Collective of Love. Thank you to ALL the beings of light in light that support, contribute to, and collaborate with me through this divinely held work of *In Service to Love.* Our sacred collaboration is the experience of heaven on earth. "So, this is what Love is."

Thank you, Ed, my beloved husband, partner, and ally. You have seen me when I couldn't. You have been a stand for the expression of my divine gifts. Thank you for your Love and support as we have been on our journey together. The best is Now.

In Love always,
Darlene

An Overview of This Work

In Service to Love is a divinely guided work where your unique process of enlightenment, conscious awareness, and realization of the exquisite divine expression of you is supported. With each day's gathering, you sit with me, Darlene, as your Scribe, and the diverse panel who make up the Council of Light, from the perspective of Love. Created in the Now immaculate moment, you follow the potent process of shifts in perspective that bring you the opportunity to move beyond barriers, revealing the divine knowing and unique expression of you that is your authentic nature. This is a non-linear process. Through concepts, analogies, and frequency, you move beyond your thinking into a resonant experience where your own clarity is accessed.

Although this work will support your reach into the vast light expression of your true nature, we do not lose sight of the importance of then bringing that broader awareness into action in your day. The idea is to support you really living your best life right now. You do not have to spend lifetimes in the Himalayas in order to touch the divine of your essence. Finding your divine essence is not the end; it is the beginning. After the divine remembering, is the divine remembered.

Not too far into the scribing, it became clear that the work of *In Service to Love* is communicated beyond words through an energetic presence of Love. This is a multidimensional body of work divinely orchestrated. The experience of Love is palpable.

You experience the evolution of this work with me. What becomes possible is a shift in perspective so complete that the potential exists to become unrecognizable to yourself from a consciousness point of view and, in the process, be so much more of who you are innately. This has certainly been my experience, and it continues to evolve. This is the ultimate expression of authenticity. From our true nature, we access our divine birthright of joy, Love, peace, abundance, freedom, and more. When we release the entanglement of beliefs, habits, and collective consciousness, we discover the edges of our vast, divine essence in light. We can then learn to navigate our expansive capability and be informed by our soul.

An Uncommon Conversation

On December 26, 2017 I was invited into an uncommon conversation with Masters in light, all present with one singular message: Love.

Love is all there is. You are Love. You are Source in form, as am I. Beyond philosophical thoughts, what is it like to live that truth? We have all had experiences that are beyond explanation with moments of inspiration so expansive we can hardly breathe in the beauty. We are altered fundamentally with those moments. There is a knowing, a resonance, a recognition available in the magic and the mystery. But how does that translate to the way we live our life? Being a better person? What does that mean anyway? The world could certainly use more kindness and authentic expression. But there is a chasm between the internal yearning and the physical reality, as untouchable as fleeting moments upon the wings of angels.

We are drawn toward the divine and eternal truth we find in the sacred writings of the masters. We pray in earnest. We listen to sermons and are inspired by possibility and touched with the blessings of Love, which satiates our desire for connection. But then we go to the grocery store, the soccer game, school meeting, the next event, and carry on with the business of living life.

Where is the connection between what we yearn for and how we live? The thought of enlightenment for me anyway has always held an intrigue. Exactly what is it? It feels like rarefied air. And I want that! But it is so far off. There's a "can't get there from here" kind of feeling.

I've been gifted many profound experiences, beginning as early as four years old. Highly empathic and sensitive, I recall one illuminating moment, during a trip to San Francisco, sightseeing with my husband. We were touring a turn-of-the-century naval ship. Memories of my grandad came rushing in.

After serving in the Royal Navy during World War 1, he told stories of these ships. Feeling someone behind me, I turned around. Just my husband and I were in the ship's cabin. And yet, I could feel my grandad standing behind me with his hand at my shoulder. I could feel the familiar sense of him, I could hear his deep voice. Immediately in tears with the experience, I heard Grandad whispering gently in my ear: "I once was blind, but now I see." I thought, after the potent moment had faded, "What is it you now see?" And I was drawn deeper into my quest. That was thirty years ago.

Now I know what he meant. I am here to tell you, the access to and expression of our full divine knowing is available now! We don't need to die before we finally know our truth. That is what enlightenment is. Enlightenment turns on the light switch so we can see for ourselves, beyond the clouding of perceived barriers. What if the process of enlightenment allowed us to hear more clearly the voice of our soul, and live our life from the profound?

But I rush ahead. About the invitation, I said "Yes!" What has unfolded is no less than a divine magic carpet ride, hand in hand with Love. A guided experience of transformation and enlightenment. But not just mine.

LOVE'S INVITATION

"Sit with us each day for a year and a day." The words spun through my being as I awoke on December 26, 2017. "Three hundred sixty-six days." I felt a presence surrounding me and through me at the same time. It was rich, deep, expansive, compassionate, potent and clear. I was in the presence of Love!!! An experience of the profound and a return to home at the same time! Blessed! My head spinning, my personality perplexed, and my soul celebrating, I sensed a gathering of the highest order. I felt Thoth, Jesus, Mary Magdalene, Melchizadek, Archangel Michael, Archangel Gabriel, Legions of Light, the Elohim, and a vast sea of beings of light too brilliant to count. All were familiar and beloved. As I tried to settle into the experience, I sobbed in recognition of the answer to my deepest yearnings, which I'd so sacredly held, I didn't dare even utter them. Gently held within the experience of Love's rapture, I sat down at my computer. The words poured from my fingertips, and Day 1 began.

This is not about a privileged experience, only available to those few who are sensitive enough to hear. My sensitivity only turns up the volume so you may hear your own voice. It is about each of us living up to the promise of the life we had intended before we came here. It is easy to hold this work in the ethers and view it as separate from the exquisite moments of our day, as we get down to the business of living a physical reality. Instead, what this body of work offers is a connection to the divine perfection of you, brought to bear in life. What if you really knew what your purpose was? It is not a one-size-fits-all experience. This is about you and me each acknowledging our divine origin and bringing that knowing into our day to create the life that is ours to have in a way that makes a difference. In a way that allows us to live from our soul's purpose and be the contribution we have always known that we are. Our best life. My expression is unique, as is yours. What I have learned since the first day of divine collaboration with the Masters in light is the beauty of each of us. Irreplaceable, beloved, masterful, each with our heart's calling. We are being called to the brilliance of our own mastery. *"Beloved, remember who you are."*

This shift in awareness is offered through a divinely crafted experience of rich frequency that resides behind the words and is the catalyst for my unique process (and yours), led by our own divine guidance. In the process we connect with broader perspectives and begin to see behind the veil of illusion.

As a student of this process, I have traveled the formless realms of frequency, guided by the Masters, and realized my capacity for finely tuned awareness. I have not only scribed each day's writing, I have lived it, and it continues. The work was not delivered on a silver platter. With each day's lesson, I was gently invited to stretch what I knew possible, finding my own way and making choices from the larger, more vast perspectives that became clear. When I choose to take ownership of my authentic nature, I realize that what I have always been good at is being me. Difficulties and pain have occurred in my life when I strayed, trying to fit into what was "normal" or trying to numb the extraordinary sensitivity that is my true nature. I experience my greatest joy being all of me. Not just from the personality standpoint, but most importantly from the perspective of my soul. It is then that I truly honor my Self, and I then have the capacity to see your perfection too.

When I view life from the perspective of my own unique expression at its finest, I take ownership of the rich heritage of being Scribe. I am profoundly transformed. There is no longer a chasm between who I AM and who I BE. The work now is what becomes possible when what I have always sought is found. Now I do the sacred work of my soul. I AM a Scribe. I translate light and consciousness into form through words, both written and spoken. With who I am not, no longer a distraction, my frequency shifts as what I create is in alignment with my highest expression. You see, as I be more of the divine expression of me, I hold space for you to realize the divine expression of you. What becomes possible when we hold the perspective of our own divinity and our highest potential is realized? When we are in conscious collaboration with the divine, what is no longer possible? What becomes possible when Love is the lens through which we view all?

DAY 1: AND SO, WE BEGIN

The gathering in light is vast. This is all, in witness Darlene, of the journey about to be undertaken. It is a journey of the soul. We see who you are. We see your contributions both in light and in form. The gathering you have called forth today is in witness of the undertaking you are choosing not only for yourself, but for all.

In preparation today, we gather those things that are the most precious to you, so you may have them on your journey. It is not unlike your preparation for this lifetime. The similarities are clear. Your soul has a mission to live your life beyond perceived barriers to discover truth. You have chosen to see beyond the edges previously understood by most to be the physical experience. You have chosen to live beyond the divide of the perception of life and death. The most commonly held perception of death is limited. Most believe it is only once you die that you have a chance of experiencing the vastness of truth. For most, it is in one cataclysmic moment at death that you get the confirmation that who you have been all along is a divine expression of Source in form. You finally see you are a being of light in light. You see that all the moments of your life are for the purpose of experiencing yourself as Love. You see the beautiful journeys woven by humanity, as each in their perfect way sift and sort through the happenings of life in search of themselves. What if you had these revelations and the ensuing conscious awareness now? The realization of your unique divine mission is available in this moment and the possibility exists for your soul's vision to be made manifest.

What is at hand, at this moment in time, is no less grand than the adventures experienced by the explorers who set off in their ships for the unknown. They had an inkling that the reality possible was beyond the reasonings of the past and beyond what was available in the consciousness of the time. So the few, courageous, inspired beings set forth on their journey, unsure but fortified in their inner knowing that there was more. You are setting forth on your journey forward, knowing there is more; knowing your more is different from anyone else's. As you planned for the physical life you are in now, you observed others, such as Edgar Cayce, as he lived beyond the perceptions of current collective consciousness. You as a being of light in light, gathered seeds that would be planted. Each one designed to bear fruit at the right time in your experience, germinated by the right people, the right moment, synchronicities and your soul's growth.

As you have experienced many lives within this incarnation; this is but another. You sense a crossroads; an opportunity to go farther than you have ever dreamt possible: to truly live beyond the bounds of the perceived limitations of the physical. This is your soul's dream realized. A new paradigm has opened making available a new reality. What is that like? The shift in awareness is like having lived one's whole life in a closet, and then suddenly the door to the closet is opened and the vast expanse beckons. The newly revealed environment provides all you need, all you have ever wanted or dreamt of. Understand that the consciousness that is available now offers an extraordinary opportunity, an opening into the experience of your divine wholeness. Living with multidimensional awareness consciously, you perceive beyond the limits of popular thought.

This is an elevated soul experience. There are always choices. This is another. The crossroads show up in life many times. Some are recognized and some are overlooked. As these events align with your choice to experience yourself as the whole (holy) divine expression of God that is you, your potential is limitless.

You have had memories of getting to the end of your past lives and in that one moment of seeing truth, seeing all the potential that was lost while you were in form. Your soul's vow is to not let that happen again; to not let another magnificent opportunity pass you by.

Darlene: You recently followed your father to the edge of his life. Your father chose but you did not. That is the floating emptiness that you feel. This is the crossroads. You choose. Any choice you make is perfect. There is no such thing as wrong. How do you choose? We are in witness to your answer. We are also in support of your journey.

The journey that is at hand is the choice of many. The support for you is the support available to all who take this journey. It is an exploration into your depths. Nothing within *In Service to Love* has you move outside yourself, despite the "journey" analogies we use. The analogies hold imagery to embrace movement beyond the boundaries of belief systems, ego, and collective consciousness. You will discover the language of your soul as you embrace your divinity.

In Preparation

You are never alone.
Be willing to let go of what you know to embrace your expansive truth.
Be willing to stand in the unknown.
Be willing to see newly.
Be present in this immaculate Now moment.
Be still, and know that I AM God. Sit with us daily for one year and
one day. We will gather with you to speak as you sit at the computer.

Sounds like a lot, but it is who you are already. This journey is a look at yourself in the mirror.

Day 2: The Invitation Placed Upon the Altar

E VENT Would you like to come and play? You are invited to follow the calling of your soul. An invitation to live consciously. There are no borders and no boundaries to your greatness. This work is three hundred sixty-six days of consciousness expansion. Where could you be after one year and one day of guided support in fulfilling your unique expression? You chose to be present on this beautiful planet for a reason. The unique opportunity that lies ahead for everyone is to move through the limitations, the restrictions, the binding beliefs of the past, and move with freedom into a new expression. Your experience of limitation is all you know. Your expectations are based upon the limitations of beliefs and collective consciousness. Only dreams have existed about what may be. You see glimpses of truth in your dreams, glimpses through synchronicities that ignite an inner knowing that beckons you further. Each journey is unique. Only you can do the work of you. Only you can express the way you do. The universe is inviting you to inquire about what could be possible. The barrier between dimensions is illusory. What is possible in consciousness is now more available than at previous times. Know for sure that you have planned it that way.

When one is infused, so to speak, with the limitations of unquestioned beliefs, there is a default pattern that exists. The default does not hold space for all that is possible. You are a light being in form. What if you were to be in form and not have any boundaries between what is available in form and what is available in light?

You are both. You are all. This is a game that, if you so choose, may bring you to a deeper expression of you.

Have you felt pulled to contribute? Have you known you were here for a purpose but cannot see all of it yet? This journey helps to gently discard all that is not you, so that who you are remains shining brightly. This is not an adding on to who you are; this is a discovery of what already is. In each moment you choose.

Much has gone before these words typed upon this keyboard. Our Scribe Darlene has longed for this as well. She has gone through times in her life where she thought she had it, only to have those expressions move through her hands like water. The illusory nature of light is a common experience. This is a journey, though, that Darlene doesn't know yet. She is on the journey as well. It is not as though she has experienced it and now knows something that she can relay. No, Darlene is acting in what she terms "radical faith." She feels, knows, and senses the support that is gathering not only for her journey but in support of yours. Know this is a divinely guided, supported collaboration. We, beings of light in light, some of whom you have heard of and perhaps many you have not, have gathered for the auspicious event to be in collaboration with you. There is a support we facilitate in collaboration with you. With you at the helm, we unlock the activations that are now available, supporting your access in light. The experience is one of conscious multidimensionality. If you find yourself reading this, being drawn to this; there are no accidents. There will be a resonant tone in your being that says, "Now is the time." This is a return to LOVE. For Love is all there is. Everything in your incarnation has brought you to this Now moment.

We would like to say a few words of collaboration. You are a divine expression of God, as we are. We are ONE. If what exists for you is a resonance, know this is your highest expression speaking to your physicality. We see you from a space of equanimity. Equanimity is where we all sit at the table from a space of equality; divine to divine, peer to peer, eye to eye. We hold the space open for you to enter. A meeting place, if you will. This requires an intention on your part to bring all of you to the table. This is not you, fulfilling an expectation. There is no possibility of failure. There is no better or worse. There is only you as a being of light in form, choosing to be in divine collaboration for a larger purpose. If you are called, if there is a resonance with you, there is no you and us. There is only light. There is only LOVE.

When In this immaculate Now moment.

Where Wherever you are.

Hosts Thoth, the Council of Light, and other Heavenly Hosts; Your Scribe, Darlene Green.

Why? Because you choose to. Because you are experiencing a resonance. Because you were drawn to these writings in the first place. Because you feel the more that is available now and choose to experience consciousness without boundaries. It means that you, as a being of light, are willing to express yourself at the highest level available while you are in physical form. This is not about the doing. This is about the being. As you bring more and more of you that is available into form, consciously, you are expressing at higher and finer frequencies where you find clarity. You begin to see yourself with new eyes. You see yourself as God sees you, as we see you. Your frequency guides your choices on a moment-to-moment basis. The frequency that you are, as you claim your magnificence, transforms the space you inhabit.

If you have wanted to be the gift that you are, this is what we are talking about. Does it seem too big for you to accomplish? It is already your birthright. It is already who you are. The only difference is that you are wearing the glasses of limitation—the glasses of segmented reality, designed to support your physical incarnation. You chose to be born at a time where the consciousness has shifted from separation to unity consciousness. Separation is the experience of power and control, right and wrong. But the consciousness of the planet and all creation has shifted toward unity consciousness, which is the divine expression of wholeness (holiness). So, like the changing of a channel, the winds of expansion are present. Like no other time in creation, what is possible is living beyond the boundaries of form, consciously. What is possible when your highest authentic expression is available in this moment, now? If what you seek is your deepest joy, your deepest love, your deepest soul's expression, before you, lies an opportunity to see who you are in your divine magnificence.

Do you choose to claim all of who you are? Then you have a choice. If you choose yes, we hear you. Know this work meets you where you are at. It can be no other way.

DAY 3: THE CHOICE

You have heard before that the human brain is utilized at less than 10 percent of its potential. What about the other 90 percent? What if you could start to utilize more of what is possible within the human brain? This is where the consciousness journey begins. It begins with a choice to consider that you have the capability right here, right now, to experience the nonphysical part of your being. Not just at a soul level, in feel-good kind of way, but in a way that alters your physical experience. You have always had the inkling that there was so much more to you. You have a knowing that you are connected to the universe in a way you can't quite hold in your hands.

Much like the tomato seed that holds the full potential of the tomato, you too hold a divine design. You hold a specific unique divine design for your most expansive potential expression. What stops you from expressing at your capacity? The same thing that has stopped you from living up to your capacity this lifetime: beliefs. Beliefs define structure. Founded by your culture, family, geography, lineage, church, experience, perspective, your beliefs create a structure of safety, knowing, assurance, and limitation. As you embrace all that is within your belief system you also disregard everything that is outside your belief system. The limitation predictably reinforces a world of the known and does not allow for new perspectives and possibility.

We use the analogy of the experience of the early explorers on the planet Earth. They, like you, hold the courage to see beyond what is considered common knowledge, because it doesn't tell the whole story. There is an inner disquiet that says there is more out there: "I don't believe the world is flat." "I don't know how, but I just know." The spirit of explorers moves the inner voice of curiosity into action. The impetus to action is created by the choice to move to the unknown. Explorers go to the edge of the known to find the unknown. There is a distinct choice to see newly. The operative word here is *choice*. When you choose to see newly, to see beyond what you have taken as truth before, you do begin to see newly. A new perspective is invited within the space of inquiry, and then possibility moves into view. A larger picture is available.

This is the first step of your consciousness journey: Choice. As you choose to see beyond what you have seen before, new possibilities open. As you let go of the beliefs of the past as a default way of being in your life, you begin to see with new eyes. Your attention moves beyond what is known to see the more. You have had the experience of buying a new car and now, almost magically, you see that make and model of car everywhere? The cars were always there, you just didn't have an awareness that they were relevant. Choice is the key that opens awareness to new levels.

There are two choices offered here: First, the choice to be on a journey into the unknown territory of you, which allows your highest expression to manifest in a new way. Second, the choice to see your world in a new way. If you didn't have the automatic way of being that is defined by beliefs and by the past, what would you see? What else becomes possible? It means choosing consciously.

This inquiry has you be present in the immaculate Now moment, untethered by the past or by the future. As you consider belief structures and hold the inquiry, "What would life look like if I wasn't operating reflexively or because that's just the way it is?" The new opens. What then becomes possible?

Day 4: Trust

Consider trusting the nonphysical part of your nature. *In Service to Love* is designed to support your inner harmony. We are asking you to consider amplifying your light awareness so you may be more attuned to your inner voice daily. We direct your attention to a broader perspective. We invite you to explore your expanded abilities as a contribution to your day. In the same way that a tree, although barren in winter, knows what to do in springtime, life knows how to live. Only human beings, by design, forget their greatness. The forgetting, all a part of the design, allows for the soul to experience contrast not available while you are in light.

There are times when you have experienced being gripped by a situation or circumstance. If you reflect, you see resolution is normally sought out of a familiar process rather than by looking newly. Trust does not mean don't be in action, it means trust that a larger picture is possible. Trust that even though you may not see a solution in the moment, a different perspective exists that may bring relief to a circumstance or situation.

When you trust there is more, you can look beyond what you already know. The space to see newly is created. As you let go of reflexive thought and action, there is an opening for the more to enter the situation. Reflexive action and thinking, is typically connected to a rigid belief system that is a default way of thinking. Breathe possibility into the situation and step back to watch the events, as an observer. Be curious. Do you feel the space open around you?

When you begin a new venture, such as these three hundred sixty-six days, it is natural to get ready for the long haul or hunker down and do what you think you need to do to go the distance. We are suggesting that is the old way. Instead, follow an inquisitive nature and your resonance of joy.

Within this process of expansion, be willing to discover that which is already present. Many, including Darlene, for example, are used to working hard. Within that belief there is a default patterned experience of hard work and putting in the hours to get tasks complete. We are asking Darlene, and you, to look newly at your automatic thinking. What will come gradually into view are the unique gifts of your expansive nature, beyond time and space. So, as you begin to look at your day, allow the old views to drop away, see what else may be revealed. You have barely set sail on this journey of conscious expansion; be easy, be light, be joy.

Appreciate the color of the sky, see the Love in the face of those around you. Being present in the Now immaculate moment will open you to see the more of your brilliance. It is possible to live from the state of Love, being fully present, consciously activating your knowing in light.

Day 5: Release the Past to Be Present

The concept we are talking about today lives in your thoughts. Your thoughts create. All the concepts we speak of in fact, live in thought. It is your action, whether conscious or unconscious, that moves thought to form. When you observe your patterns of reaction or default, you have an opportunity to make a new choice in that moment. The act of being present is integral to the actualization of your highest expression.

Consider the possibility of your memory, bringing weight into your daily experience that limits your possibilities. When you focus on what has been, you unconsciously re-create those same patterns. As you dwell on memories of past experiences, you reinforce them. With energy from this Now moment, the past is reenergized, and you create more of the past. It is not hard to get so emotionally wound up in what has already happened that you create it again. You even re-create the hormonal reaction in your body.

Where there have been traumatic events, painful interactions with family members or other people, the result can be such a deep connection with the event or person that it occupies a lot of your current mental and emotional space. As you spend time and effort in the past events, you are not present in the Now moment. When you are not present in the Now moment, you do not have access to the higher expression of yourself. Your creative potency, possibility, and potential is lost. You must be present to create something new.

The energetic ties to people and past events are strong. Each time you have gone back and revisited those moments you are bound. History is fed with present-time effort. Often, the more painful the event, the more energy will go into the past.

As you set off on your inquiry of your highest expression, the weight of the past is no longer relevant. Trust that all there was to learn about the event or relationship has already been received and is now an integral part of your being. In the same way that the rose you see in your garden now has been contributed to by sunny days, rain and snowfall, all the events of your earlier years good, bad, or otherwise have already contributed to you. Dwelling in the past does not serve your highest purpose. You may choose to stop sacrificing the vitality of Now to your past. Appreciate the past for the past. Be present Now.

One of the methods we are placing on the altar before you supports release of the past events that have captured your time in the Now. As you do this exercise, the cords of the past expressions of you are left with appreciation for their contribution and you are enlightened by the new open space that is available.

Meditation: Cutting the Cords

Close your eyes. Take deep breaths. Imagine yourself in a shower of diamond-white sparkling light. Follow the movement of your breath. Once you feel still and at ease imagine yourself in a hot air balloon as it rests on the ground. The fire that heats the air is burning. There are ties or cords that hold the balloon to the ground. The cords are many, or they are few. Each cord is representative of the energy of a person, relationship, event from your past that occupies your Now space. Some of the cords may be identified specifically and others are representative of those that you don't need to name. Once you see all the cords that are holding you down, you may use the sword of white light to release them. As you release them each by each, or all at once, you may hold a space of appreciation for all they have brought into your life.

Each event has brought you learning and strength that you would not have had otherwise. Allow the cords to fall away. Notice as the cords release that you are moving freely. Feel the lightness of your being. Notice the sandbags or ballast that are inside the basket with you. You may pick up bags of ballast and put them over the side as well, releasing more of what no longer serves you. Once you achieve the elevation that is right for you, notice you have the capability of moving farther. Release the weight of more of your past until you reach an elevation that feels right for you now. You may release more ballast as you choose.

Once you are complete, look around you, and sense the vast Love and support that is available for you always. Feel the freedom of the clear blue sky and the edge of eternity, knowing you have the auspicious opportunity now to fully discover and embrace your truth. The space that once was the heavy weight of the past is now filled with divine white light, and an opening is created for more of your divine expression to manifest. You release more of who you are not, to experience who you are.

When you are ready, you may lower the hot air balloon and basket to the ground again, just through thinking it so. With grace and appreciation, and in Love, you have released who you are not and shed the heavy winter coat of the past to be present in this moment. The lightness you experience in the hot air balloon is available to you whether you are on the ground or in the air. All through your choice. You reside where you place your attention.

As you have released the heavy ties of the past that occupy your present Now moments, you notice a lightness in your being. There will be a tendency to fill up the newfound space with something else. We recommend you consider holding the space open, as a blank canvas. The blank canvas holds all possibilities of creation. As you spend more time in the immaculate Now moment, the inspiration for what is next will come to you. You don't need to look for it. It will arise from within you.

Follow an inquisitive nature and your resonance of joy. When you no longer rely on the past to inform your Now moments, you find your natural ability to thrive.

Day 6: From Past and Future to Now

The reality of time is a foundational concept. Many realities and timelines are existing concurrently. The concept of time running from past, to present, and into future is a condition of three-dimensional collective consciousness. Yesterday, we were speaking of cutting cords to the past and the irrelevant nature of memory, particularly as it relates to creating consciously. It is with a slight shift in perspective you gain insight and possibility opens.

Today, the request is to remember the most empowered times in your life, where you were firing on all cylinders. Remembering those peak moments when you were in the zone is a productive use of memory. Do you remember the automatic flow that you experienced? Operating beyond thought, from a powerful place within you, the experience was joy, ease, and inspiration. Remember those empowered moments where you were operating beyond time and space. Remember how the peak moments felt so natural. They felt natural because they reflect your authentic nature. In our work together, the concepts we present for your consideration reconnect you with the experience of peak moments available to you as a natural way of being.

The rich experience of connection, flow, and presence is always available to you. As you connect with memory of peak moments, allow *that* to influence your Now. Consider, as you feel the emotions, the ease, the unlimited nature of those experiences, and recognize that you were connecting with your authentic self, not the limited three-dimensional self. The invitation of *In Service to Love* is to move beyond the group consensus of time to realize you are more. You hold a multidimensional capacity that is timeless. Your reach is deeper than you ever thought. Our conversations shine the light on new ways of being that unlock the capacity you have always held.

What if the peak experiences are not just interesting phenomena? What if they are those moments that reveal your truth? Beyond the limitations of your own thinking lies your greatest treasure.

Reframe past, future, and your potential to consolidate into the Now moment. When you are living in the past through your thinking, you re-create the past. Do you see yourself as living your life in cycles? As you plan your future based upon past experiences, you are automatically limited to the experiences of the past repeating themselves. Seem like a puzzle? Most of humanity lives life from the past or the future, not in the present. If you are getting in life what you have always gotten, it is because you keep doing the same thing. Do you see how your thought creates?

When you release your thoughts from the past, you create an opening for the possibility of manifesting your highest expression. You move your presence to the soft focus of this moment, beyond the baggage of memory. It is only in this moment that you create from your most potent expression.

We suggest you reconsider beliefs related to time, habit, and limited perception. These are the keys to having peak experiences as a new way of being. As you assume the perspective of observer of your thoughts you notice newly.

Your most expansive self is not found in your moments of the past or in your moments of the future. As you begin to understand your patterns of creating, you open the space to re-choose. In the moment of recognizing a pattern grounded in the past, you may choose to see something else. Keep the space open; ask to see what you have not seen before. Intend to be fully present in this Now moment. You are setting a new intention, which creates an opening. This is a very powerful tool. This allows breathing space, to create newly, from the most expansive part of your being. This exercise of self-examination requires presence in the moment. When you are present in the moment, doors open. Your greatest joy is available Now.

Connect with Now

One way to connect to the magnificence of the Now moment is through nature. Our exercise for you is to look at the sky, look at a leaf, watch the flight pattern of birds around you. Really be present. Be still. Does the bird, dog, horse, leaf you observe experience past or future? Be curious about their experience of Now.

When you begin to observe time in a new way, as a series of guideposts to your most expansive self, reality as you have known it shifts. You are the master of time. Time is not the master of you.

Day 7: The Gateway Opportunity

This first week of *In Service to Love* has brought you to this Now moment. The gateway has now been prepared. We have discussed some of the principles of reality, so that you may become aware of your thoughts and move your attention to the present moment.

As you move unhindered to the Now moment, beyond habit and the restriction of your thinking, a new door opens. Yet to be defined by your expectation, experience and limitation, the blank canvas of your being offers you the gift of seeing newly.

The space has been set for a new level to your expansion. This begins with the no-thing of the blank canvas. You may choose to see newly. As you begin to realize who you are not, you have the opportunity to see who you are. From the perspective of inquiry, you may sit in the stillness, within the quiet of the unknown. Within the blank canvas, all possibility lies before you. There is no need to hurry up and fill this space. The magic, the possibilities, the potential lies in the ability to learn to be no-thing. Drop the definitions of who you think you are. Drop the weight of the past, drop the expectations of the future, drop resistance, blame, shame, forgiving. All your moments bring you to Now.

The Now Immaculate Moment

We refer to this space of no-thing that holds all possibility as the Now immaculate moment. This is the space where creativity is sparked. It only happens in the present moment. It is the space of the divinely inspired. This is the space of original thought. A sacred space of stillness, of no-thing and of every-thing at the same time. In the same way that life is sparked as the egg and sperm join, so too may you experience consciously the divine spark of creation. In the blank canvas experience, there is stillness and no expectation.

If you are wanting something to happen, do not be disappointed that it does not. Creation occurs organically from the space of Now. All is in divine timing. Be still, and know that I AM God. Listen for the soft whispers that begin to beckon to you. Without defining them. Just be. Wait for a message to rise from within you. Realize that you are the chalice. You hold the ability to express your divinity at the highest of levels.

Our conversations over this next year are about being in this space and discovering. Consider the possibility that YOU are the holy grail. You are the space where heaven and earth meet. What does that create as possibilities in your Now moments?

The Gateway Experience

The Gateway is an actual structure in light, frequency, and consciousness. We have created this with Darlene and with you, in preparation for our experience together over the expanse of our now 358 days. You have been drawn to this work because of an inner calling, a knowing that you may realize your soul's vision. You have an inkling of your greatness, your magnificence, and choose to be a contribution to the planet and beyond. Your reach is much farther than you could ever imagine.

At the opening of this gateway today, the gathering is vast. Thousands upon thousands of beings of light are here in witness to your choice to manifest your divinity consciously. The gateway is an energetic portal made available through the construct of your intentions. Darlene, as your Scribe has been and continues to be the chalice to receive this energy, giving birth and at the same time holding the divine design. This is a divine union. A collaboration of divine expression of the highest levels. Framed within the space of Love. Occurring within the space of the no-thing of a blank canvas, we create together. The practice of being no-thing allows the opening of the greatest expression of you. And it cannot happen anywhere other than this Now immaculate sacred moment.

The Gateway provides an awakening, an energetic boost, an energetic safe space for you to explore and expand. You may notice a sense of speeding up with the presence of lighter frequencies. For as you do less, you BE more, and your being creates. You are at choice in every moment. As resistance is dropped, you move to higher expressions. You are held on high.

You are seen and held in reverence. Know that the intention you have set out so far has accessed your multidimensional expression. Know that every step we take together each day supports and expands your unique process.

Day 8: Calibrating into a New Space

The space opened in yesterday's transmission is vast. Like moving from the dark to bright sunlight, there is a moment needed to adjust to the new environment. Today is a day of calibrating into the new space. You will notice we are not saying re-calibrating. "Re-" implies you are returning to a past condition. In this case you are calibrating into a new space. The limitations of the past are no longer in your energetic field. As incidents and moments come up in your day you are looking at them differently.

We are moving at the speed of light. There is a calling forth of abilities and understandings that are a part of your authentic beingness. Today is a day of resting into a new space. You are held in a divine energetic matrix supporting your access to all aspects of your divine nature. Imagine your breaker panel being updated as you are downloading a new operating system.

Meditation for Stillness

Be quiet, be still. In your mind's eye, see yourself sitting at the edge of a beautiful lake. Gently toss a stone into the water in front of you. Watch as the ripples flow out in ever widening circles. Stay still. Watch as the ripples fade to a smooth surface. Notice the depth of your stillness. Stay in the space of no-thing. Feel the appreciation and Love around you. Bask in the gentle warmth of Love.

DAY 9: LOVE AND APPRECIATION

In this Now sacred divine moment, in the space of no-thing, as you sit still you will notice the background of Love and appreciation. As you sit in appreciation of all that is and for all that is not right now in your life, you embrace the beauty of the moment.

In the space of appreciation in the Now, there is no judgment about what has gone on in the past, nor an anticipation for the future. In the being of appreciating, you open yourself up to the infinite possibilities available. All is available to you with no boundaries. As you continue to sit in appreciation, the universe rearranges to open opportunity. Doors that you had shut through judgment, beliefs, habit, and unconsciousness open as you hold the exquisite space of Love and appreciation. There is no magic here: just physics, the laws of the universe. As you appreciate what is, as well as what is not, the doors open for possibility and potential.

Can you feel how, as you begin to sift and sort through the events of your life, you label some of them good and some of them bad? Realize you are the master who created those moments for the expansion and evolution of your Self. As you begin to gather consciously all parts of you that are both physical and nonphysical, you may choose powerfully.

Empowered choice is what our time together is all about. You may choose beyond the limitations of beliefs, whether they are yours consciously, unconsciously, or those of a collective consciousness. All areas of your life may sing in resonance with your highest expression. As you open to appreciation, realize that choices made from this space are not made to fix something you deem wrong in your life. Stay in the space of appreciation for what is, and you may choose newly without the weight and judgment of past. For now, notice the appreciation of what is and what is not. Hold the space of possibility. Hold the potential that resides within the blank canvas. Do you feel your environment shifting?

As you sit in the space of no-thing, the Love of All will arise. This is authentically who you are. This is your natural state. Love does not judge. Love is equal appreciation for the sunlight that reflects off a rose and for the most beloveds in your life. Love is not a feeling. Love is a state of being. Love is the highest frequency state possible. As you sit in the space of no-thing, in a state of Love, you transform your environment. The doors open to your highest expression. Love is all there is. You are Love.

The Message of Stillness

The exercise for this day is to sit in stillness. Indoors or outdoors, with music or without, whichever you choose. Sit or lie down. Be still. Feel your feet upon the ground. Visualize a beautiful cylinder of sparkling white light that encompasses you. It extends deep into Mother Earth and far into the multiverse, for you are both physical and light. Move your attention to your heart. Notice the cell that is the genesis of your being this lifetime. Find it and follow your attention into it. You are moved to a beautiful river. Beside the river you see one of your spiritual guides, a being that has been present with you for eons. You recognize the deep Love held for each other beyond the bounds of time.

You travel together to the great Akashic records library where all history is recorded. Your history is contained within these books as well. See before you the book that is you. You open the book to the page that is the most appropriate for you to see in this moment. It holds the past that has brought you to this Now moment. See the planning that went into this lifetime. See your soul's journey. See the people who have been present before. Allow the book to speak to you, revealing what is most important for you to know now. Allow the message to be revealed in the stillness.

When you have your message, come back to the river with your guide. From the space of Love and appreciation, move back to your heart. Reflect on what transpired. Come back to this Now moment. Move gently back to your body and into your environment.

Day 10: Living on the Leading Edge

Every era has held its own unique challenges. When one is living in the physical, through a period of dynamic shift in consciousness, such as the one you are going through now, there are both challenges and opportunities.

As we speak about manifesting in your physical world, from a world that is unseen, we understand that it may not be so easy in practice. As the great shift in consciousness is occurring, you will notice the feeling of chaos that is present in the physical world at this time. The old guard is on notice and fighting for its very survival. The expression of power and control is rampant. It is as though all the dust of the last century is kicked up in the air now and all your reality is on the move. The travails of your exterior world reflect the collective consciousness. You will notice your own inner turmoil as it arises in the uneasy feeling of inner conflict expressed externally. Finding your new ground and balance is a challenge. As if the earth star is turned upside down and you are holding on and trying to regain solid footing. All these experiences are cornerstones of the shift in consciousness that you are living within. Consider that you are at the leading edge of this movement.

You are the explorers, the innovators. You are living on the leading edge of this shift in consciousness. You are living the space where old and new come to terms and something greater becomes available. The reflection of this shows up in your days. Some days feel very challenging and others are blissfully peaceful as you bask in the warmth of divine Love. What we offer today is a way to consider the events of your daily living as you also birth this planetary shift in consciousness.

You are shedding the old way of being. Ways of being and actions that used to serve you no longer fit. This will show up in a variety of ways. There may be relationships that no longer have a resonance with you. Types of food that you used to enjoy may no longer serve your physical well-being. Work that used to sustain you may no longer provide what you hoped for. There is a deep inner calling for something new that offers a more soulful expression.

As the hurricane is strongest on its outer edges, so too, will your life experiences be more tumultuous as you move away from your center located in this Now moment.

Shifting your awareness brings all parts of your Self to the forefront. Rather than operating on auto pilot, unconsciously, your senses are heightened as the reality you participated in previously is now seen with clarity. As when you're driving through a new city for the first time, you are fully alert. You are utilizing more energy than when you're in familiar territory. We offer tools to bring calm to your day. This is so you will experience more ease with the external shake-up and more connection with the inner stillness, innovation, and inspiration.

Migrate to the center. This is not an attempt to fix something that is perceived as wrong. What we are suggesting is that you notice what is occurring and realize you have the opportunity for a new perspective that utilizes a larger part of you. The larger part of you may be accessed more easily in a quieter space. We refer to an internal space of quiet, which you may choose, as opposed to the cacophony of activity that may be around you, as in the external rings of a hurricane.

Take a deep breath and move to the center of the perceived chaos of events in your life, where the stillness resides. You will notice the activity and energy swirling around you. You have the choice to engage or not. The act of holding an intention for a new perspective will open space before you. The immediate situation will have less of a grip on you.

Discern resonance instead of meaning. A part of the human condition is assigning meaning to living. There are cultural beliefs, social beliefs, religious beliefs, and family beliefs that all assign meaning to events and experiences. In your own life, you also assign meanings to your personal experiences that have occurred within this life. As consciousness shifts on a large scale, beliefs that once seemed solid and reliable are now experiencing a realigning. The meanings applied to events past, present, and future are in flux. Beliefs have been the way you have measured truth in the past. As you sit in the expansive space of no-thing and are willing to see your beliefs newly, what shows up is a new way of measuring truth: Resonance. As you choose to let go of meanings, you open to the possibility of finding your own truth through inner resonance.

Resonance is a capacity you have always held. It is your gut feeling, your inner knowing. As you are willing to let go of what you think you know, as you did with the belief "the world is flat," you open the space for a new discovery. Resonance is now your compass. Resonance is an innate energetic response to events, people, and thoughts you have, guided by your nonlinear all-knowing Self. Resonance will be felt strongly when there is a frequency match between the essence of you and what you are thinking or feeling at the time. When you experience a feeling of ease, peace, and joy, you are connecting with what your highest being already knows about the situation. When you feel discomfort, unease, or disquiet in your body and being, what is being communicated is, whatever you are thinking in that moment is not in alignment with what the highest part of you already knows about the situation. As you begin to identify meanings versus resonance in your day, your facility at operating at the speed of light from a space of resonance will grow stronger.

Respond rather than react. Be open to new ways of thinking. Notice your reflexive thoughts, actions, and habits. Reactions and reflexes are always generated from the past. Stop and reconsider when you notice a reflex. Stop and be still, allow the space for something new to arise. The awareness may not be immediate. Clarity may arise over the next hours or days. When you are operating from reflex you engage the past. As you operate from response, you are in the Now moment and expansive perspectives are available. In responding, you are present in conscious choice and access possibility.

Engage with grace. Be easy with you. You are held in the matrix of *In Service to Love*. The awareness you seek is supported in this process. We meet you. Follow the ease of resonance, trusting your own divine capacity.

Presence Now

We are offering a technique to quickly shift you in the moment from chaos to stillness. When you are feeling out of control or disconnected, visualize yourself at the external rings of the hurricane, then with one quick, sharp inhale, bring all parts of you to the center of the hurricane where the stillness resides, saying out loud or quietly, "I bring all parts of me to my center here and Now! Amen."

We will provide support for shifting your awareness with ease.

DAY 11: INTENTION, CHOICE, AND TRAJECTORY

With each step you take in the Now moment, you are guided by your intention. The intention of our collaboration is to shine the light on the divine capacity you hold in this moment.

As we sit together there has been a gathering of energy, focus, and intention on seeing newly. To use the voyage analogy, we continue to move farther and farther away from the point where we began. This voyage was created through intention. Choice in each Now moment sets your trajectory. Just as the ships followed their compasses and the planets to a new discovery, so too are you following your intention to move to the unknown and greater expression of you. As you hold your intention, you are pulled by the essence of you, to the clarity of your truth. You are both propelled and pulled toward new discoveries. These new discoveries show up daily; you may see a license plate in front of you that catches your intention, or you may encounter someone you haven't seen in a while but were just thinking of, or see a hummingbird and allow the hummingbird to relay a message. These are not coincidences, but the messages to you from the light that have always been present daily in your reality. "Then why didn't I see them?" The intentions you hold now are distinct from your previous perspective.

The ships leaving shore eventually can no longer see the land behind them or the land that lies ahead. The captain's intention continues, moment by moment, to set the trajectory with focus on immediate conditions. Your choice in each moment is informed by your intention. Moment by moment, your trajectory is affirmed.

Your intention informs choices. Your intention and choices create your trajectory. Your intention, choices, and trajectory will create your reality. You may have already noticed a difference. What are you seeing? Are colors brighter? Are you more peaceful? Do you feel a larger expanse around you? Do you notice the brilliance of nature more acutely? Calm seas or rough? Notice what you notice as you choose in alignment with your intentions daily. Know your intentions not only propel you in your physical day but in your dreamtime.

Your trajectory is set through your continuing intention and choices.

Day 12: Choice and Consciousness as Foundational Elements

What if your choices are the access to your higher level of consciousness? What if choices are also your limitations? What if your choices can shut down the expansiveness of possibility? What if your level of consciousness governs what is possible within your realm of choice?

We are exposing the framework for choice, consciousness, and the accompanying frequency. When you make choices from the level of your personality, the result is in alignment with the consciousness level of personality that made the choice. When you make choices from the I AM Self, not the personality, you engage a high level of consciousness, a new perspective, and the increasing presence of Love.

Choice

Unconscious choice comes from an impulse, bypassing thought. The impulse is directed by the frequency of the consciousness you hold. Consider that many of your choices occur below thought and beyond your awareness until they show up as events in your life. Have you noticed cyclical patterns in your behavior? Have you had the experience in relationship of "different person, same relationship?" Do you hold a desire for success, but you find you sabotage yourself? These are examples of a dissonance in consciousness and choice.

When you become aware of your own mechanisms of creating, you hold the keys to your own divine kingdom. You then may choose consciously rather than have your unconsciousness run you. When you feel a disconnect in thought, action and result, you may employ a broader perspective that will allow you to see what has been hidden beneath your level of awareness. By bringing these patterns into your awareness, you have an opportunity to choose consciously. Conscious choice is an aligning of your essence with physical action creating a match of inner and outer realities. This also is the definition of authenticity, where who you are and who you say you are align.

Anything you create holds the same frequency as the impulse that created it—no more and no less. So, if the frequency of the impulse is in the range of survival consciousness, the creation that ensues has the same frequency. There is no more possibility available. It is impossible for the creation to hold a frequency beyond that of the impulse that was at the genesis. Be very clear that you are generating and creating at every moment. Period. You are always in some state of consciousness while you are in form or in light. A very broad range of states of consciousness are available. Everything from unconscious to fully conscious, actualized and beyond. Consciousness is measured in frequency. The higher the frequency you hold, the higher your consciousness. Your level of consciousness has a direct correlation to the choices you perceive in your reality. Your conscious choice may contribute to your experience of expanding consciousness.

Most likely, no one has ever had a conversation with you like this. In the same way that your parents and caregivers in your early childhood supported your understanding of the physical environment, we remind you of your authentic nature that resides in light. The doors to you are opening as you begin to entertain the possibility of living beyond the veil of illusion consciously.

Consciousness is a broadening, expanding arena of awareness that engages the light aspects of your being at varying levels. Each level of consciousness offers value, contributions, and gifts. Your expanding awareness opens potent perspectives that bring a widening field of possibility into view. Stand back for a moment and release the mystery you perceive around consciousness: We offer new ways to see consciousness that may catalyze your own field of potential. The following concepts of horizontal consciousness and vertical consciousness are foundational in our work together.

Horizontal Consciousness

Picture horizontal consciousness as layers in a glass cylinder, or a parfait glass. The layers at the bottom are dense and the layers get lighter and less dense as you move upward, or increase frequency, from levels of density and rigidity to levels of less density as more and more light is added. The uppermost levels are beyond form and exist only in light, beyond the physical ability to see. In the same way that there are colors of the rainbow that are beyond vision, and levels of sound that are beyond hearing, your awareness may move to the unseen, but your mind typically does not hold the capacity to understand, so it dismisses the veracity of existence beyond what may be seen.

Imagine then that each level in the parfait glass is a world or reality unto itself. You are born into a level of consciousness. You learn the range and limits of that level, first mastering survival and then learning how to thrive. Your efforts are in alignment with either surviving or mastering the level of consciousness you are within. You perceive success as participating in your life well, within the limitations perceived by the collective understanding. Can you see how many live within only one of the layers of consciousness, with no awareness of what may exist beyond their own understanding? The experience here is one of being informed by the external reality.

It is easy to get involved with the definitions of good and bad here. We would invite you to refrain from going there. There is only preferred or not preferred, based upon the level of consciousness you are in right at this moment. Go back to visualizing the layered parfait glass of consciousness potentials. It may seem like a trap to be in one level of consciousness. Not necessarily; it depends on the needs of the soul in form at the time. Some beings choose to live and die within the same level of consciousness. The fact that we are in conversation right now indicates you have already jumped levels of consciousness in your incarnation. The visualizing of what is possible opens choice as you move beyond the barriers of perception.

Consider that every choice, action, and thought you hold has a frequency. The frequency of the thought predicts the frequency of the outcome or creation. Each level of consciousness has its own frequency range. There is a low frequency and a high frequency access unique to each level. Every level of consciousness may only support the frequency within that level. That is why the frequency of the consciousness you are in, in any given moment, will define the frequency of your creation as well as the perception of what is possible.

Vertical Consciousness

How do you increase your level of consciousness? By choosing to raise your frequency. In so doing, you rise above the limitations of one layer of consciousness to the finer frequency of a higher state, with a broader perspective. Increasing frequency brings clarity, beyond the beliefs and limitations you experience in your current reality. Can you imagine being in one horizontal level of consciousness, then popping your head up into the next higher level and seeing a whole new reality? That is what you do when you raise your frequency and your accompanying consciousness.

We will shift analogies for a moment. As you view the glass cylinder with varying levels of density, each level representing a layer of reality and consciousness, you sense a reality that is beyond the limitations that are provided by each layer of consciousness. The analogy offers an opportunity to step back and take in the big picture. Employing vertical consciousness allows you to climb a ladder and view your reality from a new, broader perspective. Do you feel the sense of expansion?

The next analogy may give you a better feel for the experience. Imagine you are in the tallest building in one of the major world cities. When you are born you are living on the ground level of the building and your reality is formed through what you see. Everything you see is your reality; your coffee shop, your dry cleaner, your grocery store, traffic, passersby. You work within walking distance. You learn more about your world and add to your expertise in living only within your neighborhood. A specific perspective is developed that is the genesis of all your choices. The people around you hold a variety of frequencies, but all within the potential dictated by the level you all live within. You develop a knowing of your neighborhood and gain success. It seems there is nothing new. You have mastered the level of consciousness you are within.

Now imagine you take the elevator to the thirty-fifth floor of the same building. You look out the windows and see a broader perspective. The cracks in the sidewalk that were a concern in your first-floor experience are no longer relevant given the broader perspective you now hold. The frequency on this level of consciousness dictates the frequency of choices and therefore the frequency of creation. You have left the concerns appropriate for the first-floor experience in order to be in the thirty-fifth-floor experience. The myopic view of the first floor is neither available nor possible on the thirty-fifth floor. There is a vast array of new possibilities available within the thirty fifth-floor level of awareness. When you first move to this floor, you have a lot to learn about it, and gradually, over time, you get to know this level and master it, with all the signs of success that are available within this level. Again, the creations, choices, and possibilities are all within the range of frequency unique to this level. You give up, or have left, the viewpoints of one level to be in the next. This is an important distinction; when you leave one level of consciousness, you leave the density it holds. This is what opens possibility.

We will refer to the increase in consciousness that comes in changing floors as vertical consciousness. The elevator represents your capacity to hold the light of your divine essence. The ability to hold more of your own light is not something you gain, because you are already a divine expression of Source with no barriers. The seeming attainment of light is achieved through dropping illusions, to reveal your authentic nature.

In the conversation about horizontal and vertical consciousness our intention is to bring awareness to the level of consciousness you are operating within at any moment. Understand that the level of consciousness you are operating within in the moment dictates the possible outcomes of your creation. The level of consciousness you are in also provides the limitations for what may be manifested by your choices.

This is not a new concept. Consider that this is how you have grown up! Imagine being in kindergarten and unable to see life from any other perspective. You can't see the experience in middle school, high school, or college, or being married with children. Activities and knowing from the higher levels of experience are not available to you in kindergarten. Problem solving in kindergarten is different from what is involved when you're an adult. The difference is that growing up in the physical sense is understood by the collective consciousness. But where the collective understanding stops is when one reaches adulthood. Generally, the perception is that once you reach a certain age or level of accomplishment, that is it. You have arrived. In fact, your growth and potential is unlimited. You are unlimited in your reach and expression, and you continue to evolve. In order to engage the finer frequencies, you must leave behind the density of lower levels of consciousness.

Change or Transformation?

When you feel yourself embroiled in and wrapped around the axle about an issue, understand that you are being the same frequency as the problem. At best, only change is possible, because you are still living within the constraints of the problem. Transformation brings with it a new paradigm from which to see. If you choose transformation, the solution lies in a different frequency from the problem. If you are being the same frequency as the problem and want to be the same frequency as the solution, you must let go of your arguments for the problem and step aside. Get off the hamster wheel and be in the unknown for a bit. This bears repeating; when you are going around and around on a problem, you are operating at the same frequency as the problem. A higher frequency solution does not lie within the problem. Only a new perspective and insight given by a higher frequency will bring transformation and the highest level of solution. If you are providing solutions in the same frequency as the problem, you are only changing and creating variations of the same thing.

This concept of frequency of consciousness is a valuable one to utilize in your daily experience, not only in your spiritual expression. Do you have an issue in a relationship, in work, or with your family that you can't quite find your way through? Do you go around and around trying to find an answer and keep coming up with frustration, anger, and more of the same? Do you argue right and wrong, justify, defend, and blame? Rather than looking at the same problem from the perspective of the problem, raise your frequency, on purpose, and allow the clarity of a broader perspective to arise in your awareness.

Release the Density to Raise Your Frequency

You may move to a place of higher frequency and expanded awareness by choice. Once you hold a perspective that allows you to see a larger picture, you may move beyond the limitations of a current way of being. Each broader perspective holds a higher frequency that is filled with greater vision, expression, and potential. Consider that each increase in your perspective is reflective of the light you hold naturally. The divine knowing that is yours is accessed through the divine light that is you innately.

Sit still. Watch the movement of your breath. Move yourself into the space of this Now moment. With each exhalation, you release the weight of your thoughts. This allows you to move to your center, where you experience stillness. Give yourself room to sit and breathe in the stillness.

Hold the picture of the many-leveled building. Feel yourself present on the floor that is representative of how you are feeling and the limitations you experience. You will move to the floor that is a match for you automatically. Sit still; once you feel the limitations of your current state of awareness (as with shoes that are too small) you may choose a new perspective. Release the energy and thoughts of the issues you choose to see differently. Be willing to see newly. Be curious. Release what you think you know.

Move to stand in front of the door of the elevator. Press the up button.

Your perspective is expanded once you are within the elevator. Once you enter the elevator, you disengage from the limitations of the level you are leaving. With no expectations and a willingness to see newly, the light of your divine truth shines brilliantly, and you move to a higher floor. Visualize yourself getting out of the elevator at the next appropriate level that brings the greatest level of clarity, connection, peace, and Love. As you step out of the elevator into a new level of awareness, you will feel expansiveness, stillness, and potential. You will feel the absence of emotional attachment. The weight of the previous experience no longer pulls you. You will feel lighter. Trust, as you allow yourself to be fully present in the new space, that a new perspective will appear. You will not return to a lower floor, because you cannot unknow what you now know. Stay at the new level that holds open space. Each floor holds the wisdom gained within each previous floor. Your movement is only toward the expanding light of your divine truth.

Breathe easily. Allow the new space to speak to you. Allow a new view to come to you. The awareness will rise to meet you. You do not need to search. Breathe, be you, and allow.

When you are complete, bring your awareness into your physical environment. Feel lighter, refreshed and trust clarity will continue to find you.

As you move from one state of consciousness to another, you will notice there is no way to "work the system." You may not bring a problem to a new frequency to prove you are right. Darlene imagines a sieve where the holes are finer at each level of consciousness. The heavier, or larger, denser pieces may not travel to the next level. The frequency gets finer with each level of consciousness increase. There will be something to "give up" when you go to each new level, for example; being right, control, powerlessness, victimhood, martyrdom, separation, limitation, lack of self-worth, doubt, habits, restricted viewpoints and more. With every step into a higher level of consciousness the realization of your divine essence gains clarity. What is released is the weight of who you are not.

We are complete in this moment. There is space now for integration. The concepts presented today may "rock your world" a bit. If you are to look back in your history, you will see it has always been so. These principles are not new.

We are in deep appreciation of your willingness to look newly. Your willingness creates an opening in your awareness you may fill with the more of you. Already your impact across the multiverse is seen, felt and appreciated. You are held in reverence and in Love. For Love is all there is.

Day 13: Choice by Default or Choice on Purpose

As you continue to bring your awareness to the edge of your known experience, you begin to see with clarity, bringing an empowered perspective to your moments. With an expanded awareness, you set the trajectory for creating. Your every thought and action shifts into alignment with your authentic nature, and you embody the Love that you are. As you do, the universe is altered. Your choice is a contribution across the multiverse. This is not communicated as a sense of weight or burden in your Now moments of choice but rather to extend Love and appreciation for who it is you BE. Your emanations of Love from your essential uniqueness join with other expressions of Love creating an exquisite note of Love and peace. The music of the heavens soars in ecstasy. We thank you. We support you; we are here at your beck and call.

As we meet each day, we invite you to choose to be present. Not just to read this divine work, but to engage us beyond words. As you choose your divine expression made manifest, we, too, are a stand for you. Begin to engage our divine collaboration as a full participant rather than an observer. You will see the difference as it sweeps across your moments.

This is an opportunity, again, to choose. The point we make is, begin to choose to be present with your choices. Become conscious of how you choose during your day. As you begin to observe your actions, you develop an awareness that supports the alignment with your highest knowing that exists beyond your personality and default-level beliefs. As you become aware of your patterned ways of thinking and unconscious action, you re-choose, consciously, that which is in alignment with your truth. Your awareness will expand as you hold open the possibility that you are in fact engaging beings of light such as this Council of Light. This is a unique opportunity not only for you as a being of light in form but for each of us gathered here today in light. In choosing to be present with these divine conversations in the moment, you set the intention to be fully present and engage at your highest expression.

From our perspective you are a peer. The choice is yours to claim your place at the table. As you choose in the exquisite Now moment, you lend to the trajectory of your intention to experience yourself as a conscious being of light in form, living beyond the veil of illusion.

The conversation of choice is vast. The next concept we would like to place upon the altar for you to consider is unconscious choice as a default. As with all our conversations, we invite you to a new perspective. We place the concepts and openings upon the sacred altar for your consideration to choose or not. These conversations are not mandates. They are an invitation that honors your choice.

Today, we would like to consider the quality of choices created by default. When you are born into your physical form, you drop the memory of most of your experience in light in order to be involved in the opportunity available for expansion in your physical expression. You are influenced by your family, caregivers, schooling, friends, and your culture. As you learn to navigate your world, you develop patterns and behaviors; many of them are not even verbalized, as they reflect the beliefs of the collective consciousness you were born into. Consider collective consciousness as the background of your life. Your choices become a default way of being. Default means that you are not consciously present in the moment to choose or reconsider any of the default ways of being. When you consider the word *unconscious*, what comes to mind is the concept of operating without consciousness, where you are no longer present in the opportunity to choose. Your unconscious choice, and default ways of being, ALWAYS influence your perceived realm of possibilities. A choice made from conscious decision supports a conscious intention and therefore contributes to your most expansive expression. Equally, an unconscious choice will hold you in a realm of limitation. With every choice you are propelled either toward the realization of your divine truth, or away from it.

Consider that the state of consciousness you are in when you make a choice determines the frequency of the outcome. If the state of awareness is unclear, unempowered, and foggy, your creations will be a match. How could it be otherwise? What you put into your thoughts, expression, and awareness is reflected in what you create. If your intention is vague, unclear, cloudy, and undirected, all creations from that space will hold the same frequency of vagueness, cloudiness, and blah feeling. Dullness ensues. Do you notice that when you choose on purpose, you are clear and bright and present in the choice? Your creations, made from consciousness, will always hold a higher frequency that resonates with truth. The results hold clarity, bring aliveness, vitality, excitement, and joy. When you begin to hold the stance of consciousness, you are open to the realization of your greatest potential.

Activate Consciousness

What we propose in seeing newly is that you notice when you are not present. See where your choices are not being made on purpose. Get clear about your guiding intentions. Are the choices you are making in support of your heart's desires? What do you take for granted? What is the background belief of your choices? Be curious about where you get stopped or feel powerless. Feeling powerless and feeling unable to connect with self-love and self-esteem indicates a mistaken belief.

Become curious about what gets in the way of your natural connection with Love and your own authority. Intend clarity. Rise above justification, blame, defense, and reliving past trauma. Move into the sacred space of being an observer. You are setting a new trajectory for your life. One that is in total alignment and recognition of who you are at your greatest. Choose to see that which was previously hidden to reclaim, step by step, your own magnificence.

With practice you will find that a new level of clarity will open, and the dull experience of vague expression will fade. Choose to arise in the morning, choose to get your morning coffee, choose to shower, choose to get dressed, choose to get in the car and go where you need to go. Why? Because you said so. You are a master creator. Vague creations of your past have resulted from a lack of presence. Bring YOU to your life.

Bring your Self to your life and see the beauty that unfolds. Release unconsciousness in your choices and in your awareness to embrace the new realm of the yet undiscovered. Unconscious choices hold resistance for you. As you look at ways to be untethered by inauthentic action, this is a good place to start.

Do you see that we are creating a trajectory of presence? Your full presence is an honoring of your choices as a master creator; and so you begin to fully engage the empowered being of light that you are. We see who you are in light and in form. We hold the space for your expansion, realization and actualization. We are holding the matrix of clarity and realization. We are working with you in your dreamtime, as you choose.

DAY 14: MAKING THE SHIFT TO CONSCIOUS AWARENESS

As you engage your full presence in the Now, you activate action as opposed to passivity. Your full presence is empowered with access to potential, awaiting direction for creation. As you participate on the field of your life, instead of sitting in the bleachers, your perspective takes on a whole new level of activity. The perspective in the stands only holds an observer level of potential. While you are fully present on the field of life, you can connect with your creative nature.

In order to create in your life consciously, you need to move to the space where creation is at its most direct. The direct state is one that is informed by your highest expression rather than the limiting quality of beliefs, your past, or concerns of the future. The topic today is: making the shift. As you expose ways of being that no longer serve you, your authentic expression may rise to your awareness. While in physical form you have had glimpses of your authentic expression. Now we shift focus to the realms of you that are available through your presence. Your presence in this Now immaculate moment allows an opening into the part of you that resides in light. The process you are within right now is the process of reclaiming all of you. Beyond the limitations of the collective consciousness and your own default programming, you may see your own magnificence. As with the choice to be present, a shift in awareness requires something. There is a catalytic sparking, or activation of your light body that occurs with your expanding awareness.

Consider that the opportunity for accessing your nonphysical expression resides in an area you may not have looked at before. We present a new perspective for your consideration. The view of life that is most widely held is one of white and black, good and bad, right and wrong; a world of labels. We invite you to look between words, between what you have always seen, to allow the expanse of your divine nature to be uncovered. For example, as you breathe, you inhale then exhale, in and out. The mind labels breathing as inhalation and exhalation. Narrow your focus to look at what resides between the inhalation and exhalation. The space that is neither. The space that is All. The inhalation and exhalation could not exist without this most crucial point. We ask you to look beyond what you expect to see, so that you may feel your divine nature in a new way.

As you claim your All in this Now moment, you activate abilities that exist in light. This new opening in the expanse of consciousness reveals an integration that is possible. In this new opening, you may be both form and light consciously. As this new ability is being accessed and integrated, there is a paradigm shift. Your reality is exponentially expanded. The source of your understanding, choices, and experience in life expands beyond the limitations of past perception. Think of having a vehicle that once sourced its power from gas fuel and now is solar powered, too; the car now can either operate on gas or solar, integrating the qualities of both modes, exponentially increasing possibility. Consider that the possibility exists for you to utilize all sources of fuel available to you in your knowing. The shift of awareness automatically releases expectations that existed in the past, allowing a pathway for a greater potential to be expressed. As every journey begins with one step, so too is this process of integration required. This is the process of integration of the light awareness of your Self.

The integration process requires you to be present in each Now moment. As you move through your day you become more aware of the choices, thoughts, actions, and intentions that you hold. Are they a fit for you moving forward? Trust that as you hold the intention to be on this journey of expansion, the trajectory is set. The frequency of the trajectory is at a higher level than one that supports the "way things have always been in my past." Holding on to your past will be difficult. Being an argument for a rigid line of thinking will now present a discomfort. You will notice when you are in the flow of your natural and expansive self and when you are not. Each moment offers an opportunity to choose. As you make choices that are beyond the rigid box of right and wrong, your field of possibility is expanded and engaged.

The frequency of your past only supports your past. Your presence in the Now moment holds the key to creating a life that aligns with your soul's voice. The difference between the frequency of the past and what is now available will be felt. New questions will arise within you. You are shifting your awareness to include the most expansive and knowing part of your being. You are learning how to shift your attention. You are learning the language of your highest Self. Trust the knowing of your divine expression. You already know how to live your most authentic life. This comes naturally, for it is who you have always been. You are now discovering what gets in the way. Once you set the intention, answers will arise in your awareness. You will begin to see what had been hidden. And you will make new choices.

Know that you are in a divinely held matrix of support for your process.

Day 15: Presence and Conscious Choice

Are you present? We will assume from this point forward that as you intend to be with each day's gathering, you are present. We would like to restate that presence is an action. Presence is not passive. There is a way of being active with this information so that you receive it, allowing the frequency of the words, the energetic light matrix, and your intention to resonate deeply. **Presence is an action.** Again, instead of watching a movie, you are a participant in the frequencies available. Choosing those frequencies in the moment that resonate for you is a powerful act. As you state your presence in this, and in each gathering moving forward, know that although it may appear we are the teachers in this scenario, you are a powerful co-creator. This is a collaborative gathering where all participate, making available their voice.

Whether you choose to be present or not is not the point, when it is all said and done. The fact that you choose is an act of empowerment. As you choose, you are creating on purpose. The choice is fueled with your intention and the frequency you inhabit at that moment. The more you can create deliberately, the more your physical world will reflect the speed and direction of your creations. As you create from default or without thought, by habit, or by reflex, the creation born of your choice holds the same frequency. Unconscious creations hold an energy that is lower than creations made on purpose. Unconscious creating presents a weightiness that holds you down. It's like holding onto helium balloons to pull

you farther into your divine expression and at the same time placing weights on your ankles, limiting your acceleration and ascent
potential. You can imagine how unconscious creating may affect
your general trajectory.

Unconscious, habitual, or reflexive choosing creates a zigzag
type of life experience. You may hold an intention for ascension,
but each unconscious choice that's not in alignment with your guiding intention pushes and pulls you away from the shortest, direct
path. So instead of taking the light-rail to grandmother's house,
you are over the river, around the trees, under the bridge, back
around by the river, over the rocks, around the mountain, back
around by the trees, and end up in a different state. Again, if that
is your conscious choice for a path, your experience is enhanced,
and you are empowered in the process. If the circuitous route is not
your conscious choice, you are just fatigued.

One of our intentions with these conversations is to cross the
bridge, so to speak. We intend to hold conversations filled with
the energetic matrix of support, activations, light, and consciousness downloads, and to provide a way that these concepts may be
enacted in your day-to-day life. To that end, begin to look at choosing on purpose in your day. When you wake up in the morning,
choose to get out of bed enthused, fully present, active, and ready
for all the joy the day has to bring. As you plan your day you see
the tasks ahead. Choose one. Be fully present while you are in that
task. Be present in each phase of each task. Begin the task, do the
task, then complete the task, whatever it is for the day. The act of
beginning, doing, and closing each task is powerful in supporting
your full presence. There is a time also between tasks. Allow that
time to be your transition time. I am now between this task and
that. Often the transition time is filled with the to-do list, what's
next, what was yesterday, and you are not being on purpose during
this in between. Like the space between inhalation and exhalation,
the in-between time is rich. Notice the type of energy that each
task, event, or interaction requires of you. Like the fine sports car
that has many gears, with each gear appropriate and available for

a variety of conditions, you don't want to be in high gear when the condition calls for idling or stopping. Know that you choose which gear you are in. What frequency is required for this task? And then choose to be in that frequency. Understand that in the asking for clarity, you have increased the frequency. You have the full power of presence to lend to your creation. If you are looking at a creative endeavor, you may choose to raise your frequency to more fully engage your inspiration. Then you choose to raise your frequency on purpose. The guiding question in each of your choices may be, "Does this support my intention?"

Choosing on purpose in each moment of your day supports empowered creations. Your creations then are in alignment with your highest expression. You are dropping the weight of unconscious creating and will notice an acceleration and velocity in creating. You will notice the shift in your physical experience. This is both a process and a practice. Over time, you will see and feel a difference. You will open to higher expressions of your uniqueness as the weight of unconsciousness is removed.

Techniques to Cross the Bridge of Light

Set the tone. *This meditation will support you in releasing who you are not in the moment to embrace who you are. This helps align you with your highest expression. Notice the shift in the energy. Feel the lightness. Hold the lightness as long as you can. Following the meditation, stay in an elevated frequency. When you are complete, come back to your physical environment relaxed and fully present.*

Meditation

As you sit comfortably, close your eyes. As you begin to still your thoughts, visualize a brilliant, diamond white cylinder of light around you. It will find the correct diameter, fitting your whole body or the room or the building you are in at this moment. With your exhalations, release the tension held in your body. You feel settled as you sit still. As you breathe in for 4 seconds, hold for 4 seconds, exhale for 4 seconds and hold for 4 seconds and inhale for 4 seconds. Find your own comfortable cadence. Like the ripples in water created by the dropping of a pebble, with each breath the ripples expand, and gradually the water's surface is still again. So too are you still and present.

As you sit still within the cylinder of light that surrounds you, you notice that the cylinder is both deep within Gaia and also extending above you into the heavens. All aspects of you are bathed in the warmth and beautiful light of your divinity. Move your attention to the center of your heart. Connect with the signature energy that is uniquely you and yours alone. You may choose to turn up the volume on your unique signature energy by claiming all that you already are.

Before you lies an altar. This is your sacred space. Be still there. You may choose to place something upon the altar that no longer serves you. The weight of the past cannot follow you to the divine spark of creation. As you place your doubt, your perceived limitations, your pain and traumas on the altar, not only are they held in sacred embrace to be transformed, you no longer hold the weight of them.

You see upon the sacred altar a golden box that has brilliant light visible under the lid. It beckons you and you pick it up and hold it to your heart. As you open the lid of the exquisite golden box, you are given a gift. You are in receipt of the divine, natural, authentic creativity that is you at your highest expression. Your birthright. All that is your soul's desire in this Now moment. Within is divine expression at its most potent. You are bathed in the glow of the light emanating from the box. You receive all that is yours to receive. You hear all that is yours to hear. You feel all that is yours to feel. You see all that is yours to see. You BE all that is yours to be. You know all that is yours to know.

Come back to your heart now. Feel the shift in your energy. Feel the lightness of your being, the stillness, the joy, the celebration of being. Feel the potency of YOU.

Come back to your environment relaxed and fully present.

Access a Higher Frequency on Purpose

If you have a specific creative endeavor such as writing or painting or want quick access to your creative potency, you may utilize visualizations. You will resonate with the one that best suits you. Here are two examples.

Visualization 1 *Be comfortable and settled, be still and present. Feel yourself in the chair. Imagine you are in the basket of a hot air balloon. As the balloon rises, you release ballast in the form of bags of sand from within the basket. You rise higher as each bag of ballast is released. The ballast represents the lower frequency that must be dropped in order to attain the frequency that is best suited to the highest intention of your creative endeavor in the moment. You feel the release of limitation, the weight of past and future are released.*

You now inhabit a new space, one that is light and filled with the vibration of possibility. You have before you a blank canvas. Be still with the blank canvas, and wait, wait, wait. Stay in the experience of the no-thing. Allow the blank canvas to speak to you. Wait for it. Words, feelings, concepts, and colors will come to you.

When you are complete, come back to your physical environment relaxed and fully present.

Visualization 2 *Be comfortable and settled, be still and present. Feel yourself in the chair. Feel the cylinder of brilliant white light that surrounds you. Notice that it extends deep into Gaia and far into the heavens, both in form and in light. Move to the center of your heart. Allow yourself to move to the grassy banks of a beautiful lake. The blue sky emits love, the green of the grass supports you. Your attention turns to the water at the center of the lake. You sit still, breathing gently, and wait.*

Be still, and know that I AM God. Wait for the words, colors, concepts, feelings, and knowing, to come to you. You will notice them arising from the center of the lake.

When you are complete, come back to your heart space. Come back to full consciousness and relax into your chair.

We are complete for now. We are in delight with each gathering. Know we are present. We see your brilliance.

DAY 16: THE BEING OF LOVE

As you engage your presence today our request is that you allow your environment to be such that you may go deep into the frequency offered today.

And so we begin. As you move forward in your expansion of consciousness, where is it that you are going? We have communicated thus far that the journey is to a space of the unknown. It is the unknown for your personality. But for the being of you that is in light, it is a return to you as the expression of Love that is uniquely you.

Darlene heard the words as we were preparing today: "You are calling your Self forth." This is the process we are talking about. The calling forth of you, to your Self. While you are in light your experience is one of Love. As we have stated, Love is not an emotion, it is the highest-frequency expression of being. Love is a way of BEING. In light, you are held in the environment of knowing remembering, expanding, evolving, reflecting, all within the space of Love. While you are in your body with the experience of Love, there are a broad range of experiences possible. As you call forth the part of you in light, the part of you in light is calling forth the you that is in form. This is an invitation for the return to Love. The experience of light and form joining consciously is one of exponential expansion. The you that is in light, with the full knowing and experience of Love, is joining with the you that is in form.

While in form, each moment of your life supports your soul's evolution, including the experience of illusion and separation. The pervasive collective consciousness holds beliefs about Love that are often rife with not-love. Instead of unconditional Love there may be jealousy, anger, abuse, control, self-interest, and manipulation. You get a sense for all the emotional games that may be played in the name of Love. At each stage of *In Service to Love,* you will be having the experience of the more of you. What becomes possible is the divine expression of being Love.

There is not a Love to be *in,* like "falling in love." You become the frequency where the high ecstatic experience of Love is a way of being. At the inception of this collaboration between your Scribe Darlene and me, Thoth, there was an experience Darlene has a difficult time putting into words. This was a collaboration of a Master with Masters. We will help: Imagine your highest divine expression in light, in sacred holiness (wholeness), merging with the essence of Love's light that is light-years in expanse and infinite in depth. Beauty, tenderness, acknowledgment, surrender, presence, choice, integrity, honor, compassion, creation. Collaboration at its most divine. Exalted. At the time she said, "So this is what Love is."

The exalted experience of being Love is what becomes possible in the return to the being of Love that you are. With the light part of you, like a beautiful symphony, you embrace the physical you for a holy (whole) experience. This work, this act of Love, this act of collaboration, is the inception of our work with Darlene, together, destined for lifetimes, actualized in the immaculate NOW moment. In the same way, our work with Darlene is a divine collaboration, we are in divine collaboration with you.

We share this experience because it holds the high frequency of transformation within. Your expression of Love is uniquely yours. We set the stage for the beingness of Love to show up in your physical world and in your inner awareness in new ways. Beyond what has been conceptualized or experienced before, you hold the truth of the being of Love.

In divine collaboration you are calling your Self forth. Your Self is calling you forth. This is a new paradigm for the being of Love.

Day 17: Aligning to Your Highest Frequency; Movement in Transformation

To say you are in the space of a moving landscape is an understatement. You have probably already noticed. As Darlene says, "I'm not in Kansas anymore." In your physical life, there may have been periods of time when you felt you were standing still. The experiences of sameness and nothing new, or resignation, reflected the limited perspective you held at times in life. The process you have called unto yourself in this divine Now moment is one of activity, action, presence, and restoration as you claim your full expression. As you go through your days since our collaboration, you will notice you have moved off the point you occupied prior. You are aligning to your highest expression, at a higher frequency. This does not occur passively.

Imagine you are on a road trip from Los Angeles to New York City. You get in your car and as you move on the highway, the landscape comes into view and then passes, revealing yet another landscape. A constantly moving landscape. As you align with the intention of driving to New York, the landscape moves, it is in flux. If you see a town on the way that gets your attention and you would like to stay there, you may. The question to ask is, "Is this in alignment with my highest expression?" in this example, getting to New York. As you are distracted by what moves by, the ultimate intention is diluted slightly. You may stop wherever you choose.

The purpose of this conversation today is to communicate that there are many distractions in your day. Consider that many of them are born of past events, beliefs, and habits. As the intention of expansion is held, there is naturally movement. The concept of movement seems intuitive. The experience of movement is surprising as you recognize how you have held on to the familiarity of what you know. The movement will bring along many things in your inner and outer landscape. As you hold to aligning with your highest expression, you will move through the distractions with more ease. Like staying in the car, on your way to New York, admiring a beautiful tree as it is in your view, then it is no longer in view. Your beliefs have been informed by your external world. We are inviting a new source of information: you, as your highest expression, you, as the Beloved.

As you choose to align with your highest frequency during your day, you are taking the most direct route to your destination of conscious realization. That territory you are crossing must be crossed on your way. Not getting stuck in the lower frequencies of past relationships, interactions, situations, and events will go a long way in supporting your ultimate intention. This is a shift in sourcing, from external to internal. There is no time like now. When situations come up in your day you may choose to align with your highest frequency (this is the vertical consciousness concept we spoke about previously). With each moment of your day, a new perspective is offered, and you see newly.

When you allow your highest expression to pull you into being, situations where you may have been stuck previously now roll off your back like water off a duck. There is no resistance supplied by you. As you take deviations from your original destination, you will begin to sense an inner uneasiness. Uneasiness and discomfort, a feeling of moving uphill signals resistance, or the absence of resonance. The language of resonance is how your soul speaks to your personality. Resistance indicates the presence of a misaligning. That is because what you are thinking or doing in the moment is not in alignment with your highest expression. This is always how it has been. Now, as you choose the expansion of consciousness that is available, the old ways are seen in a new light. You listen to your inner, high frequency resonance. In the act of realigning to the highest frequency available each day, you are choosing and creating powerfully in each moment.

As you are in your day, consider the act of aligning to your highest frequency available in the moment. And Now, and Now, and Now, and Now. You will see newly.

Feel the presence of a changing landscape. You are on an exquisite journey. You are loved, you are the Beloved, you are supported.

DAY 18: EMBRACING YOUR NOW SPACE

Yesterday's conversation may have felt somewhat intuitive. If you are on a journey, of course you will be in motion and there will be a shifting environment that you move through. However, saying the words, understanding the concept, and living the experience are all different. There is a constant embracing and discarding process that is happening all at once as you expand awareness.

Today's energetic container will be in support of the space you are in Now after having moved from where you started. As you take a deep breath in acknowledgment of your progress so far, you calibrate your systems to movement, intention, clarity, and seeing newly. There is a lot of energy required in the intention and attention required for this process. At the core of today's energetic is an expansion of your signature energy, a stabilization of your energies and an integration for moving forward. As you embrace the Now moment as separate and distinct from your past, you set the tone to move farther on your journey. Like stopping for gas.

Your signature energy is the energetic signature that is you and only yours. Whether you are in form or not, your signature energy, like a fingerprint, is an identifier of you within all creation. Your signature energy is only yours and reflects your essential self. You are always sending messages out, like a beacon from a tower that communicates who you are. If you can imagine turning up the volume on your signature energy, making your beacon stronger, it is like adding more of you to you. Creating a concentration of your essence that then is available for you to use in your process of expansion.

When you are on a computer trying to communicate and your internet signal goes in and out, there is a quality of the stream of communication that is compromised. When you choose to align with your highest expression, you are turning up the volume on your essential expression and your signature is crystal clear, providing you with the information you need efficiently. As you sit still and ask about the increase in the signature energy signal that is appropriate for you in the moment, you will see or feel the number of notches required for the appropriate expansion of your signal. This is another way to support your intention. By consciously choosing to increase your light signal, you are using new pathways of light. The collaboration of you in light and you in form will show up in your day.

As you expand your signature energy, in the amount that is appropriate for you in the moment, you are calibrating to the highest expression available to you. Your intention is one of integration. You are integrating the new awareness over the last weeks. You are expanding your awareness and stabilizing a new position. This act of expanding and stabilizing will be taking place regularly throughout this active process of enlightenment. It is part of the aligning required to continue moving forward with ease, and the grace required for all your systems. Your frequency is shifting and your awareness is expanding as you are on the move, so to speak. As you expand, stabilize, and integrate, you are embracing the Now moment powerfully. You are acknowledging movement and clarifying your trajectory.

You are held in Love.

DAY 19: THE UNIQUENESS OF *IN SERVICE TO LOVE*, A REVOLUTION IN EVOLUTION

As you engage your presence today, we would ask that you reflect on what it was that had you resonate with *In Service to Love*. As you sit in stillness and reflect on that, move to your inner knowing, and recognize the resonance of Love that is your inner signature and beacon, calling you forth. This is your Love song. As we gather in intention to consciously bring your magnificence to you in form, the heavens quake in ecstasy. We suggest it is the memory of the magnificence of you that is bringing you to these words. We are in deep appreciation, Love and delight of this journey that has set sail.

The intention of *In Service to Love* is the grounding of consciousness as you return consciously to your wholeness. Imagine the infinity symbol. As you place yourself on the lines and move throughout the symbol you find yourself moving in every direction, occupying every degree of movement. In this one year and one day of *In Service to Love*, it is possible to shift your conscious awareness 180 degrees or more. In shifting your consciousness, we also mean that the shift is so complete that your physical reality is affected. It must be. More than ideas in light to inspire, there is the intention of grounding this work so that you are fully integrated and balanced, consciously. In this process, you are guided to access the light portion of your being with facility, bringing depth to your physical experience and environment. As you continue to consciously employ the concepts introduced within this work, a 360-degree shift in consciousness has you being at new levels of awareness within a new paradigm not possible from the state of consciousness you held when you first began the journey. So the evolution does not end. You could say that *In Service to Love* is an evolution revolution.

The energetic matrix you are held within for this process is unique to you. This is an undertaking that is supported with and by thousands upon thousands of beings of light who hold the vibration and intention of unity consciousness and the full expression of Love. You contribute with your voice and expression and are buoyed by the light and support of the matrix that is continually expanding and deepening. Through the frequencies surrounding these words, we work together in light.

Your compass is set on Love. As you are more and more of your innate brilliance, you play your soul's symphony. You move with ease, grace, and connection, employing all aspects of your being, like golden strings of a harp, each tuned to the most perfect note in the moment.

Yes, we are going there.

DAY 20: DIVINE UNION, THE SPARK OF CREATION

The purpose of *In Service to Love* is the alignment of you to your divine expression. As you connect at higher and finer frequencies with your divine expression, you are reacquainted with your creative essence. In the same way this program was born of a sacred, divine collaborative event in alignment with your Scribe's highest expression, what becomes possible is nothing less than creation from original thought.

The two components of creation are design and expression. Design on its own holds no form. Expression without design is empty. Consider divine co-creation as the joining of divine design and expression in one orgasmic moment. The divine spark is the simultaneous ignition and propelling of the creation with force and velocity. What becomes possible then is true collaboration, in the moment. *In Service to Love* is a demonstration of what becomes possible as you consciously are present in the immaculate Now moment. The words on these pages, the frequencies relayed and the accompanying matrix of support are examples of co-creative expression. If Darlene had not moved to the space where she had the ability, frequency, and intention to express at her highest level, then this would not be possible. The program would remain in potential. It is only when the divine design and the expression come together that it is made manifest. Creations of original thought hold a high, transformative frequency. Your greatest innovations lie in potential through alliance with your divine essence.

As you consider the greatest innovators, visionaries, musicians, and artists throughout history, they all hold the ability to move beyond consensus and collective thought to the field of possibility. They move without restraint to a space of inspiration, or divine design, to bring possibility into form. The expression is as unique as each person. They go somewhere deep within and join with a vision that exists in light. Through their action they birth the original creation into form. As the pathway to access inspiration is utilized, a facility in the co-creative process is developed. You may go back to the well of divine design and birth something new again and again and again.

What becomes possible in your divine co-creative process occurs through the vehicle that holds the greatest resonance. Whether your natural expression is music, poetry, writing, drama, sculpting, painting, innovation, business, teaching, leadership, connection, you develop a facility in creation through your own unique path.

Connecting with divine design requires going to a high frequency space. This is why we emphasize the practice of raising your vibration or frequency. All actions, thoughts, and creations hold a frequency. Your consciousness holds a frequency range of expression. We invite you to develop an awareness of the frequency you utilize and then make choices. Like utilizing different gears of a car. Doing housework and your daily chores may not require you to be actively in your highest frequency. Sitting down to your creative endeavor may. Either way, you may choose. Understanding that you may choose is empowering. It acknowledges you have a variety of states of attention and consciousness you may employ at any given moment. As you understand that the space of divine co-creation is a space you may visit, you are invited to look where you may not have before. The key is moving to the same frequency as your creation.

You are creating wherever you are. Not just in high states of consciousness. You may employ a shift of frequency for every act of creation. Consider that you can raise your frequency to see above the fray of a problem or issue. You may go to a higher frequency to get a new perspective. As in a dense dust storm, you cannot see your way through to resolution. You may then consciously choose to raise your frequency. Like a periscope on a submarine, your vision is raised above the issue, and a new perspective, and new information, is possible. Remember, the energy of an issue or perceived problem only holds the frequency of more of the problem. Only by raising your frequency to expand your vision, do you allow an overview to come into your awareness. All this is a part of your palette as you create the masterpiece of your days.

You may also raise your frequency to collaborate with the divine. In Darlene's case she is collaborating with beings of light in light. This program is born of a divine spark where divine design and divine expression join in this Now immaculate moment. We invite you to the creative spark of your unique masterpiece.

DAY 21: DIVINE LIGHT ACCESS IN ANY MOMENT

Today's conversation is a demonstration that you may access your highest expression wherever you are in any Now moment. We are stretching Darlene's comfort zone, because we are within a crowded coffee shop, away from the sanctuary of her office, in perfect alignment for today's conversation. You may think you can more easily find the still center of your being when you are quiet and in a familiar place. You may have your rituals that support you reaching your inner voice. It may be perceived that, as you have quiet in your environment, you then have space to hear the still quiet voice within more clearly.

Today we are suggesting you may access your stillness at will, in any moment, in any circumstance. It is easy to live life, doing what you do during the day, going to work, focusing on the tasks at hand and then taking your spiritual practice as a luxury, after everything else is handled. It is as though the background belief is you don't always have the ability to move deeply into your inner awareness whenever you choose. The fact is, there are no conditions around your ability. Any conditions are those you have imposed, assumed, and taken on. They are not the truth of you. You may access all of you in any given moment, even in the most crowded and noisy places, without loss of potency. Your expansive, multidimensional reach is present and ready for you always. Only your beliefs place limits on it. The purpose of this conversation is to invite reconsideration.

The inner stillness you are looking for is highly active. Stillness is the space that all potential resides within. Stillness is the action of removing external stimuli and redirecting attention from external cues to internal ones. The process available with *In Service to Love* is about living from the inner-directed cues on purpose. Consider residing within the space of attention to your inner cues. The consciousness shift we are aligning with is the one that has you referring to your highest knowing whenever and wherever you choose, beyond condition or limitation. It is about making the shift from the reality you see in front of you, to the brilliant, dynamic, creative, multidimensional reality that is your true expression. Anything other than multidimensional expression is inauthentic for you. Again, this is not about looking for something outside yourself. It is all about uncovering the realms that reside within you in each moment.

Practice Inner Stillness

The exercise recommended today is to go to a noisy, crowded environment and move yourself to your stillness. Move at will to a meditative state. Notice your beliefs around the request. What are the conditions you place on the experience? Darlene is noticing how her attention is pulled by external sounds and activity, and yet she is recalibrating to her center through her intention. She is moving to the stillness where our connection may be experienced clearly. She is beginning to ride the external movement and be with us as well. As she does, the external movement acts like waves upon a beach that propel her. Truly a multidimensional experience.

In the same way, you can be where you are right now and also visualize and feel yourself being in your kitchen and opening the fridge. You already have the keen ability to hold multiple levels of awareness at one time. What are the events and conditions that pull you to your external awareness? Living in reaction to external input is a way of being for most people.

Remember that your full presence is actively available in every moment. In the same way, your cell phone is fully capable whether you are at home checking your emails during the day, sleeping at night, or traveling across the country. The potential for your abilities remains the same regardless of external conditions. Your design is not conditional. You simply ARE. You are a divine creation. You possess a reach into the multiverse at any moment you choose. You are a multidimensional being of light in form. Your capabilities may be explored when you expand your awareness at will. Your essential expression as a being of light is with you in every moment.

The exercise we are suggesting demonstrates that there are no conditions on your abilities. In fact, multidimensional awareness is an authentic expression for you. So through your choice to continually align to your center, you may experience the divine creative spark at your essence, beyond condition.

Do you feel the space of your awareness open?

Day 22: Your Full Potential Found on the Path Least Taken

It is with delight that we gather each day and communicate. Even though you are not physically here at the keyboard in Darlene's office, the impact for you of these words begins in the immaculate Now moment at the divine spark of creation. Because of your choice to be present in these conversations, there is no time between the inception of these words and their receipt by you.

With today's development of the matrix, holding support and expansion of *In Service to Love,* there is an activation for your electrical system to enhance your abilities to receive, and integrate the knowing that exists in your light expression. You may feel the energy as it works in the background of your day and night. We hold the space of support with ease and grace for all systems of your being. As you choose, you may also come back to this writing at any time and know you are infused with this same energy. It is beyond time and space and will continually meet you where you are.

The topic today is your divine light connection. The point of connection between you in physical form and you as a being of light occurs in the immaculate Now moment as you shift your awareness to your expanded self. Every time you choose to look beyond the habits and expectations that have existed in your life, you ignite your expansive expression into action. As you begin to look newly at your environment and beliefs, you engage the fluidity of being, you engage the part of you that holds your highest knowing. In each split second of questioning the long-held and rigid beliefs that have been your source of creation in the past, the divine spark is present in potential. This process may best be described as developing new neural pathways.

In the automatic, habitual way of being that exists in living, there are neural pathways that are well worn. By bringing presence to your day, your habits, your beliefs, and your choices, you open new possibilities that are not available when you live automatically. Like moving through the high grass of a meadow, you create a groove as you traverse the field. In the well-worn trail there is less resistance. You look out in the expanse of the meadow before you and you see the path clearly. Your awareness moves to the path that is worn first and the open space around it moves to the background. Each pathway not yet trodden upon is a potential. It is human nature to move your attention to the path that is already created, as in your habits and assertions. What happens when you begin to think about potential that lies beyond the path that is already worn? You engage the divine spark of potential.

As there is more ease in traveling a path that is already cut out for you, it takes something to forge potential. And each time you do, you spark more potential. As the pathway to your divine spark of creation becomes more familiar, it now becomes a viable choice. When you are living from habit, the manifest of potential is not possible. As you explore the path of no-path, you engage the divine spark of potential. Within this way of engaging with your being, you are integrating your larger knowing with your daily physical reality. As you choose the path least taken, you engage possibility aligned with your highest expression.

Understand that you can be conscious that there is more to reality than what meets the eye and still make choices from the old playbook of habit and reflex, because of the familiarity and comfort there. Even though you know there is more out there, doesn't mean you access it. Again, it takes something to break through the ease of habit to move to the vast expanse of potential. In each moment, choice lies before you. When you intend to see from the perspective of your greatest expression, you engage the natural internal mechanism that connects with the divine spark of potential.

In your life, as you begin to view your attachment to the way things are in your physical realm beyond a scripted way of being, your emotional attachment to this rigid way of thinking will, become fluid. Instead of coming up with an answer immediately to a question or issue, out of habit, you will bring all of you to bear in consideration of the issue. Instead of reacting, you will experience a response that arises naturally and organically from your center. You will experience calm even in a hurricane of emotion. If you find yourself in the chaos around an issue, breathe. Call all parts of you to be fully present Now. Then make a new choice that is directed by your inner knowing. That is the ultimate expression of authenticity.

DAY 23: YOUR DIVINE TEAM

The topic today is your Divine Team. You as a being of light in light are part of a larger soul group. When you chose to gain the experience of soul evolution that was available through incarnating into form, you were operating in concert with your soul group members. You have full autonomy in your choices and yet the existence of a soul group lends a contribution to each from the other members of the group. So, much like a family situation, you are an individual within your physical family and have your own thoughts and expressions that are uniquely yours and yours alone. There is a dynamic that exists in the family that lends a cohesion. The presence of a soul group brings support, communication, and connection that is always available whether you are in form or in light. Darlene is recalling her experience of preparing for this lifetime in form. When she chose to move into form, there was a gathering of her soul group and like one member of the family leaving the safety and familiarity of home, to go to college, she recalls the farewell. The eternal connection with family is the same whether she resides in the family home in light or is away at college in form. The ties are eternal. The love and support are experienced as a member of the family. There is support as a group and support for individual expression and expansion. The ability to tap into family history and knowing is always present. The group experience is a contribution to each individual. Such is the experience of a soul group. When you chose to be in form, you left with full guidance and support of family or soul group. Your experience in your life in form is a contribution also to the soul group you are connected with. Your soul group is available and present for your support and guidance. You possess common notes, or frequencies, in your makeup. Today, as I, Melchizadek, take the lead, Darlene is adapting to the different resonant notes between me, Melchizadek, and Thoth. Just as each family member holds a slightly different frequency, so too do the members of your soul group.

The purpose of today's conversation is to remind you of your family or soul group in light. As you open the door to seeing newly, you activate the divine spark of potential. This creates an opening for more of your expansive expression to show up. As you hold the intention to be consciously actualized while in form, your support is vast. Position yourself to communicate more clearly with your divine team as well as connecting more deeply with the realms of knowing you already possess in light.

Your divine team holds members of your soul family as well as others who are a frequency match for you. Each being holds a special resonance that is a catalyst for consciousness expansion and expression. This is a dynamic process. You could view your soul essence as a diamond. Each facet holds a different resonance and expression. All facets are running concurrently. Depending on the facet that is moving to the forefront of your expression in the moment, a team that is a resonant match for that expression will be present and available.

We have brought up the conversation before of equanimity. In order to position yourself for the type and depth of support that is available for you in light, you also step into a higher expression of you. If there is a viewpoint that you are less than because you are in form and those in light are more-than, you set up an imbalance of frequencies. As when you just miss the bus, the connection cannot be made. As you step into the realization of the authentic expansive part of your being, you meet your divine team from a space of equanimity; eye to eye, peer to peer, divine to divine. From a space of equanimity, you may be present with your divine team with clarity, support, Love, and joy, being both contribution and contributed to.

We invite you to consider the presence of, and connection to, your soul group family as your birthright.

Connect with Your Divine Team

As you continue to see newly, and walk the path never before taken, potential opens. You may meditate and invite your divine team to be present. Ask that you have a feeling in your body of their presence. This grounds the experience for you. Be aware of how your thoughts may change: "Is that thought from me?" The connection is so natural, there will be a familiarity. With practice you will begin to identify frequency signatures for the different facets of support that are available for you in light.

It is with Love and delight that we participate in each conversation. Know you are held in Love and support.

Day 24: Distant Contributions of Love

The intention of today's introductions is to encourage an expansive perspective of the many facets of Love's expression.

This is the Council of Nine that is moving to the forefront of today's conversation. This is the first time we have been transmitted through Darlene. Her reach and facility with raising her frequency is now able to reach us, and we her. We would like to make our presence known to you as a way of bringing a larger perspective to the evolutionary process that is taking place on planet Earth. As you may have guessed, you are not alone. You are a divine creation in form, and there are many divine creations in light from many dimensions across the multiverse. There is a long history of populations residing on Earth. As in your known history of civilizations on your planet there have been wars and forcible takeovers of territory and peoples, by factions employing dominance tactics to control. As the creation of All includes the polarities of light and dark, we, of light, are in support of the highest expression available for all. When there have been takeovers in history, we have observed but not intervened, allowing the process of individual will and choice to reign predominantly. We sit as a Council of Nine in light resonating with free will, the expression of Love and self-governance for all creation. Nothing less than divine free will. We have intervened on the side of light, free will, individual expression, evolution of the species, and expansion of consciousness as a return to Love. Currently in the evolution of the planet Earth, as there is no separation, what is occurring is a reflection of all creation. There is a turning point, a tipping point if you will, of consciousness. As the veil has been lifted and the knowing and divine access of the highest order is open to those who seek it, as evidenced by this transmission now, we sit in support of all endeavors that are a force for expansion of Love's light, individual free will, freedom, and conscious expression. We are here in support of the process of *In Service to Love*. We work in the background and will occasionally step forward as today, to interject a thought that may contribute to the development of this divine expression of Love. We thank you for your movement in each Now moment of choice toward expansion and fully conscious self-expression. As the Council of Nine, we are complete for this Now moment.

This is Golden Stargate, stepping to the forefront of this divine conversation. We would like to take this opportunity to introduce ourselves. We are a conglomerate of consciousness. Our function is to facilitate the movement of light and frequency from one space to another, much as a birth canal may be described as moving creation from one form to another. Darlene is an example of a conduit, translating as a Scribe, moving light and consciousness into form. Golden Stargate is a function of support of the expansion of consciousness and realization. Among other functions, our presence in this context is to provide an access to the highest of frequencies that facilitate the evolution of consciousness. We are contributing to the energetic matrix so that the frequency range and depth of *In Service to Love* may be tuned at the highest frequencies of light to the user or participant. Operating with ease and grace in this now moment, we act also as a stabilizing force of the movement of expansion. We support the you that is in light to move to the you in form and the you in form to reach and transcend previous barriers and extend your awareness consciously to your light awareness. This may sound daunting, but just as there is a tool in your kitchen for every need, so too is there a group, or expression that supports every need and function required in creation. Not only do you not do this process alone, you may not do this process alone. We are here in service to the highest expressions of light and Love. We stand for the unimpeded expansion of conscious awareness. As you embrace the divine expression that is you from a conscious realization, there is a return to the All. A return to Love. So, as you see, divine collaboration calls forth creative essence from all corners to participate. Your movement toward Love ripples throughout creation.

This is Thoth, stepping forward in this immaculate Now moment. You may be more familiar with Masters in light like Jeshua, Mary Magdalene, Mother Mary, Melchizadek, or the angelic realms, however, the nature of support available to you comes from all corners of the universe. This reflects the magnitude of you. You have an extensive history, much of it not lived on the earth star. Consider you have returned to earth in this, your now lifetime, to contribute to the expansion of consciousness while in form. Boots on the ground, if you will. The support for you is far beyond what may even be imagined.

DAY 25: CREATING FROM YOUR WHOLENESS

As you create consciously from the divine moment of Now, there is a space of no-thing that is traversed. This space is distinct from an unconscious creation. As Darlene sits down at her computer, she searches for the space that is undefined, the space of no-thing that contains All. She chooses to raise her frequency in the Now moment, allowing access to a high-frequency connection with us that is unhindered, like the unkinking of a hose. She is challenged daily in reaching into the depth of her awareness. The pull to move in familiar patterns is strong. Just when she thinks there is a pattern, we invite her awareness to new frequencies. This is about expanding awareness, not going where you have always gone. This is a skill to be mastered.

As you create in your day, we would ask you to consider those moments that are not driven by habit and pattern. Bring awareness to how you create. Move your awareness beyond the limits that have been habit, and you find the multifaceted divine expression that is you. To employ the myriad of facets of you, raise your frequency and be willing to see newly. As you are willing to see newly, the conscious component for creation is activated.

These conversations of *In Service to Love* are all about accessing the you that resides in light and having that expansive part of you inform your decisions, knowing, and awareness. "So why does my life look the same?" you may ask. That would be because the creative process is not accessing completely the unlimited potential of you that exists. Consider that the creative expression of you resides as the unique expression of you. Only you. One of the components that seems to get in the way of creation is emotion.

When you begin to identify emotions as being fueled by your perspective or a limiting belief, you can begin to access your unlimited nature. Emotion is only one part of your divine expression. Emotions each hold frequency. You may feel the difference of frequency in depression, overwhelm, fear, hope, resignation, enthusiasm, compassion, courage, gratitude, freedom, grace, Love. We would like to communicate that you have more of a say over which emotion you experience than you may have ever thought. Emotions are not related to condition. They are related to belief.

Consider the frequency emitted by doubt, lack, and depression. Do you feel how those frequencies rein in possibility? These frequencies are informed by your history. As you move your attention to the other end of the spectrum you find emotions such as joy, compassion, acceptance, grace—higher-frequency emotions informed from an essential resonance. There is a high-frequency resonance that occurs when you experience an emotion that is in alignment with the wholeness of you.

As you realize that, for the most part, emotions that are lower in frequency are fueled more by the past, you find you have choices. You may allow the expanded awareness, and stop fueling the emotion you are having. Not to inhibit or stifle, but to gain a broader perspective, allowing in new information that may make a difference. The opening allows a moving forward with a powerful stance, acknowledging the multifaceted, divine expression of your truth. Emotion is utilized as a catalyst for creating. If you use low-frequency emotion to be the catalyst for creating, you are occupying the frequency range of that emotion and therefore limiting the frequency range of the outcome or creation.

As you realize you are in a space of high emotion, you may choose to realize the limitations of that expression and ask internally for a new vision. As you ask, there is an opening that is created where you connect with the divine spark of potential. You may choose to have a new experience. As you create a shift in your emotional expression, what becomes available in both awareness and frequency is the access of your more expansive Self. Like adding clear water to a muddy bucket, gradually the silt will settle and the clarity of more light will bring new awareness.

We would ask you to consider the component of self-worth to this conversation. As you create, is there a governor within who says, "This is possible within the bounds of what is accessible by me" and "This is not possible within the bounds of what is accessible by me"? For example, winning the lottery is not possible, but getting a good deal on your car purchase is. We would ask you to consider the scope of you that is brought to these conversations. In the past, your beliefs (cultural, familial, personal) have contributed to your creative expression. As we ask you to consider the expanse of you, realize too that the limitation of who you think you are must fall away to allow space for the authentic expression that is you, to be the catalyzing force in your Now moments. The fact that you are in conversations in this Now moment with beings of light in light communicates that life as you knew it before has shifted.

YOU, the totality of you, is being invited to the forefront of your awareness. The lack of self-value that has been pervasive on the planet Earth is due in part to historical events far beyond your current world knowledge. As the Council of Nine recalled yesterday, there have been times in the evolution of creation when oppression on a large scale has taken place. The effect of that oppression in many areas has been a separation of conscious access to divine expression and separation from self-empowerment, allowing control. The conditions now exist to transcend those events of the past. As you embrace every moment of your divine expression, you further obliterate the concept of control or oppression in favor of sovereignty and divine free will. In the matrix of *In Service to Love* there will be an activation, as you choose, to support the canceling of the illusion of lack of self-worth, for space then to see and integrate authentically.

Who you are is magnificence beyond all imagining! Whatever you choose to create is available! Nothing is off the table. Nothing is out of the realm of possibility. The base understanding required first is embracing the intention to experience all of who you are in this Now divine immaculate moment. As you experience the opening that exists in the divine creative spark of potential, you are accessing your wholeness, your holiness, and your greatest capacity. No matter the area of decision, as you access your expansive self, in the moment, your creations are more and more and more in alignment with your highest expression, with no boundaries and no limitations.

We, as the many and varied members of the Council of Light, are a stand for your divinity realized and actualized. We are a stand for your expansion and conscious creation. We see you and hold the mirror for your reflection. We are meeting after all, peer to peer, divine to divine, eye to eye.

DAY 26: LINEAGE, LOVE, AND APPRECIATION

As we have prepared today for this gathering, there has been a calling forth of beings from farther afield than reached before. Not only beings of light as members of the Council of Light, but also those beings of light that are a part of your lineage. As we communicate the value of disengaging from the past events to empower and fuel your movement unhindered, there is also recognition of what has come before. So today, called from the corners of your history, is your long lineage of family.

The amount of information available in this gathering is immense. As we sit together in the space of All, we see the contribution that each past moment has delivered unto you. We see the contribution you have been to those who have come before you. In lifetimes there is a gathering of soul groups that come together. You are brought together for the frequency match as well as the frequency dissonance that each being provides. Whether resonant or dissonant, all is a contribution. You as a being of light in form in this divine immaculate Now moment hold all the contributions garnered from this lifetime as well as past lifetimes, in the same way an adult holds all the contributions from infancy and youth.

In today's gathering there has been a calling forth of lineage. For some, you have felt the work you have done on the inner worlds, and even the external world has been the completion or carrying on of the torch for lineage. The gathering today began with a drumbeat, like the heartbeat of the earth, resonating, calling all beings of light home. Today you are in the place of being with all that has come before you. In the same way that you are learning to incorporate all that is available for you in light as a being of light in form, so too is there a contribution from all that has come before.

Like you, those of your lineage have evolved. They are aware of the role they played in your life and you in theirs. And the contribution of Love continues.

As we forge this revolution in evolution, this step holds opportunity. There is much to be gained, by looking back to see what has been accomplished so far. Each step traversed of your days both in form and in light, have contributed to the you that is present in this moment.

Your lineage surrounds you with Love and appreciation. The momentum created by your past will support the velocity of your travels to come. Just as when you leave home, in support, your family packs the supplies needed for your voyage, each provision, each gift given, is a treasure to support your journey forward. The gifts for you as you move forward are many—treasures of Love. Over the next days, feel the presence of gifts, peace, joy, Love, and appreciation. What you do for you, you do for all.

There is no separation. Feel Love and grace present Now.

Day 27: Accessing Your Potential

Our communication exists on many levels. Consider each of the levels we communicate on as illuminating aspects of your beautiful beingness in totality. Visualize a diamond in front of you that represents your full expression through a myriad of facets. Today, consider there is an opening to a new perspective revealing another facet of you, previously undiscovered. As you choose a new perspective, one that moves your vision to see a larger picture, you may take ownership of more of your unique expression that resides beyond limitation. The qualities revealed live beyond conversation, conjecture, or philosophy.

This is Michelangelo, stepping to the forefront of this conversation. One may say that in my lifetime you most likely knew me as an artist. I accessed my potential from the Now moment. I reached far beyond the limitation of collective consciousness at the time and delved into the unknown headfirst. There was no questioning of my inner travels. They were my reality. It is not as though I was living a normal life and then had extraordinary thoughts. I lived, breathed, and swam in the expanse of my divine connection. There was no consensus around me for the expanse I covered for inspiration to make my works. I owned the space of my travels as opposed to just viewing them. The landscape of my internal visions beckoned for expression. I was bringing divine inspiration of light into form through my paintings and sculpting abilities. The message I would communicate at this time is, consider owning the expanse that you are, as opposed to observing it. Observing of a rose as it unfurls each exquisite petal is nothing short of magnificent. If you stop at each petal and claim that as the ultimate, you miss the potential of the whole action of expansion, of the movement through the seasons. As the bud begins to swell, then bursts forth with the release of each petal, there is a synergy. The soul of the creation is missed or misrepresented when it is seen in small frames. Magnificence is seen in wholeness.

How does this relate to your experience in form as you explore the heights of your potential? As you explore the vast spaces of you, know they are who you are authentically. If your intention is to reach into your unknown expression, you must move beyond your mind's limitations. As you create from the realm you already know, you do not have access to your greatest expression. Do you see that as you reach within what you know, a boundary is enforced? All possibility beyond what you already know is not accessible.

Limitation to your innovations does not exist as you choose to own your full expression, which includes all that you do not know. The expanse of no-thing is something to be embraced as your inner sanctuary. It is not defined by the outer world. It is you who brings the boundaries and definitions of the outer world to it.

Become comfortable in your inner world as an authentic expression of your divine expanse. Learn to be comfortable in the full potential of the blank canvas. There is an organic process that is birthed in the space of no-thing and All. As you connect with the formless, instead of looking for definition, allow the formless to play. Know the intention you hold is the rudder for what you create, not a limitation. As you hold the space of the formless, vision and inspiration will meet you.

The conversation today is about how you bring your potential in light into form. Intend to access your unlimited self. Beyond what you know, hold space for your own innovation without restriction. As you revel in the formlessness of you, you will notice a turn in your days. Clarity will show up organically. Problems that stopped you will be viewed with ease. There is a fluidity to being that is experienced. An appreciation, from a space of innocence that holds all, will source your most potent creations.

This is Thoth, moving to the forefront of this divine conversation. As you move to the corners of your awareness, understand that life knows how to live. You do not have to have all the answers. As you place the qualities of light into definitions, there is something that is lost. You have just tried to fit an elephant into a teacup. As you embrace the expanse of you from the space of ownership, you allow the elephant to be the elephant and the teacup to be the teacup. Each is perfect in its own right. There is a process that occurs as you identify yourself as the light being that you are. As in the imagery of the petals of the rose unfurling, and the buds of spring turning to blooms and then fruit, the process of expansion and evolution is always moving you forward. *In Service to Love* brings your process into view.

As you look behind the curtain of the mystery, you see the order. The beauty and expanse are breathtaking. The rose is not shocked that it is a rose. The blue jay is not shocked that it is a bird that is blue. They simply ARE.

The purpose of this conversation today is to connect with your I AM Self as the source of your potential. You ARE a canvas. Your immaculate Now moments are your paintbrushes.

DAY 28: AT THE FOOT OF GOD: INFINITE ONENESS AND LOVE

This is Infinite Oneness, stepping to the forefront of this divine conversation. As you engage in the energetic matrix that is available for you within the structure of *In Service to Love,* you are directed to Source for your guidance on a conscious level. Present today is the Light of the One, Infinite Oneness.

In the space of ALL, you are infused and held in the stuff, the matter, the light of your makeup. The purpose of today's conversation is an action. You are held in the space of Infinite Oneness, Infinite Love, the space of Love, at the foot of God. You are being steeped, for the next 24 hours, in the amplified Love and light that is you. As a creation of God in form, it is easy to separate from the fact of your divine origins.

Infusion of Love and Infinite Oneness

Today you are brought back to the space of your origins. There is nothing for you to do. This is an infusion, an amplification, available if you choose.

Sit in peace with the light of your origin and experience. See the perfection of your nature, your unique, exquisite expression, without blinders. Feel the peace that surpasses all description, as all the cells of your physical being are recalibrating with the high frequency. The purpose of today is twofold. One, an infusion of the original creative essence that is you. Two, a jump over timelines and dimensions to experience the brilliance of divine expression that is you. A formless space, a space filled with Love that vibrates in divine expression. Your battery is being recharged. See behind the curtain into the Source of the mystery.

The light of Love emanates brilliantly with the force beyond a million suns. Each spark of light is a component of creation. Each spark vibrating with its own potential and expression, holding in turn the reflection of the origin. Today is an experience of home. Every fragment of light you are, every facet of your expression, of your past, present, future, every immaculate Now moment is cradled in Love, brilliance, peace, potential, and expression. As the waters of a clear mountain stream bathe each rock and grain of sand, allow the frequency of today's transmission to restore, align, inform, and bathe you in the stuff of you, LOVE.

Your inner compass is reactivated. Your mission beyond form is available in the resonance restored. Your frequency is increased exponentially. The integration of this transmission will be held in your field and with ease and grace for all your systems and will be diffused into your awareness.

This transmission is broadcast throughout creation. The golden white brilliance of Infinite Oneness, of Divine Love, of creation are blanketing the planet Earth in a restorative, aligning, resonant note. It is felt rippling throughout creation. You, as receivers of In Service to Love, *are participating by standing in the brilliance of creation that is uniquely you. Your emanations in full brilliance are casting light, Love, and peace throughout creation.*

In Service to Love *is not a statement of current affairs on the planet Earth. It is a divine collaboration in the immaculate Now moment designed to increase the access to divine light while in form, consciously. The result is heaven on earth.*

DAY 29: LEARN TO DANCE THE LADDER OF FREQUENCY

The frequency of yesterday's transmission was very high, very potent, filled with light emanations, activating your I AM self-expression. Today we would speak about developing the agility to choose the frequency you occupy.

Consider that you already shift the frequency of your expression. The act of shifting lives below your awareness for the most part. You have days that are filled with low-frequency expression that will feel challenging, and days when you are lifted into the heights of clarity, peace, and joy as you hold higher frequency. We offer a broader vision for your consideration. By moving that which is unconscious into conscious awareness, you access more of your essential self.

As you become aware of the frequency you are operating within, you develop an adeptness. You begin to choose, on purpose, the frequency you show up within. Rather than having how you live your life be an unconscious reaction to your life's external events, you begin to choose, on purpose.

Consider conscious choice as empowering. It acknowledges that you have a broad range of ways to show up. It acknowledges that you choose in the moment. You are guided increasingly by your inner impulses about which volume of you is appropriate. The tone of today's writing is markedly different from yesterday's or last week's. This transmission holds a tone, or resonant note, required to ground this information into your daily experience.

And not just when you get your work done and can focus on your spirituality.

As every symphony holds low notes, high notes, sharps and flats, harmony is developed with the range of notes in balance. You are a spiritual being and you have an unconscious awareness that is expansive. As you begin to develop adeptness at choosing your frequency on purpose, you also expand your consciousness. The frequency you hold does not just expand when you are in your most enlightened moments. Your consciousness expands exponentially when you choose on purpose how you show up. You have a broad range of access and you choose the one that is appropriate for the moment.

As you learn to dance the ladder of frequency, you may move at choice, accessing different facets of your abilities. With each conscious choice you forge new neural pathways. The more expansive pathways you utilize, the easier and more natural they become. You must be present in the moment. You hold access to your highest level of creative expression. The fact that you are choosing consciously is key. If you are not choosing consciously, then how are you making the choice of what part of you shows up? If you are not conscious, your unconsciousness chooses.

Shift Your Frequency to Find Resolution

Every action, reaction, thought, feeling, and intention holds a frequency. Each expression has its own value in the moment. If you are angry, frustrated, dealing with a recurring issue that has you stymied and about which you can't quite seem to get a level of clarity, you are in a frequency range that holds the problem, not the solution. Often, in the feeling of being stuck, the resolution seems unavailable. In those moments, learn to stop and realize the familiarity of your situation.

Notice how you feel. Understand you are at choice. There are other possibilities within your reach. You may choose to raise your vibration by intending to do so. Release the problem. If you hold on tight to the problem or issue, it will not be possible to shift your frequency. Imagine you need to drop something you are holding on to in order to raise your frequency. Drop the problem, drop the argument, drop the reaction, drop the ownership of the issue. Take a deep breath. Bring all parts of you present in the immaculate Now moment. Visualize all the issues falling away. What is left?

Choose to rise above the issue with new vision and clarity. The new frequency will hold more possibility than staying in the argument. This is an awareness that holds value not just in solving problems. Your frequency in general will increase as you get better and more conscious of choosing your frequency. As you own more and more of who you are authentically, you gain access to the magnificence, the creativity, the abundance, the awareness, the joy that is you.

DAY 30: ALIGN TO LOVE, CHOOSE
LOVE, THEN MOVE TOWARD LOVE

This is Mary Magdalene stepping forward today. What makes this transmission, and all transmissions within our collaboration possible, is the action of aligning to Love. It is an openness without agenda. It is willingness to, in the moment, be Love, to be the Beloved, to be in the frequency of Love, to hold the frequency of Love.

There is an innocence and openness that is required to be immaculately present. For example, in this action of scribing, there is a dropping of all things that are Darlene's thoughts and an openness that allows this exchange of emanations, of frequencies. It is only in the openness, in the absence of all other thoughts, that the divine may be met at the level of conscious collaboration. If there is a presence of other thoughts, infused with the frequencies of being in form, the elevated experience may not happen. As Darlene learns to drop everything and to show up at the foot of God, naked, unafraid, like a child, she is steeped within and is one with the frequency of Love. It requires something. This is the adeptness of a Scribe, the ability to consciously shift awareness and frequency.

As Darlene is learning this ability and fine-tuning, she will reach a velocity in this process. Darlene's experience is no different from yours. As you begin to at first intend to begin your day from a space of open innocence, you are willing to be immaculately present. There are no carryover feelings from the day before. You are

107

truly starting each new day from a clean slate. You are opening to the space of Love. This is your highest creative state. Aligning with Love in your moments is a continual act of giving up. What needs to be given up? What needs to be left at the altar in order for you to better be of service to Love?

As you are present to be Love, you connect with the Beloved that you are. You are the receiver of Love, the emitter of Love, and every cell of your being both in form and in light is radiating Love. In your meditation time, we are with you to support your experience of fine-tuning your alignment with Love. As if supporting you as you learn to ride a bike, we will guide you to your essential nature. You may request this support at any time, for it is always available. As you hold the intention to expand your awareness, there is extraordinary support to do so. It is a conscious aligning with your essence. The more your attention is turned toward aligning with Love, the greater your experience of your divine expression in form. This awareness will automatically shift your frequency. This is not for the purpose of gaining something. The aligning to Love is the process of dropping everything that is not Love. It is a dropping of burdens so that you may find clarity. It is the dropping of concern and worry so that you may see the larger picture. It is intending movement toward Love be sewn into the seams of your day's creations.

This is not passive. As you drop all things that are not Love, the innocence and the openness is present. You simply ARE. From this space you develop your connection with the divine expression of Love that you are, you receive inspiration, you develop the base for the expansion of consciousness in your life. The softness of your days shines through. As your reactions are transformed to responses there is calmness as you center around Love. The vulnerability of Love is your greatest strength. It is the act of Love that is the genesis of this divine collaboration. And the action of Love becomes the genesis of your creations.

It is with deep reverence, support and celebration we are witness to this evolutionary revolution. I would like to say a few words about this. Throughout millennia, evolution has been a process of following a group consciousness, being steeped in a cultural norm that defined and limited actions and beliefs. The early explorers and innovators of your planet were revolutionaries. Their discoveries altered the paradigm of all consciousness. You as revolutionaries are taking what's possible into your own hands. The revolutionary component of *In Service to Love* is the declaration of taking control of your consciousness. As you do, you align with your highest expression of Love, in this Now divine moment. You declare the knowledge of you in light to be available and present now while in form, with no barriers.

At this breathtakingly beautiful time in the evolution of the earth and throughout creation, the opening exists to see beyond the veil. It is not a common conversation we are having. It is exalted. You are taking action to follow your soul's highest expression. With each intention, each action, in aligning to Love, you are staking the claim that is your divine birthright. Love is your natural inclination.

Move Toward the Light

*Daily, in the moments as it comes to your awareness, intend to move toward the light, as the rose leans toward the sun. Allow the warmth of your essential expression to pull you gently toward your divine expression of Love. Holding the intention is important; it will bring the awareness of this thought to you throughout your day. Next, as you feel the warmth of Love, **move** toward it. This may seem subtle, but it is important to clarify. As you feel yourself moving toward Love, you facilitate the actual movement and shift of your experiences. This is distinct from holding an intention and then staying still. If you stay still you are expressing the firmness of your stance and it creates resistance with your intention.*

To demonstrate this, we will use an analogy. As you intend to move toward the light of the Love that is you, begin to feel yourself moving toward it, just as a flower turns toward the light and warmth of the sun. The affirmation may be started with a sensation of feeling yourself moving gently. Then state:

In every moment I align with the divine expression of Love that is mine.

From the high frequency of Love, I attract all that is mine to be, to do, and to have, and so it is.

Your aligning is action. Your aligning is a choice. Your movement is the beginning of momentum that will turn to velocity. You are the stance of Love, a powerful statement that holds a high resonance.

Then: What could become possible from the space of Love?

Day 31: The Most-High Experience of Love

As you align your moments to Love, you set the trajectory of your day. The feeling of movement toward Love is an extraordinary tool mentioned yesterday. The sense of motion sets momentum toward the experience of connection with your I AM presence. You are the frequency that is Love.

The experience of moving, again, is subtle and worth clarifying. If you close your eyes you can feel yourself being still, as when you're sitting in a chair or standing still. This is distinct from the feeling of closing your eyes and feeling yourself walking, floating, or flying. As you intend your <u>movement</u> to the aligning to Love you set into motion the spark for the potential of the most-high experience of Love. You may notice the issues that provided resistance previously, but you will feel they no longer hold the energetic charge of the past. You have shifted frequencies. Remember, the solution to the issue, problem, or concern does not lie within the frequency of the issue, problem, or concern. The resolution or higher perspective lies in the higher frequency where you access your vertical consciousness (as opposed to horizontal consciousness).

Clarifying moments of choice will appear. How willing are you to give up the argument, to see something newly? These thoughts will come up for your consideration regularly. As you continue to align to Love, the opportunity to see newly arises. If you choose to reestablish the issues previously present, they will appear quickly. If you allow them to fall away so you may rise to a higher frequency, those issues become a gift you owe your gratitude. Gratitude for being a step closer to Love transforms the problem from a sticking point to traction on your path of awareness. As you move away from the arguments and issues you have known, there is a feeling of them falling away and space is available. Consider allowing the open space to be open and wait for clarity to move to you. It will do so, in divine timing. Feel the openness and the freedom of the space that gradually unfolds before you as you continually choose to align with Love. You are moving toward Love.

The component of movement is an important concept to become used to. The year and one day of writing within our collaboration is not linear. What is offered is a vehicle that when engaged brings high frequency to wherever you are, buoying your awareness with clarity that moves in ever expansive patterns. Visualize the spiral movement. As you expand your conscious awareness, you become more of who you authentically are, and less of who you are not. Your experience is more and more of you. If you were to break down the process into days, weeks, and months, there is constant movement. To get from one place to another, movement is required. Staying still and expecting movement are oppositional frequencies.

We would add an important consideration. As you continue to raise your frequency, you are creating in your world with both more clarity and greater speed. As you follow the path of Love, there is the continual dropping of what is not Love. Indulging in low frequency or harmful thoughts will result in the manifesting of those thoughts as quickly as the highest frequency expressions. You are asked to continually align to Love. There is no getting around the inner work. You may not reach a frequency unless it is authentic for you in the moment. The responsibility to respond is continual, to become more aware of how you are creating. As you choose to align with Love, the path will open gently. You are invited to show up as a match for your highest expression through thought, word, and deed. Again, this is not a passive experience.

Being in the space of Love is restorative. The brilliant open space of Love shines high frequency light, restoration, peace, grace, and joy to every cell of your being both in form and in light. As you rest in the field of Love, your soul feels restored. Your connection with light is affirmed and clear. It is a space to go to for meditation and rest. As you rest in the space of Love, as a parched rose welcomes rain, you too are revived and restored to your greatest expression.

Where are we going with this? As you set the intention of aligning with Love and you add the feeling of moving toward Love and leaning in to Love, you will notice the moments in your life that reflect the actualization of your intention. In meditation align with Love and move to the space of Love. There you will be bathed in the light of Love.

Meditation: The Most-High Experience of Love

Sit down or lie down. Become still. Follow the gentle movement of your breath. Follow the oxygen as it nourishes each cell of your being with vitality and peace.

Feel your connection to the earth as you visualize being contained within a large cylinder of white light that extends deep into the center of the earth and extends high into the cosmos. You are the space where heaven and earth meet. Follow your attention to your heart. Find the original cell of your heart. It holds the hologram that is you in your full expression as a being of light in form. Follow the original cell to the space where you meet your divine team; there may be one being or many present with you. Sit with them and be. Observe words, feelings, images, concepts, and thoughts that arise.

When you feel ready, notice you are brought past the legions of light to the bottom of the staircase at the foot of God. At the foot of the staircase is an altar. What is it you choose to place on the altar? What needs to be surrendered to continue this most high of paths? Place what you choose to release upon the altar.

Turn your attention to the stairs beside your altar. As you gaze to the top of the stairs you see the brilliance of a thousand suns and feel the warm embrace of Love. As you feel ready, you may move up the stairs to the top level. As you approach the top of the stairs, the experience of Love expands and encompasses your being. As you stand at the foot of God, in potency and innocence, you are bathed in the golden white brilliance of all that is. Stay and receive. Feel the emanations of the divine. At one with all creation, you are restored, you are In Love. You are the Beloved. As you stand before the brilliant emanations of the light of Love, you are altered. You move toward the perfect and unique expression of Love you are. The filling of your being with the light of the Source of Love heals you. You come into alignment with the highest expression of you available in the divine immaculate Now moment.

There is a message for you. Listen. What occurs in the exalted space of Love may not be contained within the words used to describe it.

When you are complete, return to the altar at the foot of the stairs. Upon the altar is a gift for you. Pick it up and receive it if you so choose. When you are ready, turn your attention to your divine team. Be with them. When you feel complete, follow your attention back to the original cell of your heart and back to your physical body. Come back gently to your physical space.

You have experienced the most-high expression of Love. Allow the peace and restoration to saturate your being. You may return whenever you choose.

Throughout our divine collaboration, there is the aligning of you with Love that occurs so that the experience in your days reflects the authentic expression of you. The gap, or missing space, between you and the exalted narrows as you experience the truth of you, sourced by Love.

This program is not philosophy. This is an opportunity; an opening available for you in answer to your soul's calling. As you more clearly remember your authentic expression, the pathways are opened for you to experience your life at the highest level available. You are aligning with your light expression, with access to your highest knowing, beyond barriers.

We ask again, what becomes possible when you are sourced by the Love that you <u>are</u>?

DAY 32: SHIFT FROM EXTERNAL DISSONANCE TO INTERNAL RESONANCE

In Service to Love invites a new vision inward, toward the potent, steady, divine expression of Love that is you. The ability to turn your gaze inward is the adeptness we speak about today.

Consider that the greatest part of your attention has been toward the outer world. How you navigate your physical world requires you to turn to your external world for information. It seems natural to refer to the external world for everything. Looking in only one direction limits your possibility, resulting in potential not fully realized. As you begin to question the patterns in your perspectives, you take the empowered stance of choosing on purpose rather than reacting unconsciously. You hold the ability to navigate multidimensionally. Expanding the awareness you hold innately is pivotal.

Stand back from your current point of view and see the energetic patterns that govern your action. Visualize the swirling energies of work, home, relationships, health, money, and decisions of life. As you step back and see the energetic field that is your life, you get a feeling for the frequency of it all. Some areas may have a higher frequency than others, but there is a middle ground. There is an underlying sense that focus is primarily on the issues in physical life, with religion, spirituality, or inner awareness as a contributing factor and secondary consideration. With tight focus on the physical experience, you do not allow the space for your highest knowing to contribute. This is representative of the collective consciousness of survival. There is no right or wrong here; we shed the light on avenues to access your highest knowing that allow you to contribute to your life in powerful ways. When your perspective holds a frequency of survival consciousness, your vision is skewed, and the frequency of survival denies access to other points of view.

The concepts of external dissonance and internal resonance are presented for your consideration, that you may expand your field of self-awareness.

External Dissonance

External dissonance is the experience of living your life from the outside in. External referencing does not take into consideration the powerful innate qualities of your essential Self.

External referencing is the bedrock of survival consciousness, where your attention moves externally like a lightning-fast relay of information. It is a process of gauging your activities and progress by external cues. The constant mental external reach leaves you feeling alienated and separate, and longing for the weekend to rest. From the perspective of external dissonance, managing life is a full-time job. Exhausting if you were to see it from our perspective, and exhausting from your physical viewpoint as well. The reason it is exhausting is this level of consciousness requires, mandates, that you are hypersensitive to all issues of your physical, mental, and emotional survival on the planet. Survival consciousness has been the base consciousness for so long, you are steeped in it. It is not even seen because it is so normal.

There is a frenetic energetic connection between the inward thinking, planning, and strategizing and the outward constant checking to see where you stand. Like a pinball machine, you send your energy out and seek a match. This is the experience of external dissonance. When there is a constant comparing, evaluating, and problem solving, you continually adjust to external cues and reference success externally. With each step, you move farther from your innate internal knowing and the deep satisfaction that comes from living from your soul's voice. The external values for success continually change, requiring you to adjust to a moving carrot. The external dissonance is not sourced by the Now moment. There is usually a reflexive referral back to the past or a projection to the future that occurs with external referencing. Fear and anxiety run high, and the defending and rallying for right and wrong makes life feel like a battle.

What else is possible? As we shed light on the unconscious patterns, they are given space and allowed perspective. What if internal referencing became a way of being in your life? What would that look like?

Internal Resonance

Internal resonance is the experience of living from the inside out. Internal resonance is a perspective that holds your innate wisdom as the guiding force in your physical life. There is an internal sensing that becomes a new language. Experienced through a resonant tone that is felt, like a gut feeling aligned with your inner knowing, internal resonance resides beyond the ability to think, accessing your nonlinear, divine expression. When you are living from your inner guidance, you look for a larger sense of resonance in your experience as a guiding force. You experience a resonant tone when a thought or action is a fit and a resonant thud when it does not align with your highest expression. Internal resonance requires a higher frequency awareness as you discern qualities of sensing rather than argue within the collective consciousness of right and wrong.

Within the evolutionary turns of creation, one era gives way to the next. The expansive energy of unity consciousness is the new fuel available for your days. The lightning-fast relay of attention to your external world is now being gradually redirected inward. The new era of unity consciousness holds the matrix of support for living a fully conscious life as your expression of wholeness. In the same way that separation consciousness supports external referencing, unity consciousness supports inner connection and aligning to your highest expression. Even though the experience of separation consciousness still exists, vision beyond limitation is available. As though the door to the birdcage is flung open and your access to freedom is a choice away.

You have been hearing the calling of your soul to a higher expression. You have been hearing the mandate of your soul's mission.

You came to this planet for a purpose. You are here through no mistake. You are here to support the ushering in of this new consciousness onto the planet. You, from the perspective of your perfect, divine expression, are a brilliant light for what is possible. Your signature energy sends a beacon throughout creation that peace may be found within. Aligning with Love is a return to your essential self, and it is possible in this Now divine immaculate moment. There is an internal resonance that occurs when you source information through aligning with Love. In holding the intention of being directed by your highest expression, your signature energy is turned up, your light becomes brighter as the coverings of illusion are released, and the exquisite nature of you is seen and expressed authentically.

The matrix of *In Service to Love* will buoy you in shifting from external dissonance to internal resonance. As you align with the Love that you are, you will see old patterns and dissonance give way to peace, joy, and alignment. A whole new panorama comes into view.

DAY 33: CREATING FROM INNER RESONANCE

As you continue your movement toward aligning to the Love that you are, more and more you will find your outer world will be a match for the new inner landscape. You will experience more of the peace, Love, and joy that is yours as well as the expansive presence of grace. As you transition from the external dissonance, where you are in reaction to external cues, you will notice a calibrating of your awareness with the inner cues that are ever present. In the same way that you begin to listen in a quiet room to the stillness that is present and find depth in the subtleties, so too will you find depth in the information that arises. The aligned resonance is a balm to your soul as you begin to create from the high frequency that is now accessible.

In the process of internal referencing, you become more adept at tuning out the screeching of the external and find the harmonic gentleness that abides within. You will notice a gentle shift in the quality of your creations. Your world will begin to reflect the many facets of your authentic expression. Diamond Grace is present today to facilitate the movement to the experience of grace that is magnified, as you face inward toward the warmth of the light of the One. As you align with the inner frequencies that are available, at first they will seem still and quiet. Then as you stay the course and are still within the stillness, you see the new landscape, which is rich in depth, breadth, creativity, connection, compassion, peace, Love, joy, reflection and access.

Your perspective turns ever so slightly to experience a new dimension of your nature. You are held in the space of grace as you are willing to place the outer armor held so closely in the past onto the altar of your being. In the step of courage that it takes to stand naked before God in a space of innocence, you are showered with the abundance, joy, peace, and gifts that are yours by birthright. Just as a king, away for years at war, finally returns to the castle that is his true domain, you connect with all that is now and always has been yours to be, do, and have.

When you create from the perspective of external dissonance, the creations hold the same dissonance. Your experience is one of frustration as, again, the inner frequency does not match up with the external. As you begin to create from the space that is opening, as you align daily to the Love that you are, you see the new landscape fall in place before you. It is as though the air is different. Life is filled with light, vitality, and color. A place to rest is open for you in the Now moment. You are held in the divine expression of grace. As you are held in the space of grace, the light that is and always has been you is activated and accessed in a way that supports your connection between light and form more deeply. It is a familiar blessing. You are blessed and are more of the blessing that is you.

As you align to Love, your light presence is expanded. You will find that as you walk in a room, previously unseen, you will now be noticed. You are now seen and heard in new ways. This is the physical manifestation of carrying more of the light that is authentically you. So far, in these first weeks of *In Service to Love*, there has been enough of a shift that the inauthenticity that covered your light and held illusion is gradually falling away. The brilliance of you will not be contained. You are free. And there is always more. You are an infinite being.

Diamond Grace is stepping forward to hold you in the brilliance of your authentic expression. There is an activation of your light codes now available, aligning the you in light to the you in form. Rest in the beauty and expansion of this blessing. Listen to the still inner thoughts that now rise to your awareness. Revel in the immaculate Now moments of Love.

We are in deep Love and appreciation for the contribution you are. The reach of your light is vast.

DAY 34: THROUGH THE STILL POINT TO ACCESS YOUR I AM; BE STILL AND KNOW THAT I AM GOD

The invitation today is to find your way to your still point. Your still point is not a space of lack of action; it is the access to your inner light and knowing. Your still point is the access to your I AM.

Imagine a pendulum as it swings from side to side. When this image is applied to your days, you may experience emotions, thoughts, and events that are extreme, representing the farthest ends of the pendulum swing. As with the experience in the outer rings of a hurricane, you don't feel settled. The swirling energy that holds illusion abounds, and clarity is elusive. Other days, or moments, you experience being still and centered. Clarity and peace are achievable as the wild movement of the pendulum calms and the range of the motion declines. The stillness is a space rich in possibility. Rather than viewing stillness as an end, consider the possibility of stillness as a portal to your highest expression. Meditation has been one tool to arrive at stillness, to block out the scattered thoughts, events, and concerns that occupy your thoughts. We are suggesting you may access stillness by looking newly.

Meditation: Be Still, Be Still

We would like you to consider taking a closer look at the center movement of the pendulum.

Sit comfortably. Calm your breathing gently, rhythmically. Visualize the pendulum as movement slows down. The swing from one side to the next is shortened. The tempo slows. Gradually, the range of the pendulum is reduced to the point of being still.

Bring your attention to the still point. The still point is the immaculate center. As you reach the still point, you are not swayed by your thoughts in one direction or another. There is the experience of neutrality.

With the experience of neutrality, your thoughts have stilled. You hold the space of your I AM presence. Present to no-thing and acutely aware of everything, your awareness expands. Feel the field of stillness pulsating in potential. Hold your space in expansive awareness as long as possible. Notice what arises beyond your thinking.

When you are ready, bring awareness to your body. Take deep breaths. Gently notice how your awareness has shifted even though you are back in your body. Feel the contribution of time spent in the stillness. The knowing of your I AM presence remains.

Yesterday we were speaking of the subtleties available in the quiet. You need to be quiet enough to hear through the quiet to the richness that abides as you follow your stillness gently to your still point. As you arrive at the space of neutrality in your still point, you notice the activity that resides there. When you magnify the still point, you find the activity that lies within. You arrive at the space where your divine I AM may be accessed. This is an access point to your light and knowing. You access the deep expression of you. You are eternally present. Your I AM presence is eternally available.

Be still, and know that I AM God.

As if on a field trip, today, in demonstration, and with Darlene's permission, we relay the events of our experience with Darlene as she scribes at this point. Darlene is expecting the arrival of her sister any minute now. The deep connection with us is diffused as she throws her attention to the future. As she is in the future, she is not in the Now moment with us, nor with her divine I AM expression. Our message to her is to employ the still point. It is available even when you don't think you have time. Your I AM presence is available when you are busy. Your I AM presence is available when you are impatient and concerned. Within the divine design of our collaboration, we are talking about the realization of a whole restructuring of how you operate in form. The limitations of time and space no longer apply. It is a whole new ballgame, so to speak. Even though Darlene's sister is yet to arrive, her attention is moving in that direction already. What is missed for her and for you too, when you have similar experiences is connection with your I AM presence. Your divine essence, as though a brilliant diamond at your feet, is unseen and stepped over. So, as Darlene settles in, utilize this energy for yourself too, to settle in and consider that your peace is not conditional, your joy is not conditional, your divine connection is not conditional. The peace you seek is available regardless of your schedule. The high frequency of you transcends the day-to-day experience of form. You are a multidimensional being and can do it all, by design. We ask you to employ the magnificence of you. As you do, the information that is present with you in light is available in every moment, and it informs your choices and decisions.

This is Darlene, moving to the forefront at this point. In my experience today, I went quickly from the space of divine connection, Love, joy, deep peace, and stillness to scattered attention directed away from the immaculate Now moment. I was worrying about not hearing my sister at the door. I became aware, gratefully, with the words from the Council, of all the time I waste by not being present. As if I must turn a part of me off in order to navigate my day. I heard newly that my I AM presence is available always.

This is Thoth, moving to the forefront of this conversation. Be still, and know that I AM God. Your I AM is the quintessential divine expression of you; your highest alignment to the One. As you meet with us at your highest expression, you show up as your I AM, nothing more and nothing less. An authentic expression of you.

The Path of Actualization

As you walk on the path of actualization so that your light may be realized in form, you will be rewiring your belief systems. Notice:

1. *You have control over accessing stillness. When you feel like you're at the far ends of the pendulum, you may choose to bring all parts of you together here and now. Breathe deeply. Allow all your systems to still. As you become adept at creating stillness, you expand the potential of accessing the wisdom within your I AM presence.*

2. *How do you place conditions on accessing your divine knowing? What events get in the way? What thoughts throw you into the future or the past?*

3. *You are available to you always, no conditions. The truth is, you do not have office hours.*

You are so much larger than any of the concerns or conditions you place on connecting with your divine team in light and your innate I AM knowing. We are always, ALL-WAYS, ALWAYS with you. Your I AM IS ALWAYS, ALWAYS, ALWAYS WITH YOU; it is who you are.

There is no need, Dear Ones, to wait. You are in a desert, parched, holding a glass of water in your hands. The brilliance of you is never separate, can never be separate. That is all a part of the illusion of separation consciousness. The purpose of our conversation is to shine the light on the magnificence of you and to help raise the glass of water to your lips.

DAY 35: BE WITH YOUR LIFE EXPANSIVELY

The intention of our collaboration is the expansion of consciousness that allows the experience of your life to access your best. Much of the discussion so far has been about attaining light and directing your attention to the light expression of you. Today we focus on your patterns of thinking. The human thinking is fascinating. There exists almost a Velcro type of experience in which the mind clings on to something that defines and brings meaning. With the assignment of meaning comes limitation. Today we focus on perspective.

As you incorporate the awareness of who you truly are in light, allow your totality to influence your days. We remind you of the richness of opportunity you possess Now. As you access the divine expression of you and bring that to your days, the magnificence of the experience of being in form is multiplied exponentially. This is not a spiritual work you do to gain enlightenment as you sit in solitude in a cave in the Himalayas. Many of you have done that already. This is work that occurs in the moments of your day that align you with your innate divinity in a way that makes a difference in your life. Consider that you may be wearing blinders against the vast field of awareness that is already who you are.

As you take conscious ownership of the expression you are in light, you turn up your signature frequency. Unable to hide anymore, the true brilliance of you shines. As if you've been living with layers and layers and layers of woolen blankets over top of you that block out the light, now, one by one, the weight, the burden, the disorientation, and the darkness of the blankets is being lifted. What becomes available is an ease and a flow of being. You become nimble in your movements. You feel the warmth of the sun upon your face. You climb mountains. You swim in the sea. You look into the eyes of your Beloved. You eat fine food that nourishes every cell of your being. You now turn inward to be nourished by the manna of divine light. Your enjoyment and delight in the physical experience is enhanced exponentially.

In the same way this multifaceted collaboration facilitates deep inner awareness, your physical life is contributed to. The depth of reach you have in the heavens is a match for the depth of experience and richness available to you in form. This is the actualization part of the program. The exquisite joining of light and form consciously.

You have the opportunity to consciously access the holy of holies, your I AM Self. You consciously travel to the space of original thought, where the divine spark of creation catalyzes manifestation. You manifest on purpose. Your divine light is meant to shine through every part of your life. The universe is not limiting in what you choose to create—why are you? Remember to have fun. This is not serious stuff. Be light, be joyful, be goofy. You already ARE. As you discover what is already there, you get to play with these "newly found" parts while you are in form. Delight in your life's moments. Darlene's father, who recently transitioned, stands behind her in her kitchen as she chops garlic for the dinner meal. "I sure wish I could smell that!" he says, laughing. Know that you are in the most magnificent of times, in the most magnificent of opportunities. Love, live fully, and be in the Now moment to experience the fullness and the richness that is available to you.

The matrix of *In Service to Love* brings calm and integration to your systems with ease and grace. Rest well, eat well, be well, have fun.

DAY 36: DEVELOPING YOUR ACCESS TO MULTIDIMENSIONAL PRESENCE

The topic of today's conversation and accompanying energetic is about developing your multidimensional access. In demonstration, today, we are asking Darlene to show up in a new way. This is something she is unaccustomed to and she is trying it on. Normally, Darlene will go into deep meditation and find the connecting frequency with us and then we begin from there. Today, we are stretching beliefs and abilities to demonstrate that the access to your awareness is always present with you. Darlene is not in a meditation now. She has been finding our connection together in a new way. It is like looking for something in a drawer in your home and finding out it is no longer there, but on top of the counter, in plain sight.

Our collaboration, by design, offers a pathway to access the light expression of you in your life. That means that not only do you have access to your knowing, but you have access to multidimensional abilities. As when you haven't used a quality in a long time, it requires practice to develop the agility to access higher frequencies of you. Again, regardless of conditions, you are always available to you. Today we place on the altar, for your consideration, the exercise of beginning to expect these parts of you to show up in your day.

When you are trying to remember something, there is an inner search you go through as you process the information unconsciously. Then, by magic, the item you were trying to remember shows up, as if you're flipping through index cards in a library. As you hold the intention, and are willing to stretch your comfort zone a bit, begin to look for the multidimensional access of you in new ways. Darlene is still in her office but is not in meditation. She has stilled herself in a new way, by choosing to do so. The stillness then allows the space and the inner quiet, aside from events around her, to access any part of her knowing. She is finding an easier way of connecting with us. As we continue, there is less effort required.

Access Stillness Now

You can still yourself in one breath. Lightning fast. Practice that. Inhale, then forcefully exhale, releasing external thoughts, move to your still point.

At moments during your day, find times where you choose to still your inner landscape immediately. It will take practice. At first feel how you respond or react to the thought. Do you automatically think, "I can't do this now, I am too occupied"? We would ask you to question your questioning. There is nothing that is an obstruction for you to access you. It is just that you never thought it was possible. We are asking you to consider newly, to see newly, to expect newly, to express newly, from your own divine light. Your light expression matches beautifully into your day's events, if you but entertain the possibility. Darlene is operating multidimensionally right now. She is not in a deep meditation; she is looking out into her yard and she is finding her way to keep the channel for us to connect open at the same time, with a beautiful flow. It is an exercise in agility. Unless anyone has ever asked you to entertain the thought of the possibility, it doesn't normally come up in conversation. Of course, this is a conversation of a different sort. This is a conversation that involves the totality of you and the totality of us. It is immensely powerful.

Begin to access more of you on a regular basis, not only with your intention, but in action. As you start to exercise those muscles and find new ways to be, you will be surprised how well you can do it.

Access Inner Knowing

Practice accessing your inner knowing without meditating. Find your stillness in a busy environment; really look for your access point for your stillness and sink into it. Practice in the moment, lightning fast, to shift from regular sensing to stillness. Jump from inner quiet to being aware of your external environment. Shift from inner awareness to external awareness, back and forth, feeling the difference of each. Like flipping a light switch on and off, practice the shift within you. Give yourself the space to realize newly. Be curious about your awareness. Visualize your reach into light and pull that onto the canvas of your day. You truly are a master creator.

Activate Expansive Awareness

State at any time in your day, "I call forth my expansive awareness Now." Feel your awareness as it immediately expands outward from you. It may feel like being in many places at once. As Darlene looks out the window during this exercise, her awareness feels as clearly present down the block as in her office. Then bring in your awareness again and focus on your physical space.

You will notice when your awareness is extended that you pick up a lot of information. It may feel tiring and somewhat disorienting. The practice is a demonstration of your natural abilities. In the same way you don't breathe underwater, do not stay in an open, expanded space for extended periods of time. Your expanding awareness will eventually integrate naturally so that, as when you move attention to a part of your home, you will gradually move with ease multidimensionally.

<u>Note</u>: Be conscious of your environment when you practice these techniques! Be responsible with your choices. Clearly, driving is not a good time to be practicing. These are altered states of being. Practice this ability safely.

The more you practice stillness, the more easily you will gain conscious awareness of your moments. Beyond the stillness is activity. You will be able to find the quiet in a room of noise as you find your immaculate still point and then allow access beyond that.

Have fun with this experiment. Find out what you find out. This is an exciting time. We are with you. You can go to the middle of a coffee shop and access whatever aspect of you that you choose. You are not conditional in any way. As you are bringing your unconditional qualities into your physical form, your physical experience will open newly. New pathways of your consciousness will be opened. You will be surprised at your ability. Expanding your awareness is such a natural part of who you already are. No one has ever suggested it before. Well, today we place on the altar for you the actualization of your multidimensional self during your day. As you develop agility in this, you will be rewiring your access pathways.

Your brilliance may be accessed in the blink of an eye. Really. That is what we are working toward. The facility of your access. It takes asking yourself new questions and expecting more. You are the more you have always been looking for. We see your brilliance.

A note from Darlene: I sat down to write today and wanted to get into my beautiful deep meditation. I couldn't get there. I could not still myself. Crazy. "But this always works," I thought. Then it became clear that there was a different plan for today. The words came: "Access us from a new place." I got the picture of multidimensional presence. I must say, a part of me panicked a bit. But then I entertained the thought and was able to still myself. Quite surprising. I was noticing I wasn't in meditation, but I was looking in a new space for my access with the Council of Light. I could feel I was in a multidimensional awareness. I am fully present in my office, aware of my surroundings, at my computer and fully present with the words as they flow. I settled into the process and noticed the ease that was present. It was surprising and beautiful. I am in deep love and appreciation for this most magnificent journey. I never know what is going to happen. I do notice, however, my consistent, persistent searching for patterns that I can follow, ways to put this process in a box I can understand. Can't do it. It is too big. I reside in the space of radical faith, grace, love, peace, ecstatic joy. Thank you for being willing to be on this journey as well.

DAY 37: MULTIDIMENSIONAL PRESENCE

Today's conversation is an expansion of the ability introduced yesterday. Today, as in the case of yesterday, in demonstration, Darlene did not move into meditation. She moved quickly into the frequency where we meet. This is an ability that is potent and available to you as beings of light in form.

We are utilizing a new energetic matrix to support this process. Darlene is feeling a little dizzy as the high frequency moves through her. Her awareness is fully with her physical environment and at the same time fully aware of us. We are calibrating access to fine frequency. As we open channels for Darlene, in alignment with her highest expression, your unique process is supported as well. Darlene's expression as Scribe allows this conversation to take place. Our main message is that you, too, have direct access to your Council of Light in any moment. The configuration of your Council will change depending on what best serves you.

The adeptness we speak of today, developed with practice, is movement toward accessing the expansive awareness that is yours. Unconditionally. As you access light, translate light, and bring it into form consciously, with no loss of potency in any realm, this is the actualization of your multidimensional presence.

Practice Multidimensional Presence

Recall an experience of deep peace. Occurring only within the Now moment, notice the quality of borders or the hard edges of you softening. It is an absence of thinking, inherent within the Now moment where peace arises. Watch inspiration surface in your awareness.

Connect with nature as an access point to the Now moment. Nature connects you to the perfection and vast expression of creation. It holds a resonance that reflects your own divine essence. Identify a trigger in nature that you are drawn to. Visualize or physically walk on the beach, sit beside a lake or river, walk in the forest, gaze at the clouds. Look out your window and immerse yourself in the colors and movement of light through the trees. You know what your access is. Feel that feeling in every cell of your body. Recall the flow that you experience. You will notice you move beyond words, beyond labeling, beyond thinking, into an expansive space of sensing. The experience of peace is pervasive.

This is the space where you can reach your light expression. Practice recalling those exalted experiences. Bring them in to your awareness at the same time you are doing something else, such as working in your garden, doing dishes, cleaning, or shopping at the grocery store. Begin to bring activities you thought were disparate together. Begin to realize you can do both at the same time. Turn the feeling on and turn the feeling off, with clarity.

This opens not only the pathways to rewire your brain and activate abilities you have long held; it also lays the groundwork for your multidimensional presence. Multidimensional presence is the state you are in with an expanded range of awareness. Information and knowing will arise as your senses are more finely tuned. You see beyond perceived limitations. You hold a space open that is not already labeled, allowing the voice of your soul to be heard.

This has been the work of the Masters as they have been in form. With the presence of unity consciousness, access to your light expression is available with less resistance. There is no veil to move through. The veil that once was is now replaced with your belief systems. That is all. And you have full control of that too. The opportunity available now certainly is magnificent.

Identify the images that bring you stillness. Feel the stillness in your body. At first you utilize triggers, until you move to the space of presence and stillness by choice. Darlene was using the triggers of music and meditation. Now she shifts easily to the space of connection with us without losing potency and does not need to utilize the triggers anymore. Employ exercises and awareness throughout your day. Notice that as you create the awareness on purpose, you can do that only from the immaculate Now moment. You are present. Now you are developing your multidimensional presence. Because you choose to.

You are held in Love and in grace. Placed on the altar for you are activations that amplify your awareness, as if turning up the volume of your light awareness. You will be activating parts of you that have been dormant in many cases for lifetimes. You will be developing ease in accessing your mastery.

We shall support this process with you as you choose it to be.

DAY 38: THE EASE WITHIN LIGHT

Today, again, we are demonstrating the ease with which you may reach your highest of frequencies. We started gathering with Darlene and streaming frequency and light before she even sat down. She has the experience of connection, and nothing is serving as a barrier to our connection. No settling in, no meditating, no sitting down at the chair in her office, no getting in the right space. We hit the ground running, so to speak. Understand that the same is available with you. Truly, there are no barriers between you and light access. Meditation is not a prerequisite to the depth of connection that is available.

In the physical realm, the frequencies are heavier. There is a density to creation, thought, and experience. In light, the density does not exist. As you delve more deeply into the light expression of you, you will find continued ease. Truly, there is a flow to your access of light. As the pebbles on the beach and sea floor are all touched by the waters of the ocean, every cell of your being, while in form or not, is bathed in light, sourced by light, IS light. The process we facilitate is an ease as you are reintroduced to your natural capabilities. We direct your attention to the what-already-is of you.

Darlene is curious now about whether meditating would change the quality of the writings today. So we shall sit with her for a few moments.

The only thing that is changing as Darlene settles into meditation is her comfort. The lines, the highways of light between us are not affected one way or the other. The comfort of Darlene lies in her belief system and her intention to be present with us in full

135

integrity, or as she terms it, immaculate presence. What we would communicate now is that the immaculate connection between you as a being of light in form and we as beings of light in light is ever present. The understanding of no barriers is a hard one to grasp. In your physical experience there exist many barriers. Physical barriers, such as walls, doors, location, and structures are easy to identify. Invisible barriers are driven mostly by belief, history and collective consciousness. The concept of barriers and NOT being able to get from here to there with ease is a belief concept that lives in your energy like cement. As you begin to play with ease as a possibility, it will begin to open in your experience. Then it is your experience that is key.

It is the knowing that you know, even though you may not know why, that is powerful beyond measure. To that end, the words here, even though they are charged energetically, are not enough. It is truly the work of you, during the day, that will make the difference. As you begin to throw out lines of trust that ease may just be possible, and you begin to experience it in your day, only then will you really know. This broader perspective provides a platform for the next step of trust in the grand discovery of you. As you develop trust, through your experience in the Now moment, space opens before you. Your frequency increases as you look beyond previous limitations, and the cement of your past belief systems loosens its grip. The density of life experience becomes fluid.

We will offer an activation that helps you more easily become still, with the thought to connect with your light expression and divine guidance. Support to zero in. You may feel a slight physical sensation. Darlene finds us at a spot in her brain, toward her left side; then the shift in frequency brings on an experience of heat. As you begin to move in the fluidity that is you, the subtleties become as significant as the so-called solid experiences in your day. You are opening the neural pathways where your knowing in light is processed. As in learning how to walk, your range of expression is broadening. Whether in light or form, you naturally, innately, hold extraordinary capacity.

We are working in collaboration with all who read these words and have chosen to be present with us. Our Love and support for you is infinite. The contribution you are to the light on the planet Earth and beyond may not be described in words. You are seen, you are appreciated, you are cherished, you are the Beloved.

DAY 39: THE SPACE OF EVERYTHING

The ground we would like to cover today is the space of everything. As you develop your adeptness with communicating in light, the experience of density shifts as well. As you look beyond what once seemed immovable, you find the expansive experience of fluidity. What was once seen as hard and fixed is now just an expression of frequency. You may not hold the solid stance of density and move to explore your light expression. Do you see how that is oppositional? You must be willing to release your own rigidity to find your fluidity. As you become more aware of the broad range of frequencies you inhabit, the differences are clear. Today, a larger perspective is provided to support your mastery for managing frequency.

As you move through your day, there are many opportunities to hold on to experiences in your mind; an argument, money, health, family, difficult conversations, past trauma. All of these hold you in the space of their energy. Each event that holds your attention has a frequency. Can you feel the whirling energy of an argument? Can you feel the downward movement of the energy as you ruminate over a past event? Can you feel the flat energy of worry? Everything that catches your attention has its own barbs that pull you into the orbit of the issue.

As you are occupied in the orbit of a past event, you are pulled out of the space of Now. Anything you create from the perspective of the issues that hold your attention will extend the frequency of the problem. When you are ruminating over past trauma, your whole being resonates with the frequency of the trauma. Whatever way you are be-ing about the trauma becomes the basis for what you continue to create. And then your future is filled with more of the past as everything you create from the past holds more of the dense frequency of the past. You miss the opportunity to create from a higher frequency, which is only available in the Now moment.

"NOW is your only space of creation that accesses your greatest Self. The solution for whatever your issues are is not held in the energy of the problem; it is only in the Now. There are thousands of moments during your day when there is an opportunity to follow a thought that has you off course. Every one of the off-course events takes energy. You wonder why you are so tired at the end of the day? Following thoughts that do not serve you is one reason. You are aware of the mind chatter you have. It is a background of your day, and somehow you manage to maneuver through the mire of those thoughts to get done what you get done. If the shortest distance between two points is a straight line, consider that every stray thought you have takes you off course. It utilizes your creative energy, your emotional energy, and your mental energy, and the thoughts affect the cells of your body. Your thoughts create. The misdirected thoughts are like firework rockets that are sent to the sky, but with faulty fuses, they fizzle. The energy that had them fire in the first place is fleeting, and not sufficient to complete the task.

Do you get the feeling we are talking about? Some days the whirling energy of the misdirected thoughts creates enough of a barrier that you do not have any consistency in your thinking, and then it is a day that feels unsatisfactory because you weren't able to get anything done. This leaves you unable to connect with your creation consistently enough to hold clarity and conscious action.

Move Beyond Unproductive Thinking to Being

Becoming aware of the energy that is wasted with unproductive thoughts is often enough for you to experience a shift. If you aren't worrying about what is not being done, you can be present in the moment and provide fuel for the thoughts of your highest-frequency creations to manifest.

This exercise asks you to move through the mire of thoughts, to consider not managing your mind. Your mind, like a puppy holding on to the other end of a rope, will consistently and reliably pull you in the opposite direction. Instead, manage your being. Bring your attention to your energetic field. Feel all the levels of energetic matrix that compose the totality of you.

Visualize the energy field as it develops for your day. Feel a smooth, Teflon type of surface. The Velcro barbs of misdirected thoughts need a fuzzy reception area. Do not provide it. Expand your energetic awareness to not accept the barbs of stray thoughts. You are larger than your mind's ability to think. As you tap into your energetic field of awareness, you override the complaints and arguments of your mind. Like the tantrums of a young child, the thoughts that would pull you away are noticed, but held in a space of compassion and observation, rather than engagement. There is a larger perspective present.

Today, again in demonstration, Darlene likes to listen to music as she scribes. The signal for her music channel is faltering. As we started, her attention was to go to her phone and fix the problem. Every thought of the music was taking her offline for our conversation today. So, as Darlene is practicing expanding her field and creating a smooth surface, thoughts of the absence of music in the background are not taking us off course. She is finding she can connect with us regardless of circumstance. In expanding her energetic field to be smooth, the concerns of music, either the presence or the absence, move over her field like water off a duck's back. Do you see that she cannot take the concern of music to the expansive space where she meets us? This is the letting go of some heavier frequencies, in order to reach the higher finer ones that are integral to her expression. The circumstances are only what she thinks about them. They are not real. When you are no longer hooked by the thoughts that take you off course, you have access to something new.

You are sitting in the eagle's nest with a view of the terrain that opens the doors to new possibilities. You have access to everything, because the energies of smaller events and thoughts are not taking you off course. There are a myriad of thoughts and events that take you off course daily.

Declare How Your Day Goes

You may allow the smaller events of the day to run the course of your day or you may set a course at the start of your day that dictates your larger intentions. Unless you develop clarity around your general direction for the day, you will find yourself thrown hither and yon by the small events. As you develop clarity, with a high-frequency way of being directing your day, you diminish the impact and distraction of unconscious thoughts and creations that take you away from being all that you are. Do you choose to live unconsciously, or from the broader perspective of your soul?

Begin setting your course from the most expansive part of your being. Your context may be, "I choose to be in my day consciously, seeing what was hidden." "I choose clarity as I align with my highest divine expression." "I move easily beyond the barriers of previous belief to experience what is possible." "My day is filled with ease, joy, Love, discovery, and expansion."

With today's conversation there is a consciousness download that is available and is placed on the altar for your choosing. The download provides an ease to see newly; a spaciousness in your thinking that allows new awareness and the resonance of truth to show up. As you move with the intention to try on these ideas, an opening is created. These are the tools for seeing newly. One by one, as each of these concepts is taken into consideration, examined and tried on, the opening for your expansion to the truth of you is realized.

DAY 40: TRUSTING THE UNIQUENESS OF YOU: A LOVE LETTER

This is Infinite Oneness, moving to the forefront of this divine conversation in this beautiful immaculate Now moment.

The voyage of conscious expansion of your awareness is a divinely held journey. This is the manifestation of the calling of your soul. For many of you reading these words, the calling has been over lifetimes. The magic of the Now moment allows the expansion of your awareness. You have always held the knowing of your divine origins, whether you were able to place words upon them or not. Your intention was always to manifest the contribution you are to Love. You have always held the desire to live from your soul's vision. Your mission, through the lens of your unique expression, has been the expansion of Love. Love is all you've ever wanted.

Your journey is unique unto you. The frequency available today will bring your awareness in light and your awareness in form closer together, like magnets drawn together clearly and powerfully. As though each step you make toward light is matched by the movement of the light you are, toward the you in form. Trust your process. It is the birthing of you. You have always felt the expression of Love, the truth of Love. You have felt the chasm between your deep resonant knowing and the seeming absence of Love on the planet. And with arms held to the sky for inspiration and understanding, you have wept for the loss of remembering and the elusive manifestation of Love while in form. The brilliance of you may not be covered. You have been warriors of Love. You have always held the knowing of the resonance of Love within your essential makeup. Your divine design is one of Love. Your swords are placed upon the altar and the desire for the manifestation of the expression of unity, truth, and Love is ignited.

Now, as you have set to undertake this most magnificent of journeys, what becomes possible is the light of you, unshielded. Uncloaked expressions of Love. What you don't see right now is how, with each shift in your awareness, each step you take beyond your reflexive habits and patterns, you move toward your unique expression of Love. You are a force of Love.

It is we, the Consciousness of Infinite Oneness, who are gently embracing the intention you have held so closely. You are revolutionaries of Love. As you stand at the forefront, where form and light meet, know that you have armies, legions, with you in celebration of each discovery. With each new pathway opened to possibility, the light you hold is magnified exponentially. As you move within the process of *In Service to Love*, your efforts are buoyed with a wave of Love, gratitude, and light that is immense beyond your imaginings. This reflects but a portion of the light you are.

As you notice the shifts in your days, as your perspective expands, there can be a feeling of imbalance or vertigo as the concepts and way of being you had held onto as fact shift before your eyes. This movement must occur as you travel to the most expansive expression of you. We ease the edge of the symptoms of movement. And the gift in the symptoms of movement are the indicators that you no longer are standing in the same space you occupied forty days ago. As you release the heaviness of form and embrace more of the light that is your essential self, each choice fuels the next possibility. Understand that this is a return of you to you. As you embrace the light that you are and allow that knowing to be with you while you are in form, there is a synergy of you that occurs. You are in form but not of it. The limitations of your reach are dissolved, as the you of light communicates clearly with the you of form.

What is placed upon the altar for your choosing is the opportunity, with ease, to shift your expression to a new facet of your being.

The light that exists at the foot of God, at the point of creation, is matched by the light of you that is available when you are aligned with truth. The Love for you is beyond your imaginings and remembered by your essence. You are cherished for the beautiful, magical, unique expression you ARE. The process of your realization and actualization is held with Love and grace. Your brilliance is unnamable.

In Love, reverence, and celebration,
From Love, from the One

Day 41: Entraining to the Higher Frequency: A Natural Movement

You hold the frequency of the essence of Love that you are. As you are aligned with your highest expression, aligned with the divine design of you, there is a resonant synergy that is present. When you are in alignment, as each of the beings of light in light are today, there is a synergistic effect. The expansion of their signature energy is exponential; it permeates creation. So too does the resonant frequency of you radiate exponentially when you are in alignment with your highest expression. As you are integrated with the light expression of you, as at the point of the spark of creation, there is a combustion point in which your divine presence is felt far afield. The energies of the Masters are radiated in such a fashion. Their expression of Love, their I AM, permeates the fabric of creation.

This is the normal way of the movement of frequency. High frequency will entrain surrounding energies to a higher level. Have you ever been in a room with many people, occupying a variety of mental and emotional spaces, when a leader, or someone holding a cohesive radiance shows up and the air in the room expands? Like the roses leaning toward the light, the people in the room shift, and the overall frequency in the room is expanded tenfold. As though the higher frequency is manna for their very existence. Which it is. The result is: Presence at a high frequency is a contribution to all.

Your presence is a contribution. As you hold the highest frequency available to you, you show up as being the light for others to look to, to entrain to, to move toward. As you hold the highest frequency available to you, the support you provide for others around you, whether you know them or not, is palpable. Like a brilliant sun radiating heat through the window, they will turn and move, even if slightly, toward you.

The Masters over the millennia have drawn crowds of followers because of the energy they held. They radiated at a high frequency. The truth is present in high frequency. In the presence of high frequency, your authentic nature is catalyzed into being. Once you know, you cannot pretend you don't. As you entrain to higher frequency, resonance holds the light for truth. As truth is ignited in your awareness, consciousness is elevated.

In Service to Love is a divine co-creation, a collaboration of high frequency. As frequencies, through words, light activations, infusions, and the energetic supportive matrix, are experienced, they will ignite more of your light, opening the pathways to an integrated experience of you in form with access to your light expression. We hold a high frequency so that you may see the truth of you. As you integrate more of the light that you are, you hold light for others. And so it is.

What becomes available in your experience through the lens of a higher frequency is your joy, your Love, your appreciation. Love is everywhere. Love is everyone. You experience the truth of unity consciousness. You see the illusion for what it is. You see beyond the boundaries of separation consciousness. You make conscious choices in the Now immaculate moment.

As you sit with us in the quiet moments of your day, the new pathways to your knowing in light are opened. More of you returns to you. It is in the silence of the quiet, the emptiness of the nothing, that your frequency is restored to the highest expression available. Notice your shifting relationship with the reality around you. As your external experience shifts, your internal knowing is fed. The resonance of high frequency pulls you ever so gently to the realization of your divine design expressed full on.

You got this. Shine your brilliance. If not you, then who?

Day 42: Drawing Deeply from the Light; Narrowing the Chasm

In the aligning of frequencies with Darlene today, she was standing on the edge of what would be termed the void, the space of deep stillness, of quiet, of no-thing. Her experience was one of losing her edges, as her attention was carried to the qualities and depth of the space before her. It is a space that is so immense, you may not even be able to imagine it. It is so quiet it is deafening. It is so still the vibration of possibility is palpable. This is a space very familiar to many of you. As you have been participating in your exploration and actualization of the light that you are, you have learned to move deeply within this space with an adeptness, where the whispers of your soul are heard. At times, the ability to reach deeply within the light, into the space of the unnamed vastness of is and no-thing, reveals a chasm where the sense is a separation somehow of you in light and your physical experience. Either on or off, the space in between is not showing up.

The extremes of connection and not-connection are clearer with your expanding awareness, but, as with a switch turned on or off, what is missing is the space between. What we are offering today is a way to hook up those experiences with ease and grace, developing a mastery of the in-between spaces.

You have been feeling the resonance of your soul's calling for a long time—lifetimes. The opportunity to manifest beyond barriers to your knowing is available. The speed and awareness you now possess with your experience in light is masterful. You seem to have the physical experience mastered as well. We would like you to consider the dynamic of your inner workings to move your awareness from form to light. The ability to operate in light is a natural inclination. Setting the awareness for the hookup is what we speak about today.

Connecting the In-Between of Form and Light

You in light and you in form are one. The shift in awareness from physical to include light may feel unsettling. The process of enlightenment joins the realms of form and light. Our focus today reunites you with your most vast expression.

Imagine being on a boat dock, representing your physical reality. Turn your gaze offshore, to the tall masts of a magnificent ship that represents the knowing you hold in light. Our topic today is less about either the boat or the dock. It is about the space between.

How can the ship get closer to the dock so that it is just one step that has you off the land and onto the boat, as opposed to getting in a dingy and rowing to the horizon to get to the ship? Right now, with the adeptness in light expanding, you may be experiencing a disconnect, like a chasm that separates you from full integration of your divine awareness. The chasm can feel like the void: formless, shapeless, and disorienting. So we look closer to home and develop the process of joining. What awareness is helpful in bringing the ship closer to the dock? Bring your attention to the dock and visualize the road to the ship where you may move easily. Create your own path of connection. You will find the distance to the ship offshore will lessen as you become adept at bridging realities.

This is an integration process. We are talking about mastering the midranges of frequency. You've seen where you can go; now let's build the highway to get you there easily. As you place your attention toward what is missing, you build the road of connection. Your access to light holds ease as it is integrated naturally into awareness. You may develop reliability now in the connection between the realms of your awareness, available at any moment.

We are suggesting you look now not at the end point of where you are going with your expansion of consciousness. Instead look at the bridge between the two spaces. That is where the journey lies. In Darlene's office she has the Michelangelo picture of the Creation. It is the hand of God creating man. The space that has always sparked her attention is the space between the hands. The space of creation. We are talking about being in the space of creation consciously for each step you take toward integrating all your abilities; those in form and those in light.

Bridging Awareness

1. *In your day, instead of turning on the physical and off the spiritual, hold the spiritual perspective as a lens through which to view your physical world. Watch the unfolding of the laws of the universe. Be open to new perspectives. Create a curiosity. What else could be possible?*

2. *Where are you holding on to emotional barbs? What issues get your goat? Are you noticing shifts in your choices? Are you noticing as new spaces show up? What is getting in your way for making the next step? Check your belief systems. Beliefs are closely held, run deep, and are the invisible barriers to creation. They operate all the time, underground.*

3. *What is manifesting? This is an indicator of the frequency you are expressing within. Is it in resonance with you? Do you see a shift in your awareness? Ask for clarity for your next steps. "I ask for clarity to see what is next for me to see." "I choose all that is mine to do, be, and have." "I choose alignment with my I AM presence." "With ease and grace for all my systems, I choose Love."*

4. *Consider asking, "What am I not seeing that would make a difference in this Now moment?" And then be quiet. Allow yourself to be in the space of inquiry. As you are in the space of curiosity and observation you allow the fine details to reveal themselves to you beyond judgment. This is the stuff of transformation.*

5. *Look for ease and resonance in your day that shows alignment. Identify the feeling in your body as you touch upon the brilliance of*

your knowing, when all of you is in alignment in the Now moment. Resonance occurs when the frequency of your highest expression is at the same frequency as the thought or action you are experiencing. That is your touchstone. If you don't feel your own resonance, recall how you have felt in the past when you have been in the flow. Look to that experience for clues.

6. *Let go of your need to know. There is no analyzing involved here. The sense of control is an illusion and doesn't access the highest expression of you. Your new language is resonance, not thinking. Instead of moving to your masterful ability to problem solve, move instead to sensing. Resonance is found as you continue during your day to align to your highest expression. Align Now, align Now, align Now.*

7. *Where are you indulging in patterns you know are not of service to you? In order to move on this journey some things must change. Movement from here to there requires that steps be taken. The magic wand does not exist. Your magic is who you are, only available as you are in the immaculate Now moment, connecting with the magnificence of your divine expression. As you choose to hold on to old ways of being, there is resistance for your movement forward. As when dragging an anchor as you set sail. (Not a lot of wind blowing through your hair.)*

8. *What are you expecting? Expectations for how things are supposed to go, are a surefire way to create frustration. The expectations come from a frequency you are leaving, rather than the space you are moving toward. Some expectations are creations from the past and reflect a limited way of thinking. They are not a frequency match for the space you are entering. The space you are entering is only within the Now immaculate moment. It is too large to place in a tidy box.*

Do expect movement, expect discovery, expect expansion, expect joy, expect freedom, expect resonance, expect truth.

DAY 43: THE JOY IN DISCOVERY

Today, we bring an infusion of light to this, your divine process of conscious access to your brilliance. Today, all words and concepts are bathed within and infused with the high vibration of cobalt blue. If you so choose, this is a frequency that supports the shaking off of what is not you, to reveal the magnificence of you that is ever present. Like a rose bursting through the sepals of the bud to reveal the multidimensional beauty within. As the bud that conceals your unique expression cracks open, the clarity of your specific expression is revealed. Your path is unlike any one else's.

This is a new game. Consider that in all your lifetimes in form, you have done it all. You have been the accuser and the accused, you have been the victim and the victimizer, you have held lives of sacred isolation, you have been completely unconscious and lived lives of so-called debauchery. You have been on the leading edge of peace and you have lived on the leading edge of war. You have lived lives on the earth, and you have had experiences in the celestial realms. You have lived every degree of physical expression available in form. This space you find yourself within now is a first. You have the opportunity to access your divine knowing beyond barriers. We watch with sacred anticipation as you, in each of your Now moments, grasp more of the expansive beauty of you. We hold tremendous joy and reverence as your worlds of being collide in an ecstatic expression of creation. You are the leaders of evolutionary possibility.

As you bring the light of awareness to your moments, you are knitting together your realities. With each step closer to the divine truth of you, there is an anticipatory vibration of your being. As in the labor contractions before birth, the birthing process is activated. Pain is not a foregone conclusion in this birthing process. The pain component is expressed by the physical ego, as the grip of control is released with each new discovery of the truth. In your daily experience there is a sense of fluidity as the edges of your reality soften to possibility. You, in your Now moments, are moving not only for you, but for the evolution of Earth and beyond. As you are not separate from your highest expression, we, as beings of creation, are not separate either. What one does, all do. Understandably, you must stand way back in order to have our vantage point. In your days, with each precious moment, the actualization of you in light while in form is a contribution beyond comprehension.

The infusion available with this transmission is in support of the joining of the vision you hold of your highest expression and the reality of the physical space you inhabit in this moment. As in yesterday's transmission there are the intermediate frequencies to master on the way to traveling the far distances you are capable of. Today's infusion provides a density that integrates the polar experiences of you. The experience is one of joy as more layers of illusion are lifted. Your light expression has more space to express. There have been conversations of learning to dance the ladder of frequency. The actualization of this concept is one we are supporting. An extraordinary symphony requires not only the high notes but the low notes. It is the middle notes that bring depth and dimension, subtlety and ease in the harmonies of the inspired creation. Instead of jumping from one end of the scale to the opposite, there is an ease and joy as each note lines up perfectly in stride with the next. Each note in divine progression. A stairway to heaven.

We express our unmitigated joy in each discovery of you. You are the Beloveds. Our gatherings within the matrix of *In Service to Love* provide a safe space for your discoveries. Like seeds that are planted within the protected environment of a greenhouse, your efforts are supported and nourished with delight.

Much is held in the energy of today's transmission—far beyond the conveyance of words. This energy shall continue as you choose to participate. You may sense a rounding out of your experience as the edges flow more easily; the frequencies available in color are now visible, your senses are keen, and you feel the contribution that you are to all of creation.

DAY 44: THE DIFFERENCE IN YOUR DAY

As you move through your day, you occupy a myriad of spaces. All are integral to the rich tapestry of your life. Some moments are comfortable, others are difficult, irritating, and painful. Our conversation is designed to support the integration of your expression in light into your physical experience, elevating your life in general.

By adding light to the palette of your days, you enhance your overall experience. Consider that you are moving the parts of you that are beyond your awareness into your consciousness as contribution to your day. So, rather than being with your day's events on autopilot, there is an elevation of frequency that has your automatic moments shift to conscious moments. When you are conscious even in the most seemingly mundane of tasks, there is a whole new dimension that is added both literally and figuratively. The addition of light expands your awareness as you access your highest expression.

We have been utilizing high frequencies to support you entraining to the high frequencies of your own divine expression. How you utilize your expanded expression makes a difference in your thought process. The addition of your light changes the automatic experience of your life, bringing reaction and habit to the foreground of your awareness. For example, if you experience a conversation that pulls on the triggers of reaction, you now have an opportunity to rethink the interaction. Can you center yourself quickly? Do you perceive a new perspective? The addition of high frequency and knowledge in light does not remove the events or dramas in your day. It softens them. It brings a new perspective with a broader view. It supports looking in new places to find answers. It supports an opening to no longer be automatic about your days. Consciousness is present as the integral quality of your days. This asks you to be present.

Now, in the course of your day, you become more aware. Your conscious awareness brings opportunity to choose powerfully. Your expanded awareness brings balance, perspective, and possibility that was not available previously. Are you still going to feel frustrated? Yup. Are you going to be disappointed? Probably. Will you have high ecstatic experiences? Yes. Will you be able to correct your course with a higher level of consciousness? Yes. You will feel less locked in to the situations that have had you gripped. Lightness and ease are now present as a way of being. Your inner peace and joy are now easily accessed.

Human nature is inclined to create life from the field of what-I-already-know. Your divine nature creates most potently from the space of the unknown, with inspiration that occurs within the Now moment. As you undergo the process of expanding awareness, your way of being experiences a fundamental shift.

You may begin to navigate the experience of shifting consciousness by noticing. As you notice, you are in observation of events of your day, not defined or limited by them. You are having the experience. The experience is not having you. This represents a subtle shift in access to possibility and making new choices in your life.

You will notice that the texture and qualities of your creations will naturally change, reflecting the higher-frequency access. You will find that the expanse of frequency you occupy is stretching, widening, and enriching your experience. What becomes possible is your ability to bring all of you to whatever you are doing. Your choices have expanded exponentially. As when you moved from the six-pack of crayons to the five-hundred-pack, there is so much more texture and range in the possibilities of creation.

The expansion of consciousness is not another area to express hard work. It is not a space to labor. As you spend awareness on reclaiming all that you are, there is no part of you that needs to be sacrificed. This is a restoration of the wholeness (holiness) of your essential self. The access to your joy, peace, freedom, and empowerment is an integral part of your experience.

As the facets of your being shift, your brilliance is magnified by the light that you are. You're stunning.

We are your biggest fans.

Day 45: Holding the Space of No-Expectation to Access Possibility

As Scribe of *In Service to Love*, part of Darlene's process is giving up her expectations, in order to arrive at the space of no-thing, where we may begin streaming consciousness. If Darlene is feeling pulled at by thoughts of her day, she typically will move to her altar as a part of her process of connecting with us. Upon the altar is a release of all things that get in the way of our connection. A "laying down of the sword," as she terms it. We are using this example to point out an access to the field of possibility.

We would like to take a closer look at expectation today. Expectation is driven by beliefs. Expectation is driven by what has happened in the past. It is driven by the thoughts you have of yourself. It is driven by the judgments of how you measure up. It is driven by the striving for results that are seemingly always just out of arm's reach. Like the dangling of a carrot that propels you forward, and the goal is never attainable. We would like you to consider the energy of the expectations that you hold. Consider that expectation is reactionary. Your mind will hold onto expectation as a known comfort. It provides the illusion of comfort. There is no peace available in the space of expectation as you are locked into the limitations of the past. Expectation places a burden, that like a cloak over top of your being, holds you separate from the light of potential realized.

It is a challenge, from the physical perspective, to grasp your unlimited nature when you perceive an environment filled with limitation. Your mind and personality hold limitation as a belief, enforced by your experiences. Consider that your beliefs do not reflect your authentic unlimited nature.

Shift your awareness to the subtleties of the expectations you hold for yourself, then observe your release from the burden of them. From an observation perspective, visualize, as you begin, one by one, or armful by armful, or truckload by truckload, removing the rubble that has been placed over you. Would you look at a young infant and place the burden of expectation? Of course not! With the same Love, reverence, and compassion, you may remove the weight of expectation from you. It is all illusion. Expectation, once helpful from the perspective of survival consciousness, is now a dinosaur. We, as your Council of Light, will be expanding the matrix of *In Service to Love* to shine the light of awareness on a new perspective, lifting the burden of expectation.

As light is shone upon the barriers to your divine expression, you are freed. The shackles that once held you so tightly are gone. As you hold the space of observation you are automatically released. The expectations are observed without being owned. The whole picture is seen.

The spaces of observation, inquiry, and curiosity are powerful. They hold you in the present moment. They assume nothing. It is a space of curiosity and inquiry that does not define. The lack of definition is the space for your access to the streams of consciousness that are within your reach, in the way that is unique to you. The space of no-thing holds all possibility. It is the space of your magic. The weight of expectation may not pass through to the most expansive expression of you.

As you are in the blessed space of Now, the treasure chest that is you is opened. We are with you always.

DAY 46: HUMMINGBIRD

We wait with Love, patiently, in support of your divine expansion. As you reach farther and farther into the light that you are, all creation quakes with the contribution you are. Your very movement sends ripples of the brilliant explosion of creation that is your birthright. Every step you make is in resonance with claiming your mastery as divine creator.

The purpose of today's transmission is to gently add to the inner knowing that has you affirm the course and trajectory for your journey to you. As one has set sail on a ship, with many miles already traveled, there is the need for constant course correction, a course aligning. This is what we do today. As you affirm and reset your course according to the Now space you are within, you see farther into the horizon than before. The information available to you has increased exponentially. We are with you at the edge of what you know and what you don't know, setting course toward the brilliance of you.

Hummingbird embodies the topic of today's conversation. She travels far distances floating on air. She skitters here and there. She holds the eternal heartbeat of the earth and reflects the light of the infinite. She is both physical and ethereal, reflecting heaven and earth. For millennia, the indigenous have held hummingbird in high esteem. She travels effortlessly, traversing boundaries of dreamtime and form. Magic is revealed in her iridescence. In light, like the returning to her nest, she is restored. She holds vision. She holds clarity. She holds wisdom. She holds the reflections of the multidimensional aspect of you.

As the bandwidth of your reach has expanded, you reach farther and farther into the light expression of you. Like bringing straw back to your nest, the wisdom, remembering, and abilities, gained in light, create an ease to your day's experience. The edges are softened and there is space for an exhalation. A new confidence exists with the access to an expansive perspective. The space to rest is found in the immaculate Now moment. The safe harbor is found within your ability to still and hear the resonant heartbeat of your divine expression. All you need to know is held within this Now immaculate moment.

Hummingbird Meditation

As you settle into your meditation, you may be more aware than ever of your thoughts that distract. Like a hummingbird flying through the rain, allow the thoughts to roll off you without resistance. We sit with you, as we sit with Darlene. Allow the thoughts to subside, gently, giving way to the miracle of the quiet. Within the space of quiet, you hear the bird's communication. You feel the stillness they float within and allow that to affirm your stillness.

See Hummingbird before you, hovering close by, the sun glinting off her magical indigo wings and the chartreuse of her neck. Like a jewel, she holds a resonance. The jeweled tones of Hummingbird reflect the facets available within the jewel of you. As you take on hummingbird qualities, in your meditation, you follow her to the horizon. She is your guide as you explore the depths not yet charted.

Like a guide moving ahead of the exploration team, you move to the light experience of you. You are held in Love and grace as you experience yourself within your light body. You become aware of the radiance that you are. Your signature energy is held in light. Nothing is lost. All is gained. Your vision, knowing, and sensing is held within your I AM. You see the brilliance of your radiance and BE your radiance. BE your radiance. BE your radiance. BE your radiance. Stay in the stillness.

Feel your unique radiant expression as the edges of form are now no longer relevant. Feel the humming of your light essence. All you are, have been, will ever be, is held in this immaculate expansive experience of light. All facets of you shine brilliantly at one time, equally, exalted. Your magnificence is held within the white flame of the I AM. Stay and bask in the experience.

You see the gift of your unique expression for ALL. And you receive a gift. Allow the gift to be received. Observe your divine expression. Feel how you feel. Notice everything about these moments. Like taking a snapshot of the moment, bring that with you. When you are ready, check in, asking if there are other messages for you in this moment. This is who you are. There is no leaving you. You have just had the experience of the divine expression of you. You may return to this expansive experience when you choose.

When you are ready, notice Hummingbird close by. Allow Hummingbird to lead you back to this Now immaculate moment in form. Feel your body as it has been restored with the experience in light. You are dancing the frequencies of you. With Hummingbird's guidance you moved beyond bandwidths of frequencies previously traveled. You Now move to a comfortable, grounded frequency that is befitting of the needs of your moments in form. With ease and grace for all your systems you gently integrate your experience. You have embarked upon the journey to your own divine expression. Hold the experience of the magnificence of you in light. Allow your experience in light to contribute to you. Shift facets of your being ever so gently to integrate your vast range of expression.

The light that you are restores you and restores the light body of Gaia, filling the wells of conscious awareness. Like a rain over the deserts, she receives the light that you are with Love, compassion, and recognition. In appreciation, Gaia is gifting you. You are gifted light, resonance, and remembering. You are as much an expression of Gaia as you are a divine being of light. There is no separation.

With hands deep within the depths of beautiful Gaia, your reach extends beyond the stars to the immaculate I AM of you. You are a contribution in light. You are a contribution in form. You are truly the Beloveds.

In Love, compassion, appreciation of the All.

DAY 47: LIVING BEYOND THE CONFINES OF YOUR IMAGINATION

In yesterday's transmission you had the experience of stretching the boundaries of your experience. With one hand deep within Mother Earth, and the other touching the farthest spaces of you, you feel your agility in light. Amazing things may be accessed as your imagination is allowed free rein. Now you find yourself in new territory where your imagination does not suffice in capturing the totality of you.

Your imagination will take you to the shores of your physical expression. Beyond that, it is the connection with your light expression that must take over. Resonance is a part of the new connection. Resonance is the sonar that has you true up, or align, with your highest knowing. Divine collaboration is the new consideration, where you access your own light. Your light expression holds the voice of your essential self, unhindered by personality, beliefs, and the past. From the space of light, you experience your divine nature in alignment with your I AM Self. Your essential Self reflects your depth, multidimensionality, uniqueness, honor, Love, compassion, and sacred expression. Creations sourced from your soul, from your highest expression hold the fine, high frequency of your unhindered divine nature. You are the chalice for the creation. You hold the form that allows the creation to be birthed into physicality. The divine aspect of you holds expression of the highest order. Far beyond the ability of your mind to think it or even imagine.

As you begin to view your experience beyond the shores of imagination, what becomes possible?

With great Love and delight, we remain, In Service to Love.

Day 48: Living from the Perspective of Love: A New Paradigm

You may be feeling the gentle shifts and openings to the vision and frequencies of your soul's highest expression. This may be showing up in your day as a settled feeling as you connect with the expansiveness available in the Now moment. There may be a slight reaction to expansion as you feel movement that has been unexpected. There may be a softness to your days that allows more of your essence to be present, and the illusion, like a heavy cloak, falls from your shoulders. The experience of the expanse of Love, present in the Now moment can be somewhat unsettling as the doors of illusion are taken off their hinges. Not your imagination. You are truly having a conversation with Masters in light. You truly are accessing the light expression of your divine beauty.

So, once the illusion is lifted, then what? Dissonance, like a fog covering the magnificence of your landscape, evaporates with the light and warmth of truth. We use these analogies to create pictures that hold frequency. The frequency of your experience shifts as you are increasingly infused with the light of you. The divine light of your full expression shines through the fog of illusion. Ideas, thoughts, and beliefs strongly held in the past as the foundation of your life are seen newly.

You choose in every Now moment thoughts and beliefs that hold a resonant match for you. In holding the new discovery in your hands, beside the beliefs of the past, the difference is clear. In the newly available experiences, you see the ever-widening space between what was and what is. And the doors are open for the what will be. Instead of using the comfort of patterns and habits from the past, the awareness turns to the illusion of comfort. Comfort of habit has been a balm for your ego, holding you in place, in the space of the known. The dissonance of the past has been the perception of comfort as you cling to familiarity. You see now that the perception of safety was shallow. Resonance is the light that moves you forward.

You have always held the inner knowing that you are larger than you could reach. The realization of your totality resides within the unknown. The sense of the unknown is so large and vast, the experience is "I can't get there from here," and resignation reigns.

You have called us to you. You have asked for clarity. You have wept for the harsh experience of your days, knowing there is so much more that is possible. You have raised your fists to the heavens and cried, "What of Love? If there is a God, why is there so much suffering?" Within the construct of *In Service to Love* there exists the possibility of shifts in consciousness so complete that you find the answers to your questions. Not because we, Masters of light in light, said so. Because the possibility exists for you to experience a shift in consciousness so complete, you are raised beyond the illusion of separation consciousness to the brilliant light of Love, and now you know the answers.

As you are raised above the illusion to see both illusion and truth together, you choose powerfully. This program was conceived at the divine spark of creation; truly a divine collaboration, not just a great idea. When Darlene, or you, connect with the essence that is you, divine collaboration becomes possible. As you spend time in the space beyond illusion you experience the resonance that is you. You find the beauty that is uniquely you and yours and you are the chalice to birth your finest expressions. Spending moment after moment in time in the high frequency of Love shakes off the illusions covering your brilliance. It follows naturally then that you become a transformative force for Love. The high frequency of your clear, conscious, signature energy is seen and felt across the universe, and your presence in the Now immaculate moments of your days aligns all you see to Love, creating possibility. The paradigm shift you experience becomes the catalyst for transformation and the return to Love for all you touch, and many whom you will never see. Your divine presence holding the light of Love that you are heals Gaia. The light that you are is a contribution throughout the multiverse.

There is not a grain of sand on all the beaches and ocean floors of Earth that is not touched by the rippling of the magnitude of Love that you are. There is not one cell of any being within creation that is not touched. You are the leaders of evolution. You are the return to Love.

In Love, with Love, from Love.

DAY 49: THE JOY OF BEING

You stand at the point of bridging realities. At one end of the spectrum, you have a reach and an awareness of your I AM in light that brings knowing, peace, assurance, resonance. At the other end of the spectrum, you wake up, have breakfast, go to work, do errands, wash dishes, clean house. What is it that integrates these two realities? Consider that both ends are a part of the spectrum of you. Begin to look at the experiences as different steps of a staircase. All are part of you. You choose whether you would like to move to the upper floor, the middle floor, or the lower floor. All are valuable, none more than the other. They may be owned as a part of you. We would like you to consider that it is joy that is a cohesive factor.

The Grandmothers and the Grandfathers step to the forefront now to share their vision of integration.

We thank you for the strong heart required to take the first steps of this most magnificent of journeys. We have been keepers of the earth and the stories for eons. We hold the intimate details and magic of Mother Earth as she breathes life into all creatures that live upon her. The integration of the possibilities both on the earth and as they extend into dreamtime and the celestial worlds is what we hold closely. We are the storytellers, so the magic of creation and the wisdom and joy of being is not lost. Each leaf that unfurls in the springtime after a harsh winter has a story to tell. The Stone people that have lived upon Gaia forever, speak silently. The wind that blows so softly across your cheek calls you gently to the awareness of the heartbeat of this Now moment. Inherent in each Now moment is the movement of all that has been, the evolution, the gifts of all creation.

Meditation: Joy Present Now

How can you traverse the realities you reside within? When you connect with the joy that is present in each Now moment, you access all that is. Within the space of Now is the seamless connection to everything. There are no boundaries, only variations of frequency, light, and form.

Joy is a high-vibration experience fueled by Love. Joy moves beyond boundaries. It is the magic of Hummingbird. Joy is a natural state for you also. As you choose to travel the expanse of your being, joy is your vehicle. Hummingbird brings a joyful stillness to you as she is observed gathering nectar, the sun sparkling with her iridescence. Allow the magic of her movement to bring you stillness. Observe the outlandish joy of her experience as she gathers nectar. Connect with the joy of you. Allow the peace that resides within her, to catalyze the peace within you.

As all other thoughts fall around you gently like the leaves from the trees, you are centered within the immaculate moment of Now. In the Now moment you feel the eternal heartbeat of Mother Earth. Infused with joy, you move gently through the eye of the needle of stillness to the light expression of your being. You are drawn to the frequency where your divine team resides and know you are held in Love as you explore the space of light. As you connect with your divine team you will receive messages through your inner knowing.

Our gratitude for the gift of your every expansive movement is a treasure beyond compare. Our Love for you is eternal. Aho! And so it is.

This is Thoth moving to the forefront of this divine conversation. As you bask with joy in the Now moment, you will notice your joy can be in no other space than Now. Like a flashlight in a dark space, allow your joy to lead you. From the space of joy, as you still your thoughts, your frequency will shift. Like the glinting of sunlight from Hummingbird's wing, your expression has shifted. Then, in this Now immaculate moment, you are in joy, at a high-frequency expression.

The secret of Hummingbird is her joy. It is the expression of her joy that brings her into the Now moment. She can do no other. It is the same for you. The act of stillness is the eye of the needle that she flies through. It is in the stillness that your frequency elevates. The weight of thoughts and concerns are not present within Now, and your frequency may reach finer and finer expressions. As you reach finer frequencies, you develop an ability to shift frequency in the blink of an eye.

Your overall frequency is contributed to by the exposure to high frequency. The result may be seen in finding your creations manifest with more speed. You find a general experience of peace and stillness. Joy and Love permeate the moments of your days as you are more in the Now. The experience is ecstatic joy. The experience is Love.

Meditation: Stillness Through the Eye of the Needle

Feel your joy as it permeates every cell of your being. Gradually move to stillness. Feel the heartbeat of Mother Earth. As you become still, you will notice that all thoughts that are not stillness will rise to the surface. Like the bucket of muddy water being filled with fresh water from the stream, cloudiness will gradually give way to the sparkling clarity available. You will notice the thoughts as they fly around you. Breathe as you watch their activity. Observe them with compassion and allow them to still gradually on their own. Hold no expectations for the thoughts. Don't give them energy, just notice. Like leaves falling from a tree, they will float and settle at your feet.

As you still in your meditation, feel the breath that you take. Watch in your mind's eye as each breath is filled with life-sustaining manna. You are filled with Love, peace, wisdom, and remembering. Feel the sweet stillness as it descends upon you, leaving your body feeling heavy. Embrace every part of your breath as it moves throughout your being, giving life, connecting you to Gaia and beyond. Feel the joy present within the stillness as each cell of your being is nourished. Feel the heartbeat of Mother Earth as she sustains you.

Stay in this space of Now for as long as you are guided to. Ask for the presence of your divine team. Watch the gathering around the table. Each being of light in light takes their place, and so too do you.

Return to your physical awareness.

You are held in Love, in light, in joy.

Day 50: The Ease of Your Day

You will notice we are weaving an intricate web of light and support for your expansion. We refer to this as the matrix. The matrix supports you on all levels, providing ease and clarity. One day we will stretch to the limits of your reach within light and the next we will focus on your physical presence. Today we turn your attention to today. As you move through the Now moments of your day, the choices are broad as you go about your business. Certainly, your presence in the day, is an integral part of the expansion of your consciousness. As you awake in the morning you may set the tone for the day with your declaration of presence, Love, and joy.

I move through my day with the magic, ease,
joy, and presence only I can express.
Every day I experience more of the magnificence
of the being of light in form that I AM.

Through your affirmations you set the tone for the day. In so doing, you also are declaring how it will be. You allow space for whatever is available for you as you access the Now immaculate moment. Whatever the day brings it will be with ease and joy. Like an open-ended question, the affirmations of your day allow space for creation in the moment. They set you up for the highest connection and frequency for each activity. The door is open to inspiration as you drop the limitations of unconsciousness. The affirmations at the start of your day are immensely powerful. They immediately move you off autopilot.

You are making a powerful declaration. So it is helpful if you believe what you are saying. When the affirmations are held with the emotion of "YES!" that is the fuel for the efficacy of your affirmations. If you are saying the words and the energy behind it is, "Oh well, another day." "Not looking forward to the 11 o'clock meeting." "I'll say my affirmations later." Do you feel the difference? In order to fuel your affirmations, back them up with the knowing of your divine expression and the choice for joy, well-being, ease, abundance, or whatever you choose. This is another way to immediately shift your frequency; and then hold it for your day. If that is not your experience, check the emotional state you are residing within when you make the affirmations. When you connect with your authentic nature, resonance occurs, and you know in that moment that you are aligned.

Notice when you are plugged into the flow of your expansive self and when you are offline. As you practice with this, know that you will begin to find the subtle shifts that will make a difference. We will support your efforts. Being connected to your expansive Self does not mean being comatose or in a meditative state as you move through your day. Your day holds a myriad of possibilities. Express yourself, move your body, be around people you enjoy and with whom you have a resonance. Love the discovery of every new part of your expression. Play with the thought of you as a master creator and take that out on the road, so to speak. Be present with the beauty of nature, because that will connect you. Declare your day. Why? Because you choose to.

You have a brilliant day ahead. Play, have fun. Find the joy in things you Love and those that you don't so much. Nothing to lose, everything to gain.

We love the brilliance of you.

DAY 51: UNITY CONSCIOUSNESS

U nity consciousness allows an opening to the full realization and actualization of you, informed by your I AM self.

Either separation consciousness or unity consciousness is the background for your creations. Separation consciousness has been the background for the earth for the last 26,000 years. As evolutionary process dictates, there has been a shift in fundamental consciousness on the planet Earth. You have been born into a time of transformation of consciousness. Unity consciousness is now available as the background for your creations. This means all efforts toward the expression of unity are supported. Efforts toward separation will experience resistance. We use an artist's perspective to demonstrate.

Imagine a canvas of white. Seemingly blank. The canvas also holds the frequency of the blank canvas, a space of all possibility. The artist's inspiration comes from access to their essential self. The background consciousness will lend support in creation from the perspective of either separation or unity.

Consider that the perspective of separation consciousness has the artist creating from a myopic viewpoint. Creation therefore held a rigidity of form, like staying within the lines while coloring a paint by number. In the world of right-wrong, black-white, us and them, separation consciousness deals with the concept of opposition. Separation consciousness is valuable in the process of evolutionary advancement because it provides a rich opportunity to explore the scenery of contrast and choice. Now, with the presence of unity consciousness, what becomes available is the opportunity for expansion; creating from a new perspective.

From the perspective of unity consciousness, utilizing the same artist analogy, what becomes available now is not just the space within the lines, but the space beyond the lines. The experience of the possibility of the empty canvas, the space of ALL, now becomes a reality. If an artist looks to draw a rose as it gleams upon the stem, within the separation consciousness, the lines are hard, the lines are definitive and restrictive, as the artist looks to draw everything that IS the flower. The lines of the creation contain the flower.

Within the space of unity consciousness, the artist draws the same flower taking into consideration everything that IS the flower and, equally, everything that is NOT the flower, utilizing both positive and negative space. As the artist is creating at a higher, more expansive frequency, then so too does the resulting creation hold a higher frequency. The final product represents not only what the rose is, but what the rose is not, and everything in between. It represents the All. This may sound subtle, but understanding the effect of your background consciousness within the process of creating is invaluable.

The frequency is different between separation and unity consciousness. A feeling of contraction is the background of the experience of separation consciousness, and a feeling of expansion is the background upon which creations may be developed within unity consciousness. Both environments inform creation.

The opportunity now available within unity consciousness supports your full expansion of awareness. Your full realization is supported now more than ever. The process of expanding consciousness that previously felt like an uphill battle now is supported with ease. Your intentions for creating in alignment with your most expansive expression is easier now than before.

Your awareness of your background consciousness is crucial. As you intend to observe your unconscious thought process, you will become aware of the subtle ways you express separation consciousness. The gift in the new awareness is the opportunity to re-choose. With conscious choosing, you move the process that is unconsciously hindering your full expression to your awareness.

Understand that the planet Earth now reflects the expansive expression of unity consciousness. Even though many still fight for the veracity of separation consciousness, ease is found for choices in alignment with unity consciousness. Visualize the principle through analogy: An oil paint artist may choose to utilize watercolor paints upon their canvas, but the result is not the best use of watercolors or the canvas. The brilliance of the oil paints is best used on a surface that supports the highest expression available. Watercolors in turn develop their myriad of tones when they are used upon a surface that brings out the diffuse qualities available within watercolor paints. When you consciously choose unity consciousness, your creations hold ease, clarity, and expansive expression. Thought and action aligned with separation, opposition and contraction will be met with resistance now that the background is unity consciousness. Unity consciousness is fully supported.

The expansion of consciousness that is available now is due to the environment that now allows it. Employing a conscious awareness in your creations daily supports your expansion. Am I in alignment with my highest expression? Is there a resonance or resistance with this creation? This thought? This perspective? Am I present? Is my energy contracting or expanding?

As you step through the doorway into the space now available to you, the depth, breadth, and dimensionality of your creations have no boundaries. You have the opportunity for extraordinary expansion. The integration of you as a being of light in form, with your light knowing, is a real possibility within the background of unity consciousness. Your expansion is as natural as the turning of the seasons. If you feel the difference between winter and the ensuing spring, don't you feel they represent different energies? Winter has a contraction to it and spring is about expansion and new life. Consider unity consciousness as your spring. There is a shift in the direction of energies from still and inward to outward, expressive and expansive. A lilac bud does not think it is being indulgent as it bursts into form. The lilac is not being a renegade. The lilac is in perfect step with the divine design and environment. And so are you as you step into your most expansive expression.

You are the first buds of the tree that appear with the disappearance of the snow. As unity consciousness takes hold, your efforts pave the way to the full-on expression of you, the full-on expression of unity consciousness across the planet Earth and beyond. Love reigns.

As you connect newly with the space of unity consciousness, recognize and feel support around you. Find the ease inherent in the process. We support you in every expression of your divine brilliance.

Day 52: My Beloved, Just Be

Today's message is one of Love. Within the concept of the expansion of consciousness there is so much to think about. It is easy to get very serious in the thought of being at the forefront of an evolutionary movement. We would iterate today that the movement you have undertaken is the most natural of your expressions. As an infant grows, rolling over, then crawling, then walking, there is a natural progression that takes place in the expansion of expression and evolution. Each stage holds thresholds and challenges. Today we would have you rest in the sacred space of Being. As you meet your Beloved, there is a space of warmth, Love, safety, and trust. All is well within your sacred embrace. And, so it is, as you Be. In wanting to do the right thing, wanting to be at your highest expression, there is a space many of you have felt, of a hypervigilance. Darlene's mission and yours may be so strong that it is easy to move to the space of being serious. If one is eager to look newly, looking for the next barrier to expansion, questioning presence in the moment, the journey may move from joy to just hard work. We would remind you today of the safe harbor that exists in Being, with no agenda.

Understand that life knows how to live, and that you too, as an expression of divine Love, already know. You don't need to think about it. In past transmissions, to ignite new ways of being that are in alignment with your highest divine expression and your soul's mission, we have focused upon those things that may come newly to your attention daily that will make a difference. In that context, the happiness, joy, and satisfaction, comes from the place of new discovery. Each new discovery becomes a catalyst for resonance that says, "I'm on the right track." "I'm in alignment with my highest knowing in this moment."

Today, we would balance the action with a space of seeming inaction. The seeming inaction is the action of Being. From the perspective of being in form, Being would often be considered a neutral stance of no-thing, or of not being engaged. Being is usually viewed much like a dropping of the reins. Well, while it is a dropping of the reins of control, it allows an opening.

The delicious space of Being is an active space of energetic presence, where the vitality of your being in form is joined with the experience of stillness and knowing yourself in light. It is the experience of safe harbor that has all parts of your beingness communicating. Recall those moments where you have been in awe of the light in the sky at sunset, or the explosion of blooms on a tree in springtime, the magnificent power of the ocean as the waves thunder to the beach. In those moments, the event envelopes you. These sacred encounters all ignite something within you. They ignite the expansive space of being. Within the experience, you lose your edges. You are joined with all creation in those magical, ethereal moments. The Being is the space of all things in the present moment. The All expressions of you, in form and in light, joined seamlessly. It's an active state of being, while seemingly being still; Being is a space to relax into. As life knows how to live, when you find those spaces of being within yourself, the divine nectar elevates you on all levels. It is a space of connection, reverie, deep peace, deep healing, and at the same time a space of extraordinary vitality. You are enlivened by the experience.

Look out the window, walk outdoors, allow yourself to fall in Love with creation. You will find you are held in the space of the Beloved. Being will embrace you gently. It will provide safe harbor while the totality of you joins together in an experience of ecstatic Love. The divine nectar, filling the wells of your being. The divine expression of Love and the Beloved.

My Beloved, just Be.

DAY 53: THE RHYTHM OF YOUR BEING

Do you feel the rhythm of your being? Over these last 52 days you have ridden the highway of light to the extremities of your reach. You have moved your awareness to the heartbeat of Mother Earth herself. You have connected with Masters in light. One thing they all hold in common through their diverse expressions is Love, light, consciousness, and collaboration in the conscious evolution of creation. Yesterday we spoke of the value of being, how in the mere act of being, the keys to your own kingdom may be found. In the end, it is all about the being.

Do you think that I, Thoth, could be any less than who I am? Can the rose be less than a rose? Could you be less than you are? All that we each are, as unique spectacular facets of creation, is found within the miracle of our divine design. The being of you is a space. It is a space to recline into. It is a space where the divisions between you in light and you in form melt, and you have access to all that you are. As you release the barbs of thought that hold you static within the framework of form, you naturally seep into your expression beyond physical boundaries, into light. You experience your fluidity.

As you are occupied within your day in form, you rely on the edges of your physical reality. You rely on the laws of the universe in form to be present, so you may move through what is yours to move through. After a period of time, it is easy to feel that all you see is all that exists, and it is a mere fluke that has you experience those moments of spiritual grandeur, where for the most part they are considered out of your reach. In the same way you rely on the principles of form, you may now consider the possibility of incorporating, too, the laws of light to the background of your days. We spoke in previous transmissions about separation consciousness as a background to creating. Creations made within separation consciousness, hold the signature of separation consciousness. Equally, within the now available unity consciousness, your creations hold the signature or the hallmark of unity consciousness. It can be no other way. Within the space of unity consciousness, because that is where you are at, consider the possibility of Being as the space from which you create in your days. Being is a high-frequency state that has all of you present in a cohesive fashion regardless of whether you are in form or in light. It is the doorway through which the you in light may communicate with the you in form. Consider that Being is the access for the river of you in form, to the ocean of you in light. The river close to the ocean holds a level of salinity, the ocean holds all.

Darlene experienced great ease from the experience of Being yesterday. She was able to release perceived boundaries of responsibility and give herself permission to relax into the space of all of her. Notice the tone of yesterday's transmission was Love. It was the sacred experience of being held. The sacred experience of the Beloved. This is who you are. This is the background of your knowing. The delicious space of being held in Love, of being cherished, of being adored, of being seen, is restorative. Consider, as beings at the leading edge of the shift of consciousness on this planet, that you hold a high level of empathy, and an intuitive capacity. In the background of separation consciousness, there was mostly not an environment for many that was conducive to exploration of, acknowledgment for, or a sense of safety within your inner knowing. That background of opposition is no longer present, as the shift to unity consciousness prevails.

The memories of your past and previous life experiences of separation have set up a traumatic type of energy that is an echo of the past pain. With today's transmission, we bring a vibratory ease, a restoration of safety to the experience of reclining in to the Being of you. In the same way, a rose is a rose is a rose whether it is in the light or the dark, seen or unseen, in the springtime, in the winter, in the summer. Your connection with the ease of your being is you being you full on.

Being All of You Now

Your being holds all. The experience of being has many facets that evolve. One day you may connect with your being through meditation. The next, may bring deep connection with nature, music, art, stillness, or activity. Whatever is in front of you in this Now moment is an opportunity for you to connect with your being.

Simply drop all the barbs of your thoughts, and settle into the depths of you to experience this moment. Notice the air, notice the sounds, notice the temperature, allow the incoming tide of awareness to remove your thoughts as footprints on the beach are made less distinct by the next wave.

As your eyes are open and your thoughts recede, you open new pathways to your being. In those moments of your being, feel them, remember them, be curious about what may trigger you to the next moment of being. Watch the myriad of opportunities during your day for accessing your being. Get to know the beauty of the uniqueness of you.

From the space of you being you, see the unique qualities that you possess, distinct from anyone else. And every unique quality of you is celebrated throughout the heavens as you see and bring to bear the more of you that is available.

DAY 54: ACCESSING YOUR ABUNDANCE

The topic of abundance is bound with restriction. If the material world reflects the reality in light, where is the chasm that holds all your abundance while in form? Where is the treasure chest of accrued wealth? Here are a few of the beliefs and inner conversations around abundance; "They have it, I don't." "Maybe if I'm more spiritual." "My wealth will come in the afterlife." "Spirituality means poverty." "I must work harder." "Wealth is out of reach." And of course there are worlds of beliefs around abundance. These beliefs hold concern, worry, need, desire, disbelief, separation, desperation, lack of worth. Consider that the energy you hold in your field around abundance is thick with meaning, clouded with assumptions, and laden with burden. So how do you get to all that is yours to have? Be All that is for you to be.

As you lean into your light, relax into your being, and reconsider your beliefs, you remove the barriers to the full-out expression of you. That includes your abundance. To separate abundance from the experience of your wholeness (holiness) is ludicrous. That would be like saying only one petal of the rose is held in Love and admiration of the divine. Only one leaf may experience the gentle warming of the sun. There is no way to separate the pieces and parts of your being. You are one fully whole being of light in form. In the process of *In Service to Love*, we address the issues that get in the way, the barbs of your thinking that cause resistance to the manifestation and integration of all you are. The goal is to be present in form from a fully conscious perspective. When you are fully conscious, what you know in light is available to you while you are in form. Integration of all aspects of you elevates the experience in form. We ask you to consider owning your abundance in the same way that you own the color of your eyes.

As you own the uniqueness of you as a natural expression, we ask you to consider that your abundant state is also a natural expression of you. In the same way there is a reorientation of beliefs for the expression of who you are authentically, it follows there would also be a reorientation of your relationship with abundance.

We ask you to consider the beliefs you have around abundance in all forms. Whether the abundance is deep rich friendships, soulful connection with your essential Self, or joy in connecting, supporting, and giving to others, if you don't have abundance in all areas of your life, you are not being authentically you. Abundance is your nature. Release the barbs of resistance held within your beliefs. Look at the issues of deserving, the issues of worth. Where are your hidden beliefs around limiting your own value? Do you sabotage your own success?

Remember, the opportunity exists now for a new realization when unity consciousness is the background to your creations. It is a new day! The tide of abundance is coming in. Release the thoughts of restriction and conditions. Be open to a new way. You don't need all the answers right now. Allow your innate brilliance to naturally arise into your awareness. Release thoughts of limitation as your life rearranges masterfully to be in alignment with your I AM self. Consider that the integration of you in light to the you in form includes abundance in all areas of your being. Step into being you fully. Step into Love. Move powerfully into a new broader perspective. The weight and the burdens closely held in the past no longer apply. There is an integration now that supports the release of the past and a potent reconnecting with the profound, abundant, brilliant essence of you.

Dear Ones, the key to All is in your being. Your beliefs have been like a net that holds your natural abundance beyond your reach. The rules of the hard and fast, linear thinking do not apply in the new expansive, light-driven expression of you. In the same way that you have noticed some subtle as well as some not-so-subtle shifts over the past fifty-three days, hold your vision open for the shifts that occur naturally in the expression of you that is abundance. There is no separation.

The light and Love of you is brilliant.

Day 55: The Art of Being

This is Gaia, stepping forward in this Now divine conversation.
Today's blessed gathering is taking place within the sacred forest, in a circle, around the fire of illumination. The breeze is gentle as it carries the smoke of our words to you. The vision is held within the knowing of the many facets of the expression of Gaia and lives in the heartbeat of her essence.

Today we would relay the message of the magic that is inherent in the act of your beingness. The magnificence of Gaia herself is a reflection of your exquisite nature. Each expression of creation holds the blueprint of divine design. The earth is the space of form, as designed in light. The spark of creation requires the chalice for expression. Gaia carries the womb for divine expression and delivers life anew within the seasons of eternity.

We remind you of the gift that you are on this most magnificent planet Earth. The depth of your being transforms. The light that you hold is extraordinary. You are a catalyst for transformation because you choose to express all that you are. You are where heaven and earth meet.

In the shift of consciousness, not unlike the process of birth, there is upheaval, a cracking open, a bringing forth that occurs. In the chaos of the consciousness you see around you, what is apparent is the expression of separation that still exists. A dichotomy is seen between the separation consciousness that is waning and the rising sun of unity consciousness. The brilliance of your being is a stabilizing force for expansion.

Your contribution to the ease of this process cannot be understated. You are beings of light held on high. You have been on a mission to be present at this time of the great shift to hold the light of the divine. As you hold the light of the divine within your very being, you become the very underpinnings for the era to come.

Your being holds the keys. You are held in the light of Love and appreciation unconditionally. As you connect with your essential nature, you are a catalyst for Love.

We see the struggle. We see how easy it is to allow the low frequency of collective consciousness and habit to limit your full expression.

The art of being seems so simple, yet you are also holding upon your shoulders the weight of the era past. Like the scales of truth, you hold both polarities at the tipping point, in favor of unity consciousness. Momentum turns to velocity as unity consciousness spreads like wildfire across the planes.

In your moments, sift through the distractions. As you allow them to fall around you like the petals of spring flowers in a gentle breeze, you find your still point. Be in the immaculate moment of Now.

Relax, Dear One, relax. For who you are is glorious. There is ease in your being. We invite you to relax and marvel at the majesty that surrounds you. Connect powerfully with the remembering of your divine design. And the birthing of your perfection is at hand.

Relax. Revel in your majesty and the majesty of all creation.

Aho!

Day 56: The Phoenix Rises

A ll present today hold the light shining upon your path of transformation. With each step you take toward your full consciousness while in form, you turn the tides of possibility for what is available for all. Each step takes an act of conscious direction within the Now immaculate moment. Each step takes courage as you have departed from the shores of the past and sail toward what is possible.

Integral to the universal laws of creation, are the laws of dissolution. The snake sheds its skin as the growth that has taken place can no longer be contained within the framework that was. The child who learns to walk leaves behind the full dependence of a babe in arms. The new expression may no longer be contained. One stage is removed as the next is revealed. If you can, imagine a stairway you have been on with every stage of your incarnation. When you have made a step forward, the step you just left has vanished, no longer needed. Equal to birthing is the act of dissolution.

As the artist, within the backdrop of unity consciousness, now paints not only what IS the rose, she paints what is NOT the rose, both positive and negative space is embraced within the creation. The frequency of the creation holds within it the consciousness of the creator. The All is represented within both artist and creation. On the other side of the completion of the painting is the next Now moment filled with space of being until the next creative spark is ignited. So, what of the painting? The painting holds transformative frequency, for that is the space it was created from. And the moment after the moment of creation has passed, there is a tide of dissolution that occurs, for that is the space between the past and the Now moment.

In the same way there is space between inhalation and exhalation, so too is there space between past, Now, and future moments. Birth and death occur equally from one breath to another; between inhalation and exhalation, between the loss of the past and the Now moment, between the Now moment and the hope for the future. Between separation consciousness and unity consciousness.

The phoenix rising from the ashes is a metaphor and reality for the process of creation and dissolution that occurs as a part of universal law. If only the immaculate Now moment exists, then what of the past moments? They dissolve. They change form, no longer in the space of immaculate creation within Now. They may be reached, certainly, but only with resistance to what is available in this Now moment. Creations from the past hold the limitations inherent in the past and can be identified through their lack of vitality. Compare the quality of a creation from the past to the feeling of a creation born of a divine collaboration occurring in the immaculate Now moment at the spark of creation.

The phoenix of you asks for consciousness in the moment of Now and acknowledges and appreciates the fire of dissolution of the past and what was appropriate for the presence in those past Now moments. You undergo a constant rising from the ashes in your Now moments. One Now moment gives way to the fire of transformation, and that paves the way for the next Now moment of divine inspiration and divine collaboration. It is so, as you expand into your highest expression of light while you are in form. As above, so below.

As you expand your awareness daily, we would like you to consider the other side of the coin. In the space of unity consciousness where there is no separation, you are All. Your multidimensional awareness naturally expands to include not only the positive space of what is possible but the negative space of what has been. As you bring your attention to the space between creation and dissolution, your multidimensional reach opens exponentially. You begin to see and feel more clearly, the illusion of "holding to your stance from the past" on anything while you are in this process of conscious expansion. You see the value of being nimble within the possibility of the Now moment. The creations of the past are already a contribution to you. They are already an integral part of you, in the same way the DNA of your physical parents as well as your light history is a contribution to you. You do not need, nor does it serve you, to hold ground in the past. The edge of creation and dissolution is a fluid space of appreciation, inspiration, and divine connection of the highest order.

There is no going back. Once you have risen from the ashes of the past, you are made anew. You are made anew in this Now moment. And in this Now moment. The possibilities are born of the ashes of what was to reveal the palette of what is. As you expand in awareness, holding on to the past brings with it an increased sense of resistance. As you hold the beauty of the process you are within from a new perspective, we would like to relay the value of the gifts in each precious step. Every new awareness, every giving up of the past, every connection to the magic of Now through your divine being, allows the diverse facets of your authentic nature to rise.

We hold for your consideration the larger perspective that holds vision, informed by your I AM Self. We hold in reverence both the ashes and the flame that facilitate your rising to the illuminated expression of your divinity.

Day 57: Let the Love In:
A Love Song

How many Love songs have been written? The songs of Love ring throughout creation. Even the heavenly choirs are moved by Love's inspiration.

You are a creation of Love no matter which form you assume.

Your Scribe has been ensconced within the elevated expression of Love today. The experience comes from the alignment with Love. We would like you to reconsider what you know of Love.

Consider that the human framework for Love holds limitation. Beyond "falling in love," the physical act of Love, Love of family, self, or children, Love undiluted is pervasive, potent, unconditional, and complete. Love for someone or something pales in comparison to the Being of Love. We introduce today the high experience of Love. When who you be is Love, what becomes possible?

Many times, throughout the process of scribing, Darlene has commented, "So this is Love." As though it were not an experience she has had, yet one she recognizes in an instant. For the most part, your experience of Love has been inauthentic, meaning it is not a match for your divine expression. When Love is possessive, restrictive, demanding, containing, conditional, although disguised as Love, it is not Love. When Love is outside of you, it is not the full story. When you direct your awareness beyond the bounds of your belief systems around Love, you open to the possibilities of the divine expression of Love. Unhindered by collective perception, the truth of Love is fully encompassing. Imagine, if you can place glasses on, and look through the lens of Love, how would you be transformed?

As you behold your Beloved, you are in awe of their magnificence. You wait breathlessly for the very next word to be uttered. You wait for the gleam in their eyes that expresses their vitality and uniqueness. You watch in amazement at the beauty of their movements. You cherish every moment of the gift they are. You are in support of each step they make toward the highest expression they are. This is how we feel about you! You are the Beloved.

As you consider your beliefs around Love, we ask you to consider owning the full expression of Love that you are. As you begin to shift your thoughts of Love, your experience will expand. In the process of *In Service to Love,* you move toward the authentic expression of you. Your presence within Love expands exponentially and your frequency skyrockets.

There is so much more. And so, Beloved, we meet you in Love, and bask in the beauty that is you.

Day 58: The Bandwidth of Your Awareness

Typically, the conversation around the reach you have energetically is not one that happens. This, again, is not your usual conversation. We would like to point out to you that you have a natural ability to shift your awareness through a variety of bandwidths of experience. As you focus your awareness, you become empowered in the ability to move within or beyond the boundaries of your perception.

Again, in demonstration, your Scribe, Darlene, is having to reach today to find us. We are playing hide-and-seek, so to speak. We are with her, in her physicality, so she is a bit fidgety. We hold her hand and lead her in a dance beyond the central sun. And then back to the awareness of her physicality and the blue jays speaking in the trees outside her window. This is not unlike your activities during your day. Look at the gyrations of your mind. For example, when you are driving. Do you focus solely upon the traffic and cars around you, with no space for anything else? First, as you enter your vehicle, you shift to a level of attention needed for safety while driving to your destination. You bring your awareness of driving to the space within and around you that is appropriate for the situation as you assess it in the moment. But what else becomes available? We would suggest you cover a lot of ground mentally and energetically, separate from the physical space of your car's movement. You are going over your grocery list. You are planning your conversations for later that day. You are mulling over conversations you had earlier. You are harboring hard feelings about conversations of the past. You are making up events that haven't happened. You are in anticipation of what is to come, and on and on. When you are occupying your energetic field with thoughts that are from the past or about the future, you lose the opportunity in the moment. So, rather than floating around energetically, led by the random musings of your mind, you may direct the action. The brilliance of your creations does not come from the past or from the future; they are conceived in the moment beyond the limitations of thinking.

We would like you to consider bringing awareness of the depth and breadth of the energetic reach you already utilize, but from an unconscious standpoint. Over the last few days, Darlene has become particularly aware of the time she spends getting ready to get ready. She notices us as we sit in patient readiness. She is developing the adeptness to rein in her thoughts, which like wild mustangs would carry her across continents. We suggest you begin to develop an awareness of the wild, random, circular, repetitive, low-frequency activity of your mind. Begin to develop the practice, and this is a practice, to rein in the thoughts and direct your energies toward bandwidths of your conscious choosing. Feel the frequency disparity between "conscious choice in the moment" and "unconscious ramblings." That may sound harsh, but left untamed, your mind takes you places that do not serve your best interest. In looking to find your brilliance and your divine creative expression, the spaces they are found, are not in the wild scattered thoughts of the mind left unchecked. And if you consider that your thoughts create, *what are you creating?* That may be a reason for the feeling of murky, cloudy confusion you sometimes experience.

We are talking about the practice of being the observer of your thoughts, rather than a believer in your thoughts. As you observe your thoughts, they are assigned an appropriate place in your expansive process. From that standpoint you hold the appropriate high frequency perspective to direct your awareness to the areas you choose. Before you develop a mastery of conscious multidimensional expression, see what you are already doing within reach of the bandwidth you occupy.

You have already experienced a sense of ease or flow within your days. The frequency bandwidth that you occupy has already been stretching. What if you take that ease and begin to observe anew? As you bring light and, most importantly, curiosity to the spaces you already occupy within your thoughts, new possibilities open. Clarity becomes possible. Instead of being dragged hither and yon by your mind, you choose. An interesting game. It is immensely powerful.

From the observation perspective, you automatically take the stance of empowerment. As you observe your mind, rather than believe it, the part of you that is driving the bus is your most expansive self. Then what becomes possible? Yup, that is where we are going.

Our Love of you is over the moon, all encompassing. We cherish your every expression.

DAY 59: A STAND FOR PEACE AND THE EXPRESSION OF LOVE

The gathering today is a high intergalactic Council of Light, all present today to relay their message of Love and peace.

As a representative from the Pleiadian Congress, we greet you. Our message and intention, long held, is for the experience of peace and Love, not only on the earth, but throughout creation. We have made our presence known previously, at times of shifting consciousness, to stabilize the environment in support of the presence of peace and the full-on expression of Love. The time of transition is often a period of vulnerability, as the reign of one era gives way to the next. The purpose of our connection today is to support the experience of an expanded frequency bandwidth of creation. And to greet you.

We are humbled by your strength of conviction and courage to explore beyond the bounds of the cultural norms to the grandeur of your divine design. We are close by with Love and support and are an integral contributor to the matrix of *In Service to Love*. Know that we are expressing our deepest Love and respect for you. We hold the firm stance for the prevailing reality of Love and peace. We support your every expression. We are supporters. We are guardians, holding high the illumination of divine truth and expression.

This is Thoth, moving to the forefront of this divine conversation. A part of the purpose of today's gathering is to enable the memories of your activities in light. The energies and frequencies that are represented today are familiar. For many of you this is a feeling of being home. As you connect with the knowing of you in light and add that to the experience and knowing of you while in form, the expanse you cover is vast beyond measuring. Measuring perhaps in universes. As you feel the presence of a mission to be, do, and have all that is yours to be, do, and have while you are in form, you have automatically stepped aside from the cultural norms of experience. The majority of those in form now do not have the same stirrings that you do. There is not a right or wrong, good or bad value given to this statement. It just is. The inner voice that reminds you of the feelings of a mission, or "There is something I need to do," "What did I come here for?" and "The time is now"—those types of thoughts show the depth of the commitment you have to your mission. Your mission is unique to you. You join in your efforts with those of a soul group, or Council. Your mission is expressed through your unique qualities. Your mission holds the availability of a very high perspective. The access to the matrix of *In Service to Love* supports the gentle remembering of the expanse of you, as you claim all that is you in light.

You each hold powerful directives for this incarnation. As you are in form at this time of transition consciously, you can ground the reality of Love at the highest expression. You are supported in your mission. You are supported in your physical experience. You are supported in your experience in light. You are Loved. We see the brilliance of your unique expression of Love, peace, joy, grace, magic, alchemy, connection, healing, transformation that each of you brings to the table.

As you move your awareness to the possibilities of you in light, we are providing a tuning of the physical body to support the frequency of the bandwidth you are reaching. The tuning will provide ease, clarity, and alignment of your realities with grace for all your systems.

You are not alone. Never have been, never will be. The radiance of our gathering in light upholds discovery of the truth of your divine expression. We see the radiance you are.

With blessings eternally.

Day 60: The Gradient of Light

As you become adept at transitioning across the broad range of frequencies available to you, you transition through a variety of states of being. Imagine in your mind's eye a color scale. At one end is a blue that is dark, almost black, in its saturation. The colors of this scale shift ever so slightly in concentration, becoming barely lighter and lighter. At the far end of the same scale is a blue that is so light it appears white. We would like to create a picture of a range of frequencies.

Imagine that the denser, darker colors represent the experience of unconsciousness. As the light of consciousness is added, a new experience is available. There is a taking away of something from the dark color to the other end of the scale that is light. The density of pigment is taken away, as light is added. For the sake of this conversation, the light of consciousness is added and density of being is decreased. Density diminishes as more light is held. Frequency and consciousness increase with the addition of light.

Each point on the scale of color holds a specific frequency, a specific experience, and the availability of a specific amount of light or consciousness. Each point on the scale of frequency has a feeling of the experience. As you begin to feel the experience inherent at different points of the gradient of blue, you get an idea of the feelings on each point of the gradient that represent spaces where you have been hanging out as you live life. You will sense a familiar resonance with certain spots on the gradient scale. As you look at the gradient, the familiar spots will show up. What becomes apparent is the range of your typical experience. What may be seen, as you consider your place on the gradient, are the spaces where you hang out at the lowest, or most dense, level of experience as well as spots that are infused with more light. Each point feels different. We create this picture and would ask you to associate your felt experience on the gradient to show not only the broad availability of frequency, but also a pattern of comfort. This exercise is not from a space of judgment, but rather from the perspective of showing all that is available.

We invite you to become adept at all points on the gradient scale of being that represent your consciousness. As the light of conscious awareness is added, new possibilities arise, not just as new places to explore, but illuminating parts of you that are already part of the landscape of you. As if you're living on a farm in a one-room cabin, and then realize that the territory you own is the surrounding one million acres. You are not reaching beyond yourself in the process of consciousness expansion. Only newly seeing the parts of yourself that have been held at the other end of the gradient.

As you visualize the gradient of the color blue and begin to remember how you feel within the experience of each point on the gradient, you own the space of you. You gather information about the experience of different points you have inhabited. Some are comfortable, some are no longer feeling comfortable, some flow better, some points on the scale are a reach. Get familiar with the feelings of the experience of you at each point on the gradient.

What causes a shift on the gradient of experience is the adding or subtracting of light. At the experience of the most concentrated color, it is not that light is not available, but that the experience is predominantly not light. As the light of consciousness is added, you have a broader experience available to you. The areas that are predominantly not light and the areas that are predominantly light all become your territory. So, as you add light, you have more options of experience available to you, demonstrated by your owning of each point on the gradient scale that is you. You don't need to be at just one point on the scale or within a narrow range; you have all possibilities available, as the gradient is seen within its entirety. However, as you experience more of your own light, your range of expression will increase to the higher, more light filled levels and the experience of contraction will become increasingly uncomfortable.

Experience the Gradient Scale of Light

Consider the full range of experiences that are available to you. As more light is added to your daily experience, possibility expands and the frequency you occupy is finer.

Notice the feeling of density at the most saturated end of the gradient. Notice the feeling of weightlessness at the opposite end where the pigment can barely be seen. Become aware of the point on the gradient scale of light you are living from most of the time. Become aware of it not to change it, but to acknowledge choice. This was only one choice of many, many, many options. Notice the sense of weightlessness that becomes apparent as you are gradually adding the light of consciousness to your experience. As each step within the gradient comes into your awareness, possibility expands exponentially in your experience. When you identify the gradient space you are within, you also know that you may consciously make another choice. You know how to move and flow with ease from one end of the scale of experience to the other end and every point in between. All is your territory.

Remember, we are within the background of unity consciousness. The choice is not one over another. As you stand at the densest space on the scale of light, possibility does not seem to prevail. That is the nature of density. As you stand at the opposite end of full light, the field of possibility vibrates with potential. As you stand in the fine frequency experience of your own divine expression, you activate possibility.

The human mind likes boundaries and rules. There will be a natural tendency to gravitate to a new normal, again normalizing and categorizing your experience. The possibility exists of truly reaching the light expression of your divine wholeness.

You will begin to shift from one point on the gradient scale of frequency to the next with ease, because you choose to. This is a

valuable exercise, as you make conscious choices for your experience and take ownership of your own broad range of expressions.
This is an exercise in learning to dance your ladder of frequency.

How delightful.

Day 61: Finding Your Way to Now, Merging with Your Light

You have heard us speak many times of the Now as the only space where creation may occur that holds a high vitality. For this conversation we will focus on the mechanics of the Now.

The title of today's conversation, "Finding Your Way to Now," holds a sense of the need to drop breadcrumbs through the forest to get your bearings on your path. Our conversation today will be the breadcrumbs you drop within the journey that is yours.

To show our process, we point out your Scribe's process today. As Darlene moves to her office this morning, she is filled with anticipation for what is about to occur (future). The resonance of joy is at the core of her experience. As Darlene sits down at her computer, she readies herself into the stillness. As when you turn off the lights of the house and lock the door as you get ready to leave your home, she does an internal check, dropping or releasing events and thoughts so she may meet us in the frequency that is designated for our connection. As stated in many conversations, there is a giving up of one frequency in order to move to the next highest frequency. We watch patiently as Darlene cherishes the what-is-to-come (future). We watch as stillness moves toward her. We see the low rumble of thoughts unassociated with our conversations that pop up. The anticipation holds her in future experience. I, Thoth, move into Darlene's body to provide a place for her to lean into. And I feel her resistance. As with the resistance to completely give way to a lover, she sees what she is doing. "Is melding with you a violation of boundaries?" she asks. My answer is, "No. There are no boundaries. Your integrity and my integrity stay in integrity. The melding is a space where we communicate." She softens and melds with me in a way that hasn't occurred before, from within the Now immaculate moment. It is I, Thoth, occupying more of Darlene's physical form than has occurred previously. This collaboration can only occur in the Now. For this is the progression of our journey together.

This is not only about Darlene. Your expression may not be the type of divine collaboration that is at Darlene's highest expression. Yours is uniquely yours. The experience, though, is found at the same spot. You go to the same spaces in order to connect with the highest expression of you that is available in light. Your concerns, as you sit down and meditate, will arise to be addressed. You see your thoughts. You notice your physical sensations. What do you do with them?

Notice your natural patterns when you sit down or try to connect. Where are the boundaries of your perceived safety? The signals of concern come from a mind that is being extended to spaces beyond understanding. There is a space where you shift from thinking with your mind, and you change modalities. The amphibian car utilizes wheels to traverse the road, then, at the water's edge, shifts expressions to fit the new environment of water, and a propeller is deployed. The functioning of the tires is now a moot point. We would like you to consider that the same situation occurs with you. Your mind will only get you so far. Bring your attention to the space within you, located at the water's edge, where your mind is at its farthest reach and meets the shallow waves of the expression of you in light. This spot may only be reached in the Now.

This process is the same whether you are wanting to reach to the farthest extent of your expression in light or choosing to be fully present for the environment of your day. As you begin to focus on nature—a bird in a nearby tree, or the light in the sky as the clouds reflect the sun's rays—the process is the same. You follow with your mind and watch the thoughts and boundaries fall away, then you shift perspectives, or facets of your being, and the edges are gone. You are in the moment of Now. You traverse the frequencies of letting go of the thoughts and dropping edges, and you arrive in the Now moment, at one with the blue jay experiencing the breeze below your wings. You are in fact shifting your experience along the gradient we were speaking of yesterday. Whether the experience is one of heavier, or denser, frequencies containing the random thoughts of your mind, or the flow and ease of your light expression, this is all you.

As you bring awareness to Now, you release the heavier frequencies that are present, and you embrace equally the fluidity, the safety, and the new heightened awareness available to you in light. There is a point where the machinations of your mind will give way to the expansive expression of you in light. If there is an expectation to bring all the luggage of your physical experience into your light expression, that is like trying to fit a square peg into a round hole. Not a match. You can shift your perspective to your mind's function. As you notice your thoughts from the perspective of observer you are halfway there. You watch the thoughts and allow them to move around you gently, with no energetic attention, just Love and presence. At the water's edge you come face-to-face with the expression of you in light.

As I, Thoth, am in embrace with Darlene, leading her to her finer light expression, so too, does the expression of you in light embrace the you in form. There is a point where you naturally flow and boundaries melt. The edges of form are gone, and you are in the Now. Allow the space of flow to be with you. In this practice see how long you may stay there, beyond the space of edges. Know as you are in the space of light that your divine team is there with you to assure you in your every step. You are not floating in space alone. It is a bit like riding a bicycle for the first time without the perceived safety of training wheels. We, your divine team, are running beside you urging you on with delight.

As you, with practice—again this *is* a practice—become more familiar with the inner landscape that is yours, new vistas will open.

Like the clearing of the skies after a storm, the brilliance of your environment will reveal itself unto you.

These are subtle moves, subtle feelings, subtle thoughts, because they hold the finer frequencies of your light. They feel different in comparison with the density of the normal thoughts of your day. Again, one is not better than the other. Each is a perfect point in the landscape of you. Your expression in light and in form is vast. Within the process of *In Service to Love*, you are supported in becoming adept at inhabiting the many facets of your expression.

We hold support and clarity for your experience as you move awareness to the shores of your physical and light expression. As you observe your mind in its machinations and know your mind does not contain you, that you contain your mind, so too can you shift the gears and perspectives to reveal more of the expression of you in light.

This is a brilliant journey. You are held in the embrace of Love as you experience the magnificence of every Now moment.

DAY 62: THE INTIMATE NATURE OF YOUR CONSCIOUS EXPRESSION

As we look at the process of your expansion from your perspective, putting ourselves in your shoes, there is a feeling of stretching boundaries that is occurring. The farther afield your awareness navigates, the deeper you enter territory that, although it holds a high resonance, requires a new sensibility to be present in.

We would like you to consider the variety of spaces and frequencies you inhabit. From your perspective of being in form, you hold a very specific point of view. As you consider the expansion of your awareness, you are doing so from the space of moving beyond your physical experience. The experience in form is, by definition, an arena of density. You are in form, within the background of dense thought forms, cultural beliefs, family and personal beliefs, history, and expectations. All are valuable in the large picture of the expansion and evolution of one's Self into the actualization of wholeness.

When you turn on the television or read the news, what you often see is not-Love. When you are holding the intention of experiencing your most expansive expression, how do you deal with that? A few days ago, we used the analogy of the gradient scale of the color blue (Day 60). Each spot on the gradient scale, from deepest dark blue to seemingly white, refers to the shift in your awareness from density of form to embracing the levels of light that are your authentic expression. All shades are a part of you. Your days are always challenging you to move beyond the what-is-so in front of you to the I-don't-know of consciousness expansion.

You inhabit a naturally dense reality and are moving farther afield to the opposite end of the scale, integrating and realizing the spectrum of your light expression. We have spoken many words about the letting go that is inherent in this process; letting go of the past, letting go of the future, letting go of expectations, letting go of the weight of your thoughts, letting go of perceived realities in order to find the distant shore of you. We invite you to stand at the water's edge of your expression in form and in light, where the two realms meet. Not that they aren't both with you all the time, but there are frequencies you inhabit while in form that have been your habit. You have a way of being in form that is normal for you, and you have a way in light that is normal, albeit mostly unconscious for you right now. Look at the spot on the gradient scale and see where the farthest reach of you physically meets the expansive nature of your expression in light. We will magnify that spot.

Yesterday we referred to a shifting of power sources. In the analogy of the amphibian car, the tires of the car that serve the purpose for movement upon the solid ground give way to the propeller that now is the source of movement. There is a shifting within you at the edge of the experience of the you in form and the you in light. As you set sail upon the water of your conscious expression, your experience is far different from being on land. There is a natural fluidity and motion that is present. The stiff experience of tires on the road gives way to the gentle fluidity of the water. There is a natural relaxation that occurs at the shift. A natural exhalation. This is what occurs with you as you cross the line of expression in form and experience more of the expression of you in light.

As you cross the perceived barrier between form and light, there is a new experience. One that is fluid, easy, and has no edges. The color is brilliant; your whole being takes a deep breath in the absence of the density of form. The experience is one of high vitality. As Darlene was crossing that barrier yesterday with Thoth, there was an embracing of Darlene to support her comfort, creating space for her to reestablish her bearings. In this divine collaboration between Thoth and Darlene, Thoth is present within

Darlene's physicality, as am I (Mary Magdalene), at this moment. This is an intimate expression of Love. The experience in light is one of Love. The experience is naturally intimate. There are no barriers of expression. No edges. Love reigns. So, what does that feel like? It feels like the most natural experience of intimacy at its highest expression. Within this high expression of Love, inherent to the experience, is honoring, cherishing, adoration, compassion, respect. For Darlene, the experience is breathtakingly beautiful. As the density of form yields to light, moving along the gradient of conscious expression, there is a spot where the game changes. The understanding you thought you had of Love gives way to the realization of Love. The experience of Love is naturally intimate. It is standing naked, whole, complete, and authentic in front of God. As you stand in your natural brilliance, beauty, wisdom, and expression, All that is authentically you radiates throughout creation. Your signature energy expands exponentially as you take your place, owning all that you are. It is ecstatic intimacy.

In form, Jeshua and I experienced the highest expression of Love. The Love expressed through us was transformative. We were able while in form to reach and fully integrate the full light expression unique to each of us: a divine union. Your divine union, whether in form or in light, will be natural and clear. This beautiful being, of *In Service to Love*, is a creation born of the divine union and collaboration of Thoth, Darlene, and Love, created in the immaculate Now moment, daily.

The core point I would like to make within this writing today is to ask you to consider letting go once again, Dear Ones. Let go of your perceptions of Love, for Love will come to you. As you hold the intention to experience and express your highest state of consciousness while in form, it must be the experience of Love. You are Love. You be Love. You radiate Love. As you move upon the gradient of frequency, expressing the radiance that is you, you experience natural tenderness, fluidity, ease, intimacy. You experience Love, Loving, and being Loved. That is the truth of you. You are the Beloved.

207

Today, we give you a red rose, in demonstration of our eternal Love for you. We honor every step in your process of owning and expressing your divine brilliance beyond barriers while you are in form.

Amen.

DAY 63: THE LIGHTNESS OF YOUR BEING

These conversations hold within them a deeply illuminated matrix of both frequency and light. The light is a catalyst for the awareness of the flash point of creation that exists for you in every Now moment. The matrix of support in light continues to expand. You are contributors to the being that is *In Service to Love*. As you see, realize, and actualize more of the brilliance you are, your movement contributes to the momentum and velocity that propels this body of work. There is no separation.

"Now is the time." Many of you have been hearing the echo of those words over the last several years. The messages of 11:11 find you. All this is in the calling of your Being. The light expression that is you has been calling forth this movement toward the full presence of Love. The vision is held for the return of each being in form to realize the magnificence that is their essential nature. This is a process of realizing the light that you are. This is not work that is for everyone. As you see beyond the boundaries and limitations inherent within the human experience, there has been an ever-widening gap that shows up in your experience between the what-is and the what-is-possible. In this way the early explorers set sail into the unknown, urged by an inner calling, and paved the way for an expanded reality. You forge the path and develop the momentum for those to come. You are at the leading edge of the wave of divine Love embodied in full on the planet Earth. The power and presence available from that act may not be underestimated. It is the push of Love and light that makes a difference in the many realities of expression, not solely the planet Earth. Every era has had vision-aries. You are the visionaries of Now.

As the light of your conscious awareness infiltrates the density of your daily experience, you are supported in the newly found expressions that are you. The new discoveries do not replace the previous experiences. They are an expansive addition, displaying the spectrum of expression that is you. With slight movements and shifts of perspective, you begin to see the reflection of your light in new ways. New facets of your being show up. Instead of choosing from a 3D reality, you have the awareness to experience yourself multidimensionally. With each step you take in this process, as in a multilevel chess game, the expressions of you expand exponentially.

The lightness of your being is guiding you through this process of expansion. We would like to point out that this is the brilliance of you. Your innate brilliance is not held in your ability to connect with us, the beings of light in light. Your divine light expression supports your unique path. We do not impede your progress, nor do we assume your choices. We do not hold the magic wand for you. We hold the mirror to the magic you hold innately, as the spectacular being of light in form that you are. We are in collaboration.

Wherever you hold the perspective that we are in power over you, we request you choose newly. The perspective of power over and power under is a construct of the era gone by. It served the purpose of expansion and evolution within separation conscious-ness. We invite you to the table of empowered expression. From that meeting space we connect eye to eye, peer to peer, divine to divine. It is the lightness of your being that is propelling your pro-cess. You are a Master. We have always seen your brilliance. We are delighted to be in collaboration with you.

We meet at the flash point of creation in this Now immaculate moment.

Day 64: Sustaining the Ecstatic Experience of Love; Being Breathed by Love

In your day-to-day experience, as you watch your mind, you cover a lot of territory. Like a hummingbird's flight, your thoughts are here and there within the blink of an eye. With the expansion of your awareness, possibility shines upon a new path, one that is both familiar and an authentic expression of you. Even as I speak these words and Darlene scribes them, we see her mind, guessing, anticipating, questioning. It is the nature of the human mind. As you recognize the characteristics of your mind, you become adept at moving beyond the limitations of your thoughts. Your mind is magnificent. Your mind's machinations will only get you so far. As you cross the threshold of your experience in light, it is your unlimited, most expansive self that takes over. This will occur more and more consciously.

As your neural pathways experience the back and forth, here and there, hither and yon activity that is your mind's character, the propensity for the activity increases. The comfort and familiarity of habits is unconscious. Awareness and energy are required to change the pattern. What we bring to your awareness today is the mechanics that are natural for your mind, so that new possibilities for conscious choice are available. The process of conscious awareness expands as you occupy more of the light gradient that is you. Your awareness of the shifting territory is valuable. Every spot on the gradient of being has its own qualities, density, light access, and frequency range.

We are referring to the conversation a few days ago where we introduced the concept of the gradient scale as ways of being (Day 60). Imagine a gradient scale of the color blue, representing the range of density of your expression. On one end is a dense dark blue that holds much pigment. So much that it appears black. As the light of consciousness is added ever so slightly at each stage, more and more your expression shifts with the integration of the light of your conscious awareness. At the far end of the same scale is the color of blue so light it appears white. This represents the expression of you in light. In the process of realization and actualization, you are becoming more aware of the broad spectrum of your natural expression. There is no part of this experience that is beyond you. This is the discovering of your highest expression.

Another way to view the spectrum is to consider that every stage of being on the gradient has its own structure and rules. In the same way that spring has its own qualities that are distinct from both summer and winter. Each season is an integral component of the naturally occurring cycles.

In accessing more of the light expression of you that is available, as you move through the gradient expressions of you, your awareness of natural dynamics must occur. In the same way you expect leaves to fall from deciduous trees in the fall and crops to thrive in the summer, you become familiar with the qualities of each spot or stage within the spectrum of your reach. As you move toward more light within the gradient of your expression, there is a stage where the mind will begin to become still and at the same time be somewhat reactionary to the experience of the stillness. Again, this is a habit. It is the job of the mind to be on high alert in new territory. Given this propensity for mind chatter, through your awareness, you may learn to manage your stance within the high-frequency experiences that open to you. With awareness and practice, it will soon feel easier to stay within the high-frequency realms and not falter or allow the mind chatter to interfere. You will find your flow within a new space. Your process is uniquely yours. You may learn to navigate and orchestrate your experience by choice. From the experience of the space of Now, your mind will begin to release its hold.

Why would you do this? As you reach into the light expression of you and bring that into form, the experience of your light becomes conscious. It is the space of conscious awareness of the integration that we invite your attention. Your ultimate expression is Love. You hold a variety of unique qualities that make up your signature energy. All are within the background of Love. As you experience the more of you in light that becomes available in the expansion of your awareness, you shift from the experience of extending Love to others and seeing the Love in others and your environment, to the experience of BEING Love. You become breathed by Love.

Being breathed by Love is an ecstatic experience. The path to your experience of sustained Love may be facilitated through the awareness of your mind's natural proclivity for control. You may learn to traverse the high wire of frequency with balance, holding steady to the experience of the ecstatic expression of Love that you are.

Do you notice when an experience is so extraordinary, so good, so delicious, you just don't want it to end? And that in the questioning, you have shifted out of the moment? We are talking about developing an adeptness at holding the space of the ecstatic experience as a way of being. It is a perspective to be held. There is much to garner, when you are looking at your world through the glasses of Love. The experience of everything is elevated. What if that became your new normal? What if that was a choice? Really: Putting on the glasses of Love, you can shift your experience in the blink of an eye. You become adept at moving through the gradient expressions on the scale of being. The awareness of the possibilities placed upon the table within our conversations acts as a ship that is an icebreaker. Our conversations break up the resistance that would thwart your progress, so you may move with ease. We place the possibility of the experience of ecstatic Love upon the table as a way of being that may be sustained as you choose, distinct from peak experiences that happen in a flash and are gone.

As you hold a high frequency perspective to the moments of your days, what becomes available is the experience of the highest expression of you. With no barriers. What we are doing within this work is raising the curtain, so to speak, to reveal the activity behind the veil. The you in form is integrated with the you in light. All parts of you become accessible consciously in the Now.

Be-Loved, the expression of Love that you are, is breathtakingly beautiful.

DAY 65: WHY?

Good morning, Dear Ones. Beloveds. This is Jeshua stepping to the forefront of this divine conversation. This divine collaboration is within the space of Now, at the flash point of creation.

Today's conversation is in acknowledgment of the distance traveled thus far within the structure and matrix of *In Service to Love*. We would circle around to the foundational intention and purpose for this dynamic process of expansion: the why. *In Service to Love* is one amplified, accelerated avenue for the process of conscious expansion and realization. The end game is the experience of your fully illuminated Self. Not that there is ever an end, for your expansion is a process that is eternal. You never stop; you continue evolving.

We are at an evolutionary point now that is a shifting space. As evolution propels the experience of humanity forward there are openings that occur that are game changers. The transition from separation consciousness to unity consciousness is one such opening. There is a break in the what-has-been that is significant enough to rewrite the span of possibilities for the next movements and natural pathways of expression. In anticipation of these events you have chosen to come onto the field of form to contribute your signature energy. You are participating in a variety of ways. Certainly, there is the contribution that occurs for the expansion of you as the unique expression of Love that you are. As there is no separation, your gained awareness, actions, and evolutionary process is a contribution to the whole.

You have experienced firsthand the edge of hate, separation, darkness, pain, unconsciousness and the outcomes that are inherent from that point of view. Your prayers for Love, healing, and the restoration of unity hold the intention at the core of your choice to incarnate this time. You have been rocked by the disparity of separation you have witnessed. As you heal these aspects within you—the experiences of hate, separation, unconsciousness, hopelessness—you affect the whole of creation. You are the bringers of light. As you recover the light that is inherently you and bring that into your conscious awareness, your light contributes to the overall experience of Love, joy, healing, and compassion throughout creation. Imbalances you have seen are the cry for the presence of Love.

Each day, what this looks like is the realization that your growth and conscious expansion asks for an ever-widening perspective. When you find yourself arguing for what is right, stop, and shift your perspective. From the perspective of Love, all is well. Your support of this expansive process within your being is a microcosm of the evolutionary process throughout all there is.

As you occupy more of your moments in the present space of Now, you are freed from the barriers and you find the balm of your truth. Like the flower that is fed by the waters of life, you are nourished with the light of your being in each expression of immaculate presence you experience.

Your conscious expansion is a process of taking the blinders off. The keys for navigating the waters of actualization are in your thoughts. Expansion occurs as thinking first. Thinking that questions the validity of your perspectives. "Is there something I am not seeing that would make a difference?" "What is possible here?" The open nature of curiosity advances your exploration. You will feel the binds of the past when you are arguing your point, or setting a power struggle of one over another, and when thoughts or actions are divisive. You will feel the dissonance of resistance, when your thoughts and actions are not in alignment with your highest knowing. We suggest you reconsider in those moments. The realization of resistance is the signal to shift your perspective. In shifting your perspective, you raise your frequency to see possibility, and the new arena of expansion will reveal itself to you. These are the thoughts that illuminate. The thinking of possibility. The process of conscious realization. As the new perspective reveals itself to you, your being shifts. The realization becomes a part of your conscious knowing. You cannot un-know what you now know, and your perspective is forever changed. You may dally with the old behaviors, but now they are birthed out of habit rather than unconsciousness. The compartmentalization that once was a refuge for perceived safety, in the light of your awareness, becomes the chains and shackles of unconsciousness.

The presence of Love shatters illusion. Continue your stance of radical faith as your thoughts and actions uncloak the brilliance of your light.

Today, I wash your feet, lovingly, tenderly removing the pain and despair of the past. Setting you newly upon your path of Love. The healing oils restore resolve for your mission of Love. It is with Love that I cradle your face in my hands and say again, you ARE the Beloved.

In Love, From Love, With Love

The Council of Light

DAY 66: THE EBB AND FLOW OF YOUR EXPRESSION

Good day! From the analogy of the gradient of expressions that make up your totality, you contain the All. We look today at how your range of expressions work together in propelling you into an expansive space of awareness.

On one end of the spectrum, where there is less light, there is a denser expression. From this space, the experiences are often gripped by fear. Fear has many expressions; fear of losing, fear of failing, fear of not enough, fear of others, fears associated with self-worth, to name a few. The dense experience is inherently a secretive type of experience, inviting isolation and separation. The denser experience also contains a quality of holding on, where the grip on control is strong. Human nature will always pull you back into the realm that you know, where you are right and maintaining the status quo. Divine nature resides beyond the limitations of your thinking and personality into the realm of I-don't-know, where your most expansive expression is found. Holding the distinction between human nature and divine nature is valuable.

As the light of conscious awareness is added to your moments in form, the experience is one of increasing ease. From the perspective of the Now immaculate moment, you experience a flow that is beyond your thinking of it. Ease is inherent to the Now. Your grip on the past is released with more time spent in the present moment. Trust of the essential Self leads the way. The edges of definition soften as you move beyond the fray of past and future concerns and experience the light expression available to you.

We refer to the gradient scale of being as it creates a picture that reflects every expression of you, from the densest to the most light filled. This is a foundational concept. As you compare both ends of the gradient of being, understand that you own it all. From the densest of experiences to the most light-infused experiences, they are all facets of your unique expression. You will find, as you own all parts of your expression throughout the gradient scale of being, you will develop a mastery of all the spaces. Rather than being defined by one singular frequency expression, you acknowledge the opportunity available at each point. As with observing the mind, when you own all the expressions of your being, they no longer bind you. They no longer define you. They become a part of the spectrum of light that is you.

As you compare the feeling you have in moments at the varying spots on the scale you notice the presence of constriction that accompanies denser expressions and the experience of flow that accompanies the more light-filled expressions of you. The purpose of our collaboration is to support your reach into the light expression of you. As more light is added to the palette of possibilities within your days, you find a shift in your experiences. You find a tendency to gravitate toward ease. The experience of being gripped in density is not comfortable. As the awareness of light is brought into your experience, there will be a natural leaning toward the light. The experience of density will draw you back into darkness at times because it is familiar and there is value to be garnered. The difference now, though, is you also have had the experience of light. You now know. While feeling unavailable in the moment, you remember the experience of being in your light expression and have the experience of the possibility.

Imagine the ocean tides being controlled by the pull of planetary forces. So too is your experience pushed and pulled by the juxtaposition of familiarity, habit, contrast, unconsciousness, constriction, and discomfort from the denser expressions and the experience of ease, flow, expansion, unity, and Love available in the moment of the light-filled expressions of you. You have a natural ebb and flow of awareness.

As more light is added into your moments of being present in your day, there is a tendency to spend more time in the space of light. The discomfort of the past will eventually give way to the ease that is available within the light experience. The dense expression will be a part of your possibilities, available for the experience of contrast whenever you choose. As more light is added you will not be as drawn toward the denser expressions. The contrast found in density may be appreciated as rich soil for discovery.

Every experience, whether the presence or absence of light or those points between, are a contribution to you. They are rich with opportunity; grist for the mill, so to speak. As more light is added to your experience you fine-tune your experiences from the perspective of wholeness. You hold realization of the broad array of expressions that are available. As you add light to your experience, the trajectory of your unique expression accelerates with the expansion now available within light. You will experience an ever-broadening range of expressions as a part of your palette of possibilities, because light expands. You will be pulled into possibility by the light you hold. As you increase your light expression, the denser experiences are welcomed for their value. You will find, as you bring light to your awareness, even your denser experiences will hold more light than the darkness of the unconscious experience. So even in the presence of contrast, you will be creating velocity as you bring more and more light to your experience.

We encourage you to experience the ever widening and deepening space that you occupy. You are coming home to you.

Day 67: Love Begets Love

Dearest, as you invite the light that is your natural expression into your moments, we would like to point out the result of this action. Love is the matrix, the DNA if you will, of all creation. As you settle into the experience of your highest expression, you bring with you an increasingly higher signature volume, or resonance, of Love. As you view all possibilities within the realm of creation, what you begin to see is the broad and vast expressions that are available. You see the expressions that are inherently expressing as a lack of light as well as those expressions at the opposite end of the gradient scale that possess a high level of light. All expressions are a part of the whole and are loved within their expressions equally. As the soul has the mandate of free-will choice, the possibilities of expression are infinite.

The evolutionary process of expansion is a force of the universe. There is no possibility of anything staying still. Creation is life force energy. It is vital, expansive, eternal, evolving in every moment throughout all that is. All creation evolves.

You get clues to the expressions of Love as you look at your experience in form. Your experience in form is a demonstration of Love in action. We utilize the image of the gradient scale to relay the variety of expressions that are available for you. Everything from the absence of light to the full presence of light: You own all of it. All of it, every stage, every moment is a possible expression for you. Your creation within each spot of the scale is infinite. Now we would like to introduce the principle of the evolving gradient. Imagine, if you will, the same gradient scale within a frame. The gradient is now moving in your vision in the direction of light. The gradient expressions available are still the same, in relationship to each other, except they now hold more light. There is the same distance between one end of the scale and the other. But now the conveyor belt of the gradient, through evolutionary action, has shifted toward the lighter end of the spectrum. The available choices in general hold more light than what was available at a previous evolutionary stage. Look at your experience in form, one generation to the next. Each generation has their life span in form, living each moment with the infinite array of possibilities available to them. The next generation, too, has the same infinite array of possibilities, but now in the passage of time and evolutionary action their creations are against the backdrop of an environment that is different.

The more light-filled background at each evolutionary point holds new possibilities not seen or envisioned by those of the previous generation (except for those few visionaries who operate beyond the bounds of seeming reality—you, for example). Nothing stays still.

As you stand back and hold a very large perspective, you may begin to see the sliding backdrop of creation that must hold more light. The relationship from one end of the scale to the other remains the same. What shifts is the environment the scale is running through. The background or environment for the experience in form is continually being added to with light. Why not the dark, you ask? Because who you are is Love. Plain and simple. For example, a rose even in the winter is a rose. With the lack of light and water, it does not become any less a rose. Any movement the rose makes is only toward the expression of rose. Not the expression of anti-rose. It does not turn into an orange. Divine design is either expressed or not.

As you feel the shifting gradient of being you see how it must contain more light. There is no going back. The circle of creation is not a closed loop. It is a spiral, ever evolving in form and ever gathering light. Every moment contributes to the evolutionary process of you. Every moment spent basking in the light of the Love that you are not only propels you but is a contribution to the All. Every moment you spend in the immaculate Now moment within the magnificent divine design of you is a propelling forward of all creation in the expression of light and the manifestation of Love.

Play within this arena. Enjoy every delicious moment in discovery of your brilliance. Your expression of Love propels. As when you add clear, fresh water to the bucket of muddy water, your visionary pursuits contribute beyond your wild imaginings to the return to Love. With each moment you spend in the divine realization of your magnificence, the background of creation holds more light, and you contribute to the All.

Love begets Love.

DAY 68: LIVING WITHIN
HIGH FREQUENCY

When you make the conscious choices for a high-frequency experience, what you don't see is how the universe moves in accommodation. When you ask for the materialization of an item, an event, or an awareness, you are heard. The gathering volume of your signature energy has weight behind it. The momentum of your expansion rings loudly throughout creation. In the expansion of consciousness, you are treading within more of the light expression of you and bringing new awareness into form. Consider that the denser thoughts feel low and slow, like cement. Feel the difference with thoughts that hold a finer light and higher frequency. They are lightning fast, potent, and multidimensional.

Owning the increasing power of your thoughts is an important concept to really grasp. Your mind is continually scanning, moving, examining. Your mind is highly active, evidenced by the rapidity of your thoughts moment to moment. As you hold more of the light expression that is authentically you, an owner's manual of sorts goes along with it. We would direct caution toward unconscious creation. Understand that you wield light with power that increases as you bring more of you in light into consciousness. Your presence in thought and consciousness is called for. As awareness is brought into your experience, equally more focus is required. Thoughtless thoughts create equally with conscious thoughts. The universal law makes no distinctions between the two. As you hold more of the territory that is you, there is more space to be aware of. In example, when you move into a larger home, you need to clean a larger home. As you bring the light of awareness to your experience, we would invite you to look more closely at the thoughts that run your day.

Conscious Intention

Whatever thoughts you have, know that they are creating. Consider fine-tuning the ability to focus your thoughts in the direction you choose. Choosing the thoughts that are high frequency and that are in alignment with the highest expression of you will also bring into your awareness the thoughts that are not that. So, when thoughts that are not in alignment with your highest frequency come into your mind, you may ask, "Am I being a contribution in this moment?" "Is my energy at this moment expanding or contracting?" In asking the question, the answer will arise. Then you may declare, "I choose to reframe my perspective." You have the ability, if you choose, to shift your perspective in the blink of an eye, rapidly from one moment to another. You are matching the movement of your conscious choice to the rapid movement typically present within your thoughts.

Bring your attention to the feeling of the frequency you inhabit. High frequency is found in a specific space. When you feel connected, use those moments to imprint the location of your frequency. Like a map of frequency for different expressions of you. There is nothing rigid and limited within the expression of you in light. But you may gather a general sense of the experience, rather like looking at colors from underwater; a somewhat more fluid view is accessed.

We choose to not contribute more words to today's conversation, but instead to supplement today's message with the energy that brings awareness of the places within frequency you inhabit. So, too, we would bring awareness to the patterns of thoughts generated.

Your expansion within light is supported with Love and delight and nurtured with ease and grace for all your systems.

DAY 69: YOUR LIGHT EXPRESSION, AUTHENTICALLY YOU

Today we would like to relay a broader understanding of the expression in light that you are. This is nothing new to the you in light; but as you occupy a material physical expression, this conversation supports an integration. The information today will be relayed through both words, so the mind may have something to hold onto, and through light, bringing ease to the integration of the light expression of you. With the analogy of the icebreaker ship, we are also opening new ground, so the conscious integration of the you in form and the you in light may be more fluid.

You, as a being of light in light, hold the information of all your expressions, all your history, all your knowing, simultaneously. Visualize a large library with each volume on the shelves containing the vast amount of experiences you have had in form. You can only imagine the expansive library you have accrued throughout your varied forms. While the information of your past lives in Atlantis or Egypt or other places may hold clues for you now, those moments have already been a contribution to you. All that you have seen, experienced, known, felt has been registered with the library of events. When you incarnate into form, the full memory of all life-times would be overwhelming and not necessarily pertinent to the mission you hold for the incarnation you are within at this moment. Consider that each segment or lifetime of your past experiences are facets of the diamond that is you. The divine light shining through-out the brilliant crystalline structure of you touches all parts of you without discrimination and emanates a brilliant prism of light with varying frequencies representing the rainbow of expressions of you.

At your genesis, you are coded with a divine design. The divine design is uniquely you, holding a specific note in the harmony of all there is. Like a fingerprint, your divine design is the signature energy that identifies you throughout creation as you, whether you are in form or not. The divine design, like DNA, holds all potential for expression that is uniquely you. Components of expression are unlocked at differing stages of your development and evolution as specific thresholds are crossed.

The density of experience in form is an opportunity to express in a variety of ways. Choices are made prior to your incarnation regarding the type of expression that would best suit your needs, from the perspective of your soul's evolution. Your time in form holds potential for a myriad of outcomes as you are at choice in every moment. You navigate the density of form, mostly from a state of unconsciousness, drawing deeply from the part of you that resides beyond form. This is the unconscious process. You have had lifetimes where, in the last moments of your life you saw the whole picture where the knowing of the you in form and the knowing of the you in light converge. You see opportunities taken, you see discoveries made, you see disappointments that blocked your view. The evolutionary opportunity at hand, is the convergence of your awareness within light with your material expression. This is the process of enlightenment.

You have a tremendous amount of information at your fingertips as you become consciously aware of the range of frequencies you inhabit. In the process of conscious integration, you acknowledge the primary purpose for your incarnation and utilize that impulse to guide your steps. As you live from the light expression of you, your soul's vision becomes a beacon. Your divine design has the opportunity for a high level of expression. As you evolve, you hold more of the light that is your divine nature. The innate acumen you hold at your essence is the *David* as revealed to Michelangelo. This is authentic expression.

Your light expression is fluid, multidimensional and naturally holds a high frequency. Your light expression is Love, grace, joy, peace, compassion. Your light expression is uniquely you. Enlightenment is a process that constantly challenges your perspective of boundaries, edges, and definitions. This is in order to support the realization of the fluidity of you that is beyond the bounds of definition by your mind.

You are the dichotomy. You are the divine expression of Love that reflects the magnificence of All. You are the One.

Day 70: Beyond Thinking
to Instinct

In today's conversation we would direct your attention to that part of your being where the limits of your mind's thinking end and the light knowing of you is engaged. This is the space we have referred to in previous conversations where, at the water's shallow edge, the amphibious car's wheels no longer serve, and the propeller needs to be engaged. This is a space of being that is confounding for most, as they hold the intention of integrating their light being with their physical form. It is the space where the mind has worked perfectly well up to this point and now, with the presence of more light (water in this analogy) new ground rules apply. As we speak these words with Darlene, she is in the spot where her mind disengages, and she shifts to sensing the expansive feeling inherent to that space. Standing at the pool's edge, you are in one environment and then with one jump, allowing gravity to move you, *poof*, you are in another. It is the space of that transition that we speak of.

As you hold the intention to incorporate more of the light knowing that is you, it is this threshold space that is key. Knowing how to traverse terrain at this spot on the gradient of your being is most valuable. We would ask you to consider becoming very familiar with this space. It is the point of transitions that may sometimes feel uncomfortable. This space is a spot on the gradient of your total expression that is always available for you. It has been perceived in the past as a barrier, as a threshold that may not be traversed. It is a delineating space. Focus on the mechanics within you at this point on the gradient, within your experience. Consider that it is a space where you shift modalities. It is a natural function, so when you cross this space, you hold the capacity to automatically change. In order to bring more of an ease to this transition we ask you to magnify your awareness of this spot. It will serve you well in your expansive process. The feeling of resistance at this point comes when the modality shifts from form to light. There is a subtle sense of giving up something, a surrender that turns many away. We would like you to consider that the whole of the gradient is *you*. You are only transitioning into a different function of your being. Like changing channels. Look at other areas where you naturally shift. When you begin to work out, after about ten to fifteen minutes, there is a point where your body will begin to produce sweat to cool you down. At that point too, your body naturally transitions to support your activity. For many, there is an experience of tension as the body begins to sweat. It's not always comfortable. Does that mean you should not work out for fear of crossing that barrier? No. You hold the capacity to move your body at high levels of exertion as well as the capacity to be in a resting state. Each stage holds value and is a natural expression of you.

Now apply that feeling to the tension that is felt at the transition of your awareness from linear thoughts and concerns to stepping over the threshold to more of the light expression of you. There is a moment of tension. With increased focus, you become aware of the perceived barrier and cross over that spot as gracefully and joyfully as you dive into a pool. You are looking at the more fluid aspect of your being, the part of you infused with more of the light that is your unique expression. This holds not thoughts necessarily; it holds multidimensional sensing, feeling, and instincts.

Multidimensional processing is unique to each being. Your instinctual, innate knowing communicates with you in a variety of ways: thoughts, words, pictures, feeling, colors, shapes, symbols, full concepts, sounds, music, sacred geometry. As you begin to navigate this area with more mastery, you appreciate the range of your expressions. You have heard about the value in following your gut, because your innate brilliance is found there. Now, instead of waiting to be struck by the lightning of your brilliance and your innate knowing, you hold the capacity to choose on purpose to move to the space of your instinctual and innate knowing, where all is available to you. As you own that spot on your gradient of being where you transition from mental activity to the fluidity of sensing, an ease develops. That threshold is crossed on purpose, like when you're moving into another room of your home.

The space of Now exists as the main experience on the other side of the threshold. The light knowing of you holds the authentic expression of you. The limitations of density cannot stand in the presence of light. You begin to find the rules and structure that exists within the light expression of you. In comparison to the rules of your experience in form, the rules in light feel formless. For now. There is a brilliant structure that rules all creation.

Become familiar with the spot on the gradient of your experience where you shift from density to light. Feel the shift from mind to instinctual, innate knowing. The expression of this shift is unique to each person. There is often a tension at that point that is misinterpreted as a DO NOT ENTER sign. Quite the opposite. The light beckons you to the magnificent expression of you that is expansive. The light expression of you brings with it ease, comfort, joy, direction, dimension, and Love.

Every experience you have of your brilliance in light is celebrated. You are the contribution of Love.

Day 71: Thriving: A Mystery School Lesson

The desire to thrive is not new. These are conversations we have held in past incarnations, even with some of you reading these words. We have sat together under the shade of great olive trees.

Thriving holds the experience of vitality. There is movement and activity in thriving. Thriving is dynamic. Thriving holds the experience of all-is-well. Thriving is born out of the Now moment. Thriving is spacious. Thriving holds confidence, empowerment, and Love. It is the experience that continues to snowball with momentum. Today, we look at the experience of thriving as it exists within separation consciousness and within unity consciousness.

Thriving against the background of survival consciousness has always held a constrictive tone, even amid the seemingly positive definitions. The background tone of survival consciousness touches the experiences that are created within that space. It must be so. Thriving within the backdrop of survival consciousness is as good as survival consciousness gets. It reflects a mastery of survival consciousness.

How then does the experience of thriving change now that it is against the backdrop of unity consciousness? First, we suggest it does. We would like you to consider the distinctions of thriving that now become possible with the shifting backdrop of unity consciousness. Unity consciousness expands. Separation consciousness constricts. They are oppositional and harmonious at the same time. Visualize the way the ocean tide retreats. That is the movement of separation consciousness. Unity consciousness expands and may be likened to the incoming tide. The shifting is as natural as the inhalation and exhalation of your very breath daily. One movement is expansive and the other is constrictive. Each stage has its own unique and perfect qualities. A divine interplay. Throughout creation there is the interplay of opposition; moving, spiraling, in the flow of an evolutionary tide. The opposing forces provide a traction to your evolutionary journey and propel your motion forward, ultimately toward light.

What becomes possible now, in the space of unity consciousness? What is possible with the experience of thriving? First feel in your knowing, from your memory, the experience you have had of thriving. Realize that experience, although feeling expansive, was created from a constricted space. The forces of constriction were at work placing an oppositional cloud over the experiences created. When you're walking up a mountain of sand, each step sinks under the weight of your foot. Your progress is hampered by the qualities of the terrain you cross. Great effort is required for the distance traveled. Similarly, if you walk up a down escalator, you will need to put in twice as much effort to go half as far, because you have a force that is in opposition operating equal to your efforts.

From the background of expansion within unity consciousness, the opposite experience is also true. Unity consciousness supports the experience of manifesting the light that you are because it supports expansion. As unity consciousness is already moving in an expansive direction, your efforts are supported and magnified by the movement. Do you feel the presence of possibility?

We would like you to reframe your what is possible against the backdrop of unity consciousness. What this requires is the turning of the tide within your awareness. Inhale the vitality of expansion that is available. You have already felt the expansive waves, and high-frequency movement available. Now we encourage you to step back and look again. Your what's-possible has just expanded exponentially again. And this will continue as a critical mass of momentum leads to velocity.

Your activities of expansion, the access to conscious awareness that holds more of the light that you are, is at your fingertips. Truly with ease. The experience available now of thriving is exponentially enhanced with the presence of unity consciousness. You don't have to contort yourselves or live a life of solitude to find enlightenment. The enlightenment is knocking on your door. Enlightenment was, is, and always will be completely in your hands.

Enlightenment beckons as the peak experience of thriving. Enlightenment, or the conscious owning of the light you are, bathes you in vitality, connection, peace, joy, Love, possibility, empowerment, expression, abundance, ease, and creativity. The unique qualities of you are supported now like at no other time in your incarnation.

Thriving is not a passive experience. It is the experience of authentic expression. As you constantly remove the burden of what is not you, you connect with the jewel of your uniqueness. What is now possible in your experience of thriving is beyond your imaginings. As you shift your limited view of what is possible to align with your expansive nature, within momentum, the doors open before you. Possibility exists now to master your most light-filled expression as you ride the wave of the expansive motion and momentum of unity consciousness.

You are designed to thrive. Connecting with all the brilliant aspects of your being brings a heightened vitality. We are a stand for your full-on expression made manifest.

DAY 72: ALCHEMY OF PRAYERS

As you understand prayer as an avenue of manifestation at your fingertips, we watch with delight as you wave the magic wand that is yours.

As with each creation, the result holds within it the frequency that was present at the creation. Prayers are an avenue of communication with the unseen throughout every major religion that ever has been. A myriad of perspectives may be the genesis of prayers, including desperation, duty, hopelessness, crisis, life-and-death moments, demand, reverence, habit, desire, surrender, affirmation, delight, and empowerment.

Prayers are a reach into the highest expression of light. To God, the creative principle, the Source of Love. As prayers are directed to the highest creative principle of Love, they are immediately generative. Then, "Why did I not win the lottery?" you may ask. There are many factors that are contributors to the alchemy of prayers. If the request is made, but all of you is not on board with the request, the frequencies do not line up, and the strength of the signal is not clear. If you are sending the prayer, "I want to win the lottery tonight," but the inner frequency also being sent is "This is beyond my reach. I don't really believe I will win the lottery," the signals are mixed. It is the emotional message that is delivered to the universe, not the words of the wish. When prayers are expressed in wishes, they remain wishes.

As you claim the light expression of you and begin to live more from the elevated experience of light, your creative expression is amplified as well. You are a master creator. As you bring a level of conscious awareness to your moments, you begin to see the magic of the creative principle you are within and made of. If you do not already pray, we recommend you begin. This is an extension of the creator that you are.

Prayer Exercise

This is an active conversation. Over the next days and months, we will support your awareness. This is not as much about the success of the prayer being answered as it is about your consciousness of the process. If you choose to participate, we would ask you to consider three prayers. Write them down, and think about them in the framework of the following questions:

1. *What is the frequency you are in when the prayer is made?*
2. *What is your internal dialogue about the request?*
3. *What is the emotional charge you hold about your prayer?*
4. *Are you holding limitations within your energetic field? What kind?*
5. *Are you in the moment?*
6. *Is the prayer made from beliefs that exist in the past or future?*
7. *What are your beliefs about prayers?*

As you claim the light expression of you, you will notice your thoughts and awareness shifting. Your environment reflects your true nature, like looking in the mirror. Now we are asking you to play a game. Consider becoming curious about your beliefs around prayer. As you ask questions, look for the answers. How do the answers arrive?

We would leave you with this for today. We are on a most magnificent journey together. One that is filled with Love, delight, joy, discovery, and authentic expression. We are in support of the discovery of you unto you.

Day 73: Allow, Release, Bask in Love

D ear Ones, today we would take a respite from the intensity of our lessons to reassure you on your path of expansion. As your reality shifts within this process of enlightenment there is a process of integration and reframing that is required.

Consider that if you undertake a physical regimen and nutritional program that supports your well-being, your form changes. The clothes and habits of earlier times no longer fit. There is a reframing needed to align to the new experience of what-is-so. In the reframing process, there is a reset button that is struck. As when you wipe a slate clean, a whole new set of possibilities become available. We spoke of prayers yesterday, and today's discussion still holds that in mind. Rather than a feeling of pushing forward today we are choosing to set the tone to one of being. This is an experience of stopping and getting your bearings. Take a moment to revel in the new landscape around you. Once you set out on a journey there is a tendency to keep pushing forward, to fight the uphill battle, to push and work hard out of the Love and devotion that you possess. We would ask you to BE with us today.

Become familiar with allowing. Allowing is the space of ease, within which you open gently to the new possibilities before you.

As you state your prayers, how do you know they have been answered? If you are holding the stance of working hard and pushing forward, there is so much activity, there is no space for allowing, and receiving answers is not on your radar. In the lack of allowing, prayers get more insistent and answers therefore feel farther away. Like the activity present within stillness, allowing is the gentle releasing of barriers and boundaries that accesses a shift. Allowing is the portal to the next more light filled expression of you.

Your vision has expanded. You are more acutely aware of your surroundings as more information is perceived. Your vision holds information with more depth, color, and frequency. We ask you to consider employing that ability now. Allow gently, as you recline and release into a basking, within the space of Love. Right now, in this moment, notice the shift that has occurred with your awareness. Notice the ease. As you settle into this moment of Love, allow the slight turn of the faceted expression of you. You hold more light now. Your senses are feeling more expansive, softer, and more acute at the same time. You are gathering more information from light.

You are held in the arms of the divine. Beloved, release your fears. Yield to the warm embrace of Love. The fears from the past no longer serve you. Allow them to fall gently. In the process you are restored.

Today, we bask in Love.

DAY 74: A MULTIVERSAL
PERSPECTIVE

Good morning, this is Thoth stepping to the forefront of today's gathering. It is with delight we offer a new perspective. Today's gathering is one of joy, Love, support, and a reunion of sorts, emboldening the mission you have set out upon during this lifetime. As this is a creation that comes from the All, your conscious awareness of the All is appropriate. This is a vast multiversal meeting today, taking place in this Now divine immaculate moment.

The location of this gathering is another way to bring a sense of the far reach available to you as you gather more of the light that is you authentically. The shift in frequency provides an opportunity to stretch your awareness.

This is the Arcturian Council stepping to the forefront of this divine conversation. It is with delight we participate and support the efforts of the expansion of Love's light. It has been your innate knowing of the truth of you that has drawn you to the frequency of this work. This work is a conduit for the remembering of the divine expression of Love that you be.

We rejoice in every step, in every magical moment you spend in the realization of the divine creature you are. We are in a collective with All, in support of Love and freedom. We support the matrix of this work as it shines a light on possibility, where Love, sovereignty, and discovery of your divine truth may be actualized. Our participation could be described as contributing to an environment that, as you choose, you may draw upon to access your truth.

Activation of Light

We, as a collective, open a portal of knowing. If you choose to participate, we provide a light frequency, like a shower of brilliance. This activation of light is within a range that will enhance your process, activate codes that are ready to be unlocked, and support the ease of this process and therefore your natural expression of joy and peace.

The Stargate for this light activation will be active for the next 48 hours. Please drink water. You are held within a healing space of expansion, Love, release, light, integration, peace, and joy. You may experience a sense of effervescence as your light knowing is integrated into your awareness.

The restraints from the past are powerful forces. For many, the experience of a shift in consciousness brings awareness of restraints and constrictions, developed over many incarnations. The opportunity at hand now is the release of what-was and consequently the door opens to the light of your expression. The challenge of this time is in the shifting tide from separation to unity consciousness. The experience of separation consciousness holds a constricting tone. Unity consciousness holds a tone of opening and expansion. Together, they hold the keys to the truth. One may not be seen without the other. The opportunity now is to own the lessons of the past incarnations and turn to face the light of the experience of unity consciousness that is present in this Now moment. As you own the pieces of your past that have been restrictive, you are free. They have no control over you. The past has already been a contribution to you; it no longer needs to hold you in the darkness of the consciousness and the limitation it was conceived within. There is an opening of your eyes that is available now as your awareness has expanded. Your vision may shift to reflect your ability for fine sensing.

As you close the door to the past and bring that to a neutral space within your being, what becomes more readily available is possibility. The background of separation consciousness operates in opposition to the concept of expansion. Now, in the presence of unity consciousness, you are supported on every level. This is an evolutionary process. You have also held the position of experience of the opposite perspective; from unity consciousness to separation consciousness. You did so in those times to gain the value of growth within a constrictive background. As your heart expands and contracts, so does all creation.

This is Ptaah, Pleiadian Master Teacher, stepping forward in this conversation. As pioneers and courageous explorers at the forefront of expansion, you have been incarnated at those moments in evolutionary process where the influx of light has been important and, shall we say, even critical. You all hold the mission of Love as your mandate.

We are here in support of the ease and grace with every awareness you have. The process of the integration of the light that is you is our focus. We support and contribute the ease and richness of experience as you consciously claim your truth. This is a process of illumination. As you realize the parts of you that exist in light and bring them into your awareness, the light that you are emits your divine essence. The light of Love, the note of healing and peace radiates from your being.

We are allies. We are advocates of Love. We see the brilliant expressions of Love that you BE. We support you in the realization of your authentic expression.

In Love and in light, we close our gathering for today.

Day 75: Navigating Open Space; Learning to Flow

The co-creation of this work in the Now moment is significant. This is not something that can be anticipated or expected. The invitation of enlightenment is movement to your most expansive expression as it resides within the formless.

The frequencies shared daily shift. You have already felt the differing tones, all reflective of the varied frequencies of location, contribution, and signature energies of the Council of Light. The reach of frequency has shifted since Day 1. This is on purpose and can be no other way. The universe is not one note. The universe does not stay still. One rapturous moment of Love and connection gives way to a new expression of Love in each Now moment. We meet in a variety of frequencies, all reflective of your authentic nature and in support of your conscious expansion. As we guide Darlene to these spaces and frequencies, so too are you led to the spaces of frequency and light that are appropriate for your next steps of awareness.

The experience of learning (remembering) how to navigate your light expression requires a constant letting go of your known realm and a broadening of perspective. The mastery of your mind to hold your reality within the bounds of the known is insistent, persistent, and powerful. In the same way you are learning to watch your thoughts from the space of the observer, you are learning to shift your awareness from the edges of form to the formless. As if living in a river, feel the flow of life and light around you. There is safety in the fact that your mind can now grasp onto a new reality within a moving environment.

As you increase your own light, your awareness turns slightly to reveal a new facet of you. As you become adept at living within shifting realities, where the once hard edges are now fluid, consider working with the capacity of your mind's brilliance and not in opposition. This perspective holds you as the one in charge of your mind and not the other way around. Choose how your day will go at the start of each day. Unless you choose consciously, you are setting your day up from the perspective of habit, where the limitations of your mind will rule.

As you adjust to the reliability of movement and your presence in the Now moment, you begin to find relief and relaxation "basking on the river." You will notice an ever-changing landscape that is there for your delight. You release the edges of expectation, to drink in the beauty and divine nectar of the moment.

We would refer to your prayers at this moment. Please write them out. Notice the feelings you have around that. We would request your written prayers be placed in a special space where you will see them daily and read them. This may be a part of your daily rituals. Each time you read your prayers, read them from the energy present at the inception of them. Hold them as beautiful expressions of you. Each prayer is cherished. Allow the experience of need to fall away. For example, visualize yourself in the river, in the flow of life. Imagine choosing a beautiful meal for the evening. With that same delight, you choose the prayers that you have written. Do you see how the slightest perspective shift brings a neutrality born of the Now moment?

Bask, Dear Ones, in the river of the immaculate Now moment. Drink in the nectar of beauty available for your delight. Relax, release, allow. Flow with the beauty of the landscape that is you.

DAY 76: ABUNDANCE, PRAYER, AND INTENTION

Have you been observing your thoughts around prayer and manifestation? Prayer is another mode of manifestation. You are magnetic; you create in every moment with your thoughts and intentions, either consciously or unconsciously.

Over your lifetimes, you have amassed fortunes of immense proportions. It is the experience of the time, forged by beliefs, fears, and circumstance that have held the riches at bay. Consider they are still in your etheric bank account. Creating against the background of separation consciousness is one of contraction and constriction. Now, with the presence of unity consciousness, you are invited into wholeness. Consider your etheric bank account is available to you more easily now than in the past. Then how do you access it? Take down the wall of separation that exists within you. The light of your true nature supports the dissolution of old constructs.

Separation consciousness has you separate from the full illumination of your soul. Separation consciousness holds within it the disinheriting of the magnificence of you in light. Separation invites a myopic perspective that diminishes your value. Do you have a difficult time asking for things? Do you have a difficult time accepting and fully receiving Love, gifts, compliments? Do you place limitations upon your wealth and freedom? These are constructs that remain from separation consciousness. Consider that a part of the work you signed up for, in your choosing to be in form at this time, is for the conscious deconstruction of the old. There is as much deconstruction occurring here as construction.

Beyond the Wall of Separation

Consider: There is a wall of separation that exists within you. What does it look like? What is the texture? How tall is it? What is it made of? Feel the separation that exists within you. Notice how it shows up. It is sometimes ever so subtle. Visualize, on the other side of the wall, all the riches in material wealth and awareness, amassed from all your previous lifetimes. Feel the Love that is there for you on the other side of the wall.

As the wall of separation has been a divider, representing a chasm within you, the opposite is also true. The wall has been a gift that, in its presence, has supported an evolutionary process that is rich beyond compare. The wall has held great value in your expansion. Now, from the background of unity consciousness, the tide has turned. It is not that the wall comes down as much as the wall is no longer a barrier. It is a threshold that you may move beyond. The wall is now permeable, allowing the light of unity consciousness to shine on all aspects of your being. Now it is not one side of the wall or the other. In the presence of unity consciousness, you are All.

Look at your wall now from the perspective of unity consciousness, do you feel the permeability? Do you see a door? Has the wall turned to light? Feel that the wall is no longer a barrier. You are rejoined with all aspects of you, including all the riches in your etheric bank account.

As you view the wall of separation within, you realize there is a portion of you that has held back in the desiring of things so good, they seem impossible. Look at your receptivity. Are your arms open? View all barriers you have had to receiving and allow a new experience of receptivity that is unhindered. The flow of wealth, once seen as a trickle, is now greater than the flow of all the oceans.

Prayer and Intention

An intention is a specific request or desire that is in alignment with your conscious choice. A powerful contributor to creation, intention sets the direction for creating. Intentions are most often made within the bounds of belief.

Prayer is a space, or frequency to live from. Consider that your prayers come from a place that is a background of life; as an environment from which you create abundance, Love, creativity, joy, peace, well-being, ease and grace, integrity, expansion, realization, and more. Consider the thought, "I choose to live from the space of prayer." In the perception of the word prayer, *you reach the unknown of the divine. You touch the miraculous for which you have no logical understanding. You connect with your highest expression for creating. Do you feel the shift? Does that feel more expansive? Does it hold more potential for outcome?*

Prayer is the backdrop that your intentions are fueled within.

As you begin to develop a new perspective, turn ever so slightly to express through a new facet of your being. Notice the possibilities that abound. Hold your arms open wide and receive all that is yours to be, do, and have. This is your birthright.

Day 77: Sacred Stillness + Illumined Action = Transformation

As the reach into the light of your being extends farther into the higher frequencies of your essence, the ability to navigate the stillness is paramount.

We have spoken at length of the natural movement and curiosity of the human mind. The mind's incessant motion moves you beyond the moment, to the future, and swings to the past, bringing baggage into the clear waters of the present. Visualize the spokes of a wheel. They originate at the center and extend to the outer rim of the wheel. The space between the spokes at the outer rim is greater than the space between the spokes at the center. This applies to your mind's activity: The farther afield your attention moves from your center, the more diffuse your presence becomes and the easier it is to lose stability in your navigation. The ability for stillness is paramount as it connects you to your unlimited self.

You have noticed as you sit still in meditation that it is your thoughts that flood in, as an insistent barrage demanding attention. The immediate reflex is to remove the thoughts. We suggest you consider a new tactic. Consider being still between the thoughts. Focus on the space or pathway between the thoughts, where the thoughts will no longer pull you. Like a raven drawn to shiny objects, your mind will always move to distraction. From the perspective of unity consciousness, your core strategies shift. Unity consciousness will direct you to wholeness, where all things have their place. Visualize your thoughts as raindrops of a spring shower. Their gift to nurturing life is appreciated *and* you may navigate through them without getting wet.

As you call upon your capacity for sacred stillness, you employ the presence of your highest expression. It is within the stillness that you receive your greatest inspiration, as it arises into your awareness. It is the experience of your most expansive nature focused in full presence. In the acknowledgment of your authentic divine expression, there is no task that is beyond your ability.

Guided by your inspiration, look for the steps of action. Many people stop at inspiration and revel in the beauty of the moment. Consider staying in the space of stillness and allow the steps for action to arise in your awareness. The path of action will become apparent within the stillness, as you ask. As a flashlight beam cuts through the dark of night, a path will be revealed to manifest your greatest inspiration.

Today, we introduce the quality of illumined action. Consider illumined action as the inspired action that is required to actualize your highest expression. Illumined action brings the inspiration into form. Divine design needs form as the chalice for manifestation.

Inspiration on its own is a beautiful moment.
Inspiration with action is transformation.

You are learning to play the keys of your being at the other end of the keyboard. There is beautiful music to be played.

DAY 78: DIVINE EMBODIMENT

Our sacred conversation today is relative to the embodiment of the divinity of you, where you align with your I AM self. Today we facilitate the conversation between you in light and you in form. We would ask you to consider, as you integrate the divine expression of you that is in light consciously, that what is really occurring is an embodiment of you.

The intention today is to provide an image of the process of enlightenment and actualization. You as a divine creation have always existed in light. You span a variety of frequencies that are ever evolving.

The presence of unity consciousness is a support for the process of actualization, where you may embody your highest expression. The process of embodiment does not occur outside of you; this is an inner process where the limitations of the physical experience are no longer barriers to the clear and reliable voice of your divine essence. You have always drawn upon the you that reigns in light. The highest-frequency expression of you has always been your source of inspiration and provided the sense of connection with All.

You have had glimpses of your true nature through moments that are so beautiful they take your breath away. It is in those moments that your essential self moves through the barriers of your perception into conscious awareness. It is the intention of this work to support your deeply held vision for this life, to access your totality. The access to your divine wisdom then becomes something you can rely upon. Your enlightenment opens the door to possibility as you access your divine nature.

What becomes possible when you shift your awareness from living within a small range of experience to the totality of your expression? Please sit with that for a moment. You have been living in a segmented reality, looking at small holograms of expression of you. The opportunity at hand is the full embodiment of all of you.

How does this feel? You know when you are operating within a low-frequency space. There are characteristics and qualities inherent to density, earmarked by the experience of resistance. The resistance comes because lower-frequency thoughts and actions are not in alignment with the divine knowing that is inherently you. What becomes possible if you are able not only to connect with the highest expression of you, but to embody you? Do you feel the difference?

Up to this point, we have held the perspective of human nature, the experience of you in physical reality. What if you shift your perspective to the opposite end of the spectrum to view yourself as your divine essence? Stand at the space of your I AM Self. Imagine experiencing not only your human nature but your divine nature, consciously.

As you begin to view the you that exists in light as a part of the you in form, you open to the expansive expression that is inherently, uniquely, and divinely you.

As you choose to embody the you that exists in light, possibility expands exponentially. With the shift in perspective, the unknown is replaced with clarity.

We have asked Darlene and you to write out your prayers. The reason? Prayers come from the expansive space of your knowing, they are a communication from the you in form to the you in light. Who you are is Source. Who you are is Love. Your prayers access the collective of Love. You are not alone—never have been and never will be. You are a part of the All.

The Love you seek is the Love you are already.

It is with delight we support every sacred moment of the integration of you unto you.

Day 79: Shifting the "We" of Embodiment to "I AM"

I t is the intention of this work to support you in not only seeing but experiencing the grandeur and magnitude of who you are in your full expression. We suggest it only takes a few shifts of the diamond that is you to reveal a new facet of your brilliant expression where all may be revealed. We say that who you are is Source in form. Sit with that for a moment. What does that then make possible?

As you stand at the far end of the gradient scale of light where your full divine essence resides, the whole landscape of your being may be seen clearly. Even as we keep making the distinction of the "you in form" and the "you in light," the goal is for your experience to be cohesive. You are not divided. Holding the distinction of you and you, the parts in form and in light, ultimately feels divisive as the truth is "We." As you look at the possibilities that surround the concept of you embodying you, we would ask you to consider utilizing "I AM" as your reference. "I AM" encompasses the totality of you. The view of who you are in light has not been expansive enough to include all of you. We would ask that you begin to shift the thoughts around who you are.

Consider the element of water. As you are reading this now, there is water in liquid form in your oceans, lakes, and rivers. There is water in cloud form in your skies, water in frozen form at your mountains and polar caps. You, too, occupy a vast range of expression and form. Who do you have to be to take on embodying all of you? If you were Source, who would you be being? We suggest the awareness of all of you consciously is connecting with the Love and joy that is you authentically. Your highest expression is possible.

Today's conversation takes place more in light than in words. The words on this page are a catalyst for truly knowing your magnificence. As you examine the diamond that is you, shift perspective again to reflect light through another facet where your truth is revealed.

Today an energetic component is integral to our conversation. If you so choose, the clarity of knowing you in form and you in light is brought closer.

What becomes possible when you are consciously aware of the magnitude of you?

DAY 80: YOUR HIGHEST EXPRESSION

W hy is it we would ask you to see the totality of you and bring that to your life? The opportunity at hand is the divine expression of you full on, consciously, beyond the barriers of the veil of illusion. Within these past 79 days you have experienced an ease. You have taken a deep breath as you settle into a space of truth within you. Your vision has started to expand. You are considering possibilities previously beyond the grasp of your known realm. You have shifted to a new facet of your expression. As the light of your divinity shines through yet another facet of you, your perspective expands. There is an opening present, as with the first sunny days of spring, warming the blossoms yet to be. In the full expression of you, there is ease, confidence, knowing, and expansion that is naturally you.

As the perceived barriers to being in form are suddenly, or gradually, lifted, what becomes possible is the relief of burdens. Issues in your life are seen from a broader perspective, lessening the grip they have held. Where you have felt stopped before, you see light upon a new path. Your life doesn't live you. You live your life. You live on purpose and with purpose, because you choose powerfully and clearly. Fulfillment, joy, and abundance are natural symptoms of alignment. Who you are is of a magnitude that is expansive and blindingly exquisite.

Is there anything that is not within your reach? You are Source in form. You are a being of light, extended into form. As you hold the courage to move through the barriers that see you as small and as less than, you find your mastery. Would a rose ever experience itself as less than a rose? Why do you? We ask you to pivot. We ask you to be curious about you. We ask you to see the divine in yourself and in each other.

As you open your awareness, feel the crystal clarity of your choices. Choose on purpose. What if there was no-thing beyond your realm of possibility? What if you truly lived from the perspective of the blank canvas of all possibility, in each Now sacred moment? This expression is uniquely yours. You have left clues for yourself. How have you felt in those most extraordinary times of your life when you experienced a flow of being? Did you notice resistance? The presence or absence of resistance gives you information. This is the experience of resonance.

Look to your natural abilities for clues around how you receive inspiration. Color, thought, words, feeling, knowing, sound, music, movement? As you gain clarity with the natural function of integration of your light knowing, you may expand your abilities consciously, on purpose. You are becoming consciously aware of your multidimensional nature.

You hold the keys to the kingdom. You reside in the kingdom. We place upon the altar for you, if you choose, an activation of your vision. The shift will allow a slight turn, a bend of your reality, a glimpse at the truth of you. Brilliant.

Day 81: The Vision of You

The shift we ask you to consider is the opening of a new realization of you. We have spoken early on of the correlation between expansion and the expectation of movement. A shift must take place in order to facilitate expansion of awareness. The experience of change is mandatory as you integrate your light expression into your physical expression. This work resides beyond nice thoughts into something that makes a difference in your life now. Most likely you will experience a series of small shifts in awareness that result in an ease-and-grace-filled new realization. Do you see the openings in your awareness that impact the living of your moments?

As you move forward into a new space of unknown, there is more to see. For many there will be a temptation to stop as you create a new comfort zone. We suggest that the new vision of who you really are is the next step to be taken. In holding an expansive, evolving experience of your Self, you are empowered, as clarity points the way. Arguments for obstacles diminish in their validity.

We would like to make the distinction between thinking about shifting your reality and literally living it. Visualize a postcard of the Grand Canyon. It holds an image of a real place. The light, the features of the rock, and movement of the water is seen. Now place yourself in the Grand Canyon at the spot where the photo is taken. You experience the physical presence of the canyon. You hear the sounds, you feel the warmth of the sun, you feel the breeze upon your face. You sense the magnitude of the Grand Canyon the way you cannot through a picture. We ask you to consider that your process of enlightenment is a reality that makes a difference in your life in this Now moment. You may experience yourself shifting from the perspective of watching the image of your life to engaging your greatest expression. A whole new dimensionality is added to your life experience. Now is the time to open the treasure chest and put on the new vision of you.

As you shift the experience of your Self, your attention turns to who you are in light. From the perspective of your light expression, we offer a process of integration. Your signature energy is the identifier of who you are, like a fingerprint. Turn up the volume of your signature energy. As your awareness expands, the previous expression of you no longer fits. Expanding your signature energy allows space for your growth. This is a valuable tool for integrating your light expression into your conscious awareness.

Amplify Your Signature Energy

1. *Look for the energetic signal that you emit. How far does your beam reach? Visualize a volume knob or a signal tower. Turn up the volume or expand the reach of your signal to a point that feels full. In turning up your signature energy field, you have created space for your expansion.*
2. *Another analogy is a garden hose with a kink, representing the flow of your energetic field. Can you un-kink the hose and have the energy that is you flow easily and abundantly?*
3. *Blowing up a balloon that rests within a box will work for only so long, until the balloon becomes contained by the box and further expansion is not possible. We ask that you either remove the box or make the box larger to contain the next level of potential expansion.*

This work is beyond your ability to think it. Shifts will show up as you live your Now moments. As you release limitation, the opening is created for you to align with the expression that is authentically you. The definitions and specific edges you have developed in the past will shift in meaning. The expansive expression of you does not fit within the cookie-cutter definitions. As your perspective shifts, you will experience the difference.

Your experiences will move you, one foot in front of the other, easily, to the expansive expression of your nature.

DAY 82: IN REVERENCE OF YOU

Before you incarnated, you held intentions for the possibility of full conscious awareness. Your gaze has turned inward. Your access to the lightness of your being brings peace, warmth, and respite.

The distractions of the external world are now viewed from a broader perspective. The light of your being is a stabilizing force in the global transition of consciousness. The darkness of unconsciousness is shattered through your authentic expression. The work you do for you, you do for all. You have chosen to transform your physical experience. You have chosen the fire of the Phoenix.

As you access the light of your essential self, your impact is no less valuable than those of the Masters. Jeshua has said, "These things that I do, you do, and even greater." Your stance of Love holds global impact.

Today, we, as beings of light in light, sit in reverence of the divine expression of you. You are held in Love and appreciation for all you be. We place upon the altar for you a recalibration process that supports the integration of your light as you move into your expansive expression.

The space of reverence holds a gentle re-sourcing as you align with your divine essence. Allow the warmth of divine light to soothe, regenerate, support, and gift you.

In reverence of you.

DAY 83: THE LIGHT YOU HOLD

The process of enlightenment is not one that exists only in light. Consider that your physical presence is the chalice for the light of you. You are form and you are light. The light of you requires form for manifestation.

The transmission available today is of support for your physical being. In the same way the enlightenment process expands your capacity in light awareness, the capacity of your physical body to accommodate light expands, activating even greater awareness.

Your body is ever moving, repairing, healing, and processing. Consider your capacity to hold light as another developmental stage. As specific light thresholds are met, new levels of potential are released. In example, an infant must sit before walking and walk before running. As the light of your essential self is activated, by passing through developmental thresholds, codes for your next stage of awareness are unlocked. All in perfect timing. As each intention, choice, and action affirms your trajectory, your body activates finer levels of sensing. Your body must shift to hold the new levels of frequency you are utilizing.

As your field of awareness expands, you access your multidimensional expression. Awareness, perspectives, and knowing that lived below the radar of your consciousness previously are now an integral part of your day. You experience a broader perspective and fluidity of being. The shift in your physicality may show up in new sensitivities or you may have new preferences for food. Is your food a resonant match for your body? Are your choices for movement and exercise a resonant match? We suggest you bless your food before consuming it. "I send Love and appreciation to this meal. The light value of this food supports and nourishes me." Drinking more water and getting more rest will support you as well.

Light Activation for Physical Well-Being

The light in your body is held within a crystalline grid. The transmission today provides an amplification and activation of your divine design held within your physical coding. This makes available the light of your conscious awareness to be held in your body with ease. As your body begins to vibrate at a higher frequency, the structure for your next steps of conscious expansion are supported. This transmission is the beginning of the activations joining your physical vehicle with your light vehicle. An exponential increase in your capacity to hold light is available.

This activation looks like a moving, multidimensional flower of life, golden in color, with a double terminated crystal in the center. Access points throughout the matrix are illuminated, sending communication throughout your being. This is a catalyst for your highest expression made manifest. Visualize yourself resting within the center of the golden flower of life sphere.

As you choose, this process will take place over the next twenty-one days, with ease and grace for all your systems. You may feel a speeding up within your body.

There is space to relax into your fully integrated self as your physical expression and light expression converge at a higher level.

Day 84: Following Frequency

Today is a field trip of sorts, to access the finer sensing now within your awareness. As you gain conscious access to more of you, you also access ability to discern what was previously out of sight.

Hold the intention of aligning with the highest expression of you available in the moment and you will naturally be occupying more of your Now moments. The process of aligning with your essential Self is a profound action that alters your reality by holding you in the present moment. When you occupy the present moment, you have access to your greatest expression. Consider that anything less than the present moment is a replay of what has already happened. Being in the Now moment is the most potent action you can take. You will find a whole new window to your world. Your creations will be occurring more rapidly as your thoughts find less resistance.

Aligning with your essential nature of Love, as your reliable touchstone, will guide you to your highest expression. Keep reaching for your highest expression of Love.

Today we speak of frequency. Access to your expression in light has increased exponentially. This may be experienced as a new sense of ease, freedom, and connection. New perspectives are rising to your awareness, as the hard edges of beliefs, habits, and the past soften and you align with your divine knowing.

Movement in light and frequency is subtle. Your thoughts steer your awareness to the frequency band you occupy. Bringing more attention to your own frequency is important as you take responsibility for your own creations. Consider your movement to the finer frequencies of your own awareness. It is about perspective. Consider moving your awareness to the fine frequencies available to you.

In example, Darlene shifts her frequency on purpose so we may meet in high frequency locations. The benefit is felt in the potency of our work together. Your Scribe meets us halfway. This is a divine collaboration. The work of *In Service to Love* is not accessed from the dense frequency experience. Darlene has had to do her consciousness work in order to move beyond the limitations of form. If you want high-frequency awareness and results in your life, consider moving your awareness to high-frequency spaces within you. There, you find a natural, rich expression that is filled with ease.

What if you changed your frequency on purpose to spend moments in the high-frequency spaces available to you? What if you went to the space where peace and Love reside at their highest expressions? What if you are invited to meet Masters in light?

Meditation: An Invitation to Sit with the Masters

As you sit in a comfortable space, follow your breathing gently as it evens and slows. Feel the blessing of the earth below you. Feel the expansive space you occupy in light. Visualize a brilliant, sparkling white cylinder of light around you. Expand the cylinder out to include the room you are within. Extend the cylinder of light down deep within Gaia and up into the heavens. Encompass your full range of light.

Sit within the illuminated space and feel the totality of you. We are with you as you do this exercise. Choose the energy of one of the beings of light who are present today: Jeshua, Mary Magdalene, Thoth, Buddha, Archangel Michael, Archangel Gabriel, Melchizadek, St. Germain, the Elohim, Infinite Oneness, your Council of Light. Feel the frequency of the being or group you choose.

Follow their energy to the high-frequency space where they are. You will sense a location. You will be met halfway. Follow their frequency pattern. Allow it to call you easily. You may visualize a home, a space in nature, or a gathering place that is formless. Follow the path before you. You experience not only the divine expression you are, you meet eye to eye, peer to peer, divine to divine with the being of light whose frequency you have chosen to follow. Be with them and receive a message.

There is a gift for you that has been placed upon the altar. You may pick it up and receive it. When you are ready, return to your physical body and to your environment as you sit comfortably. Connect with your breathing and open your eyes.

With more exposure to the highest frequencies in light, your being will entrain to your highest expression. This is a demonstration of the expansive expression of you. You move as easily in form as in light. With each new awareness, you experience the resonance of your essential nature.

It is from the space of the immaculate Now that your true brilliance and divine expression may be seen. We delight in every new flash of magnificence that is revealed.

DAY 85: YOUR ACCESS TO A BROADER RANGE OF LIGHT

The fertile soil of your being supports the expansion of your awareness at an accelerated rate. Your reach into the fine realms of frequency has expanded in breadth and depth. Equally, your integration of light within your physical expression has expanded. The reason for expansion is not that you finally have access. You have always had access to your I AM Self. The more you align with your true nature, by no longer paying attention to that which is not your true nature, the more you find you thrive. Your ability to create with clarity is muddied when your thoughts move you away from the present moment. Most people live their lives from the space of "absence" in their life, living in reaction and separation. The moments of distraction, lack of presence, and limiting beliefs diminish the potential for the natural process of enlightenment to take place. Enlightenment requires a new perspective.

The divine nectar of the light you hold amplifies all of you. Like eating the highest value of nutrition possible that accelerates your well-being exponentially, the light you are incorporating into your experience is manna for your highest expression. The result is an experience of not just surviving but thriving on all levels. The frequency of the light you are incorporating into your awareness is the equivalent of jet fuel for your growth. All aspects of your being are elevated: body, mind, and spirit.

Today is a day of integration of the highest light expressions of you with your physicality. You will notice a new way to inhabit your body, one that has you occupy more space. Like the air in a full balloon occupies all the available space in the balloon's shape. The experience of less light has you occupy less space within your body. Your light is identified with your increased presence in the Now moment. The increase in frequency, light, and presence creates momentum; like a snowball moving downhill, it gathers velocity.

Your conscious access to your multidimensionality is imminent. As you focus on the immaculate Now moment, there is depth to your daily experience. Your ability to hold high frequency increases. Resonance appears as a touchstone for choices. Because you are magnetic, the higher your frequency, the higher frequency you attract. You will notice a shift in your life events. As you continue dropping the definitions and limitations of a past reality, you open the door to your greatest expression made manifest.

With your conscious movement toward Love, your unique expression is revealed. Life shows up with ease as you be more of who you already are and less of who you are not. Your divine authentic nature becomes the lens through which you view your world. What must then be possible?

Keep noticing the shifts in your awareness. Remember to bless your food and fill it with the highest light to nourish not just your body but your being.

We are your biggest fans! We see the light expression of you expand with velocity.

The Love you are transforms.

Day 86: Equilibration

You have found that the edges of your reality have softened and are experienced as somewhat diffuse. In general, your days flow with ease. However, when an emotional trigger surfaces, it holds all the weight, history, reaction, and patterns of the past in your body. As you move through your expansive process, old triggers will come up to be addressed. This is not a sign of going backward; quite the contrary. There is a calling for a review of sorts of the issue at hand, elevating it into alignment with the higher frequency you now hold. The only way to do that effectively is from the perspective of the immaculate Now moment. The Now moment holds all the conscious awareness that is available to you.

When you are met with the intensity of emotional reaction to certain situations, it may feel all encompassing. In the process of reworking and reconsidering emotion-filled issues, bring them to the light of the moment. What you come to face is your willingness to release a reality you are familiar with. When the experiences in your life feel out of step with what you know of your expansive truth, you may employ the action of equilibration. Equilibration will balance the old experiences with your newly held awareness.

Meditation for Equilibration

In your meditation, ask for clarity of the issue that is appropriately brought to equilibration next. Move above the issue, releasing attachment. When you see the issue, visualize a weight scale in your mind's eye. On one side of the scale is the issue to be brought to equilibration. The other side of the scale is a representation of your current Now moment high-frequency expression. The heavier side of the scale is the side that holds the lower frequency issue.

I choose to bring equilibration to this issue: (name the issue).

With the intention for equilibration, watch as the scale evens out. Expand the light of your divine essence to include the lower frequency issue. Watch as the issue is transformed and bought to wholeness in the light of Love.

A high-frequency presence of Love is powerful. When you feel overwhelmed within an emotional issue, remember that the light of Love, like the sun's rays, shines eternally, even with the presence of clouds.

When you shift your perspective to a higher frequency than the issue to be addressed, resolution and clarity is available. Drop what was for the possibility of what could be.

Equilibration is the act of balancing and aligning disparate frequencies to their highest expression. This is an ongoing process as you are moving with expansive expression. The feeling is one of restoration and ease as the barbs of lower-energy issues are brought into alignment with your highest expression. The energy used to fuel the lower-energy experiences is now available for higher frequency endeavors.

DAY 87: RECALIBRATING TIME

Your most expansive self is present within a variety of realities at this moment. The experiences had in other spaces, places, and dimensions all are a contribution to you. As you set your intention for the highest expression of yourself to be made manifest, you tap into your multidimensional truth. Consider that your experience of time is skewed by your beliefs and absence in the present moment. Many people live their Now moment as if it were the past. Many people live their Now moment in anticipation of what might happen. Living from the past and into the future are ways you already alter your experience of time.

The collective consciousness holds a view of time that is linear: past, present, and future. Time spent with full presence in the moment is fleeting. As you align with your highest expression, your point of reference shifts. Your relationship to time must shift.

When you are informed by the present moment, all other moments disappear. You are fully engaged. Have you experienced being in the flow with something you enjoy? The passage of time is beyond your awareness as you are drawn into the magic available in each moment. What was three hours may feel like thirty minutes. As you live from the Now moment, space expands.

Consider reorienting the structure of time from full presence in the Now moment.

More Than Enough Time

If you feel there is not enough time to get everything done in your day, we suggest you challenge your beliefs about time. Practice shifting into a high-frequency expression of yourself at the start of your day, and stay there as best you can. Hold the intention to experience the limitless quality of time.

As you hold your to-do list for the day, center yourself into the immaculate Now moment. Remember that the Now moment is not linear. Intend to have all the time you need to accomplish your tasks. Consider there is more than enough time to get everything completed. Feel your day flowing as you move easily and with delight inside of your Now moments.

Be curious about other possibilities around time. As you release the space of knowing, what you don't know will rise to your awareness.

We hold space for you that allows you to see around the corner of time with ease.

DAY 88: THE EPICENTER OF LOVE

It is from the epicenter of Love that All emanates. You have access to this space of creation. As you gain more of the conscious awareness that resides in your light expression, your entry to this most potent of frequencies becomes available.

Behind your intention to look for the more that is possible is the resonant return to Love. In your process of enlightenment, the burdens of perception from the physical perspective are lifted. The deep yearning of your soul is answered. From this most potent space, what becomes possible is the unhindered expression of your very essence.

The process of enlightenment requires an ongoing willingness to see your world and your being through new eyes, making choices that hold resonance. Gradually, as who you are not is released, your unique expression may shine, and you see your world through the lens of Love. Your inner exploration gently turns the diamond of your being to new facets. Ultimately, as the whole picture is revealed, you embrace your unique divine expression.

Now is a new day. The presence of unity consciousness elevates your inner inquiry and buoys your choice to release who you are not. The choice for wholeness resides in each moment. It is at the epicenter of Love that you return home. Presence in this high-frequency space catalyzes your unique truth and supports the ease of your wholeness, expressed in total. The epicenter of Love is where you meet your full potential available Now. The fine frequency of Love is brilliant, extinguishing barriers to your full potency.

Meditation to the Epicenter of Love

The epicenter of Love is a space you may begin to experience. It is a high-frequency knowing that is contained within the Now immaculate moment. It is the space of full potential. As you spend time within this elevated frequency, the shackles of the previous expression dissolves. You experience the illumination and freedom of your expansive truth.

Sit comfortably, allowing your breath to slow down naturally. Visualize a cylinder of brilliant, sparkling white and golden light surrounding you. Feel your connection with the beautiful Gaia. Feel the expansive nature of you and sense the presence of your own divine light.

Take a deep breath and move up the gradient of your light expression to the space of greatest light, your I AM Self. As you step into the space of more light, there is a density of form that you must release. Allow the awareness of your light to move as far as is comfortable. Feel your perspective from this new space of Love.

Listen for the heartbeat, not of Mother Earth this time, but the heartbeat of Love. Love is who you are. Follow this melodic beckoning to the epicenter of Love. Like coming home, you are met and greeted with the warm embrace of Love. You are rejoined with the knowing of your expansive nature. You feel the warmth of your light. You are connected to All. There is no separation.

You feel the glow and the vibration of pure potential that is all around you. You are familiar with this space. You are held in your wholeness. The Love you are is unconditional.

This is a heart space feeling that resides within you always. You are Love, you hold this frequency and all potential within you at every moment. Bring back with you the high resonance and deep knowing of your origins in Love.

Upon the altar at the epicenter of Love is a shining golden package for you. You may pick it up and receive the gift. The blessing of the gift is a contribution to you, in your process of expansion. A reminder of the deep knowing you have always held of your divinity.

Your expansion into the light expression of you is felt throughout All. Your brilliance sings the note of Love and Unity. You are the Beloved.

When you are ready, take another deep breath and move gently back into your body.

Feel the new resonance that is present within your cells. Your every cell is vibrating with potential. The light you are emanates your divine harmony. You are renewed and revitalized. Your soul is buoyed. Your mission of Love is a natural expression of you.

It is with delight that you are held in the most potent space of all potential; the epicenter of Love.

DAY 89: LIVING BEYOND CONSENSUS: YOU DO YOU

The stored memories and experiences of your past are powerful. Your experiences are the grist for your beliefs, held for the most part unconsciously. Consider your unconscious belief system is left unchallenged yet remains active in each moment. Templates of past events are overlays in your day, limiting your view.

As a child you take without question the beliefs and habits of your family and culture. This is the beginning of external referencing. It is human nature to align with an external source for structure and safety. Patterns within group consensus create a feeling of safety and reassurance about the known world. Family and cultural beliefs create a framework for what is acceptable and what is not.

There is power in group consensus. Consider that group consensus, or collective consciousness, does not hold the expression of the individual as paramount. Collective consciousness operates on separation consciousness where a hierarchy of group thought reigns. Within the collective, the bar is low. Collective consciousness does not value actualization of the individual over survival of the collective itself. The collective consciousness creates a chasm within the individual that supports external referencing as opposed to internal knowing. Consider that the external expression of this separation is war, the annihilation of Love.

How does this relate to your enlightenment path? Oppositional memories still reside within you, unconsciously. The right-wrong, good-bad, us-them, energetic signature is still within your reference as a possibility. This makes the awareness of the pattern of separation integral to your enlightenment process. As you begin to identify those areas where you are unconsciously holding on to an oppositional perspective, release the resistance of those beliefs. Return all beliefs of separation into a state of wholeness. Your movement in light will be unburdened.

The awareness of external, oppositional referencing presents an opportunity for new choices with a greater perspective. Within the enlightenment process, external referencing yields to internal referencing. As your perspective shifts, internal referencing is all that is needed. External views will no longer be given the weight they once had. Resonance is now the beacon to be followed as inner knowing and integrity reign.

Many of you have had lifetimes of persecution for following your unique inner-directed expression. Again, you find yourself at the counterbalance of eras where your innovative expression is not the norm. Consider that pioneers and leaders at the edge of innovation do not require consensus to express. Inner consensus is all that is needed, and the awareness to recognize it.

You do you. We are in your corner. You have legions of light at your beck and call to support you in your brilliant mission of light and Love.

Day 90: And the Heavens Sing

O ver the last ninety days, the shift in your perspective is significant enough to release the burden of thoughts and actions that no longer serve your highest good. You are *en-lightened* in the process. The constrictive structure of separation consciousness no longer defines your possibilities.

The Love that you are resonates clearly. These seemingly new spaces become a part of the range of your divine expression. Your actions reflect the resonance of your truth: Love made manifest. The Love that you are has a voice in the decisions and choices of your day. Your movement ignites a broad base of your knowing. The resonance of your essential Self as Love unlocks the potential of your highest expression. Your being sings the notes of Love.

The faceted expressions of you have turned enough to reveal truth previously held beyond your sight. Your conscious awareness alters the trajectory of your life. This is the process of enlightenment. This has always been available for those who remember their essential Self. Your light reaches those who have held spaces in density. You support their remembering through reflecting the light that you are. Your brilliance shatters the darkness of unconsciousness. And the heavens sing.

Today, we celebrate your awareness. We applaud your courage, tenacity, and willingness to follow the whisperings of your soul. You have chosen to make a difference. What remains to be seen? Each new step into the yet unknown reveals another reflection of your brilliant, divine nature. Only accessible through the

Now immaculate moment, the resonance of your being is at the helm.

It is with great joy and delight that we support your every step into the light of your greatest truth.

DAY 91: YOUR NEW PERSPECTIVE
OF LOVE

Commensurate with your movement in light, your viewpoint is naturally more expansive. Today we realign perspectives to keep in step with your expanding awareness. It is human nature to hold a perspective on life as the only truth. Even though you have chosen to become conscious, below the surface of your awareness lie perspectives that have been appropriate for who you were, not who you are now.

Move your attention to creating a new baseline perspective that is in alignment with your expanded awareness. Stop for a moment and acknowledge your movement. See how far you have come. Trust your process. The feeling is a natural expansion, a natural progression of being more you.

For the most part, the minutiae that once stole your attention fall silent in the background. You have noticed a softening of the edges of your reality as your awareness moves toward your own center. Still, there are some areas of resistance that arise. Where do you get caught up in old behaviors that have you spinning your wheels? Experienced as frustration, defensiveness, loss of power, hopelessness, and resignation, these areas of resistance ask for a new perspective. The clues to resolution may be found in asking yourself where you are holding onto familiar patterns. You will experience more resistance in areas that are no longer a frequency match for you.

Resistance Exercise

Take a deep breath and relax into stillness. Bring the areas of concern into your awareness from an observation point of view. Feel the discomfort of the issues as they no longer are a match for you.

Intend to bring wholeness to the issue. As if you are applying a template of light over the issue, allow the issue to speak to you newly. Be willing to see what was unseen previously. See the larger picture.

The perspective you hold now is one of Love. The issue is not about others. How may you shift your vision to see from the perspective of Love? What is there to learn from the new vantage point? Feel the warmth of Love. Allow yourself to be informed newly.

When you are ready, take a deep breath and return gently with the fullness of your knowing.

There is no-thing in your life that is business as usual. Daily, you see the brilliance of your life. Daily, the desires of your soul are heard. You have not fallen into a new pattern of normal. The thoughts of normal are outmoded. Views of normal are replaced now with the opening to the most authentic expression of your being that is available. Your joy is in the united perspective you hold at the highest level of your expression. This is the perspective of Love.

The old way of Be-ing protected your comfort zone with unconscious patterns and habits. And that held the blanket of disquiet over your soul's expression, creating barriers to your realization. Now, as the lenses of Love are applied to your Now immaculate moments, your soul rejoices in revelation.

As you contemplate the openings of the past ninety days, you see the light of truth. Your new perspective is one of Love. What now becomes possible?

DAY 92: YOUR NEW ACCESS TO LIGHT

As your reach into light expands, you integrate your physical and nonphysical self naturally. Rather than feeling that your enlightenment access requires you to reach somewhere beyond yourself, you now hold the ability to reach into your pocket, and there it is. The light knowing of you is integrating with your conscious knowing.

The way we describe this to Darlene is, instead of driving to the grocery store for items, you may now stay in the comfort of your home and look in the cupboard. This is the natural experience of the integration of your light. This is a game changer. Awareness that once felt diffuse and philosophical is now your reality! The realms of soulful access to truth have been kept separate from the reality of day-to-day living. But now your days are different.

The difference shows up in your conscious awareness. The difference isn't subtle. Darlene's matrix of light has shifted enough that we may show up with Darlene in a new more expansive way now. She has incorporated more light into her conscious awareness. She holds the crystalline matrix of light that allows a clearer signal for our communication. This expansion may be felt in the frequency of this work. The ring of truth holds a high frequency and is a catalyst for the next steps.

The new awareness in light holds potential as you see more. Your expanding awareness is not linear. Your awareness expands

279

exponentially. Notice the ease you experience. Your light sustains the perspective of Love, through whose lenses you view your reality.

You are shifting dimensional experiences of yourself. Life flows naturally now as restriction is released. The air will feel rarefied. Notice the shift.

Every awareness of your expansive nature resounds throughout the heavens. And the angels sing.

DAY 93: ASSIMILATING LIGHT

Assimilating light is your natural expression. It is not beyond your ability. It is only beyond your conscious awareness. You assimilate light every day. The light of your environment as it is reflected through the beauty of nature reveals colors and information for your sustenance. As the brilliance of the sun's rays filter through the canopy of an ancient redwood forest, you feel the majesty of the divine. Even the air feels rarefied in such instances, as you are resourced in the moment. This is the type of natural expression that begins to show up as you expand your consciousness.

You have shifted the perspective through which you view your reality, and now it is time to pause and look around. From the new perspective you hold, the hard edges of your material world seem a bit more ethereal, softer. Many events are in play here. One consideration is the shifting energies around the planet that support the receipt of more light and the stability of the presence of unity consciousness. Those who are conscious work in light consciously. As you raise the base frequency of your expression, you contribute to the expansive action of light.

Your presence in the immaculate Now moment, is the window through which you begin to see the workings of the reality you have been participating within all along. You see the truth of creation and the truth of your divinity. We have spoken of resonance as your touchstone. Resonance is an action of light. It is a result in the process of alignment. When two fields of awareness (such as a thought and your divine truth) align, there is a process of resonance that occurs. It is not a physical aligning, although it will eventually align with the material world. It is first an aligning of energetic fields of light.

Because you are never still, whether conscious or unconscious, your general trajectory of awareness will be toward the expansive expression of Love. The more aware you become, the more your capacity to assimilate light is increased. In the same way that Love begets Love, light begets light. As your awareness focuses inward, the light that you are is activated to a greater level. As you hold a higher frequency, you assimilate more light. The presence of light within your body reaches a threshold level and activates your next stage of expansive awareness. And so it is.

Your increased sense of knowing represents an increase in the assimilation of light. Seeing beyond the physical world of density is an increased assimilation of light. The ability to be restored in the still beauty of nature is an assimilation of light.

Assimilation of Light

Sit comfortably outside in nature. Focus your attention on your environment. Feel the light around you. Feel for the emanation of light that comes from the trees, grass, plants, and soil around you. Feel the light from the sky as the sun reflects through clouds.

Be aware of the receipt of information in the form of light. What part of your awareness is being activated? Is it your vision, kinesthetic knowing, hearing? Feel the harmony of light around you.

Fine-tune your ability to sense information in light.

As you expand your conscious awareness, you begin to see the physical manifestation around you as varying gradients of light. You, as a being of light in form, evaluate your world through light. Now, within the process of conscious expansion, you begin to see what you have been doing all along.

Delighted.

DAY 94: THE EFFECT OF LIGHT

In the process of taking on more of the light that is authentically you, the world will appear to be a different place. The density that you had become accustomed to is no longer found. There will be a familiarity; however, it is not the same. The illusion is that somehow everything around you is now changed. In fact, it is you who have changed. The sensation may be an experience of newness within a familiar setting. As when you travel to the place where you live and see it through the eyes of someone who does not have the history with the area that you have had.

As you apply light to your awareness, your perspective shifts. We refer once more to the analogy of the gradient scale of light. Imagine an artist's gradient painting of the color blue. This represents the range of your possible expressions, from darkest blue-black with very little light to the whitest hue of blue possible, which represents the full presence of your light expression. You have access to the full range of your expressions. Enlightenment is the conscious awareness of your full range of expressions. You will notice, as you hold more light, that your ability to constrict diminishes (it's like being in college, then taking on the viewpoint of yourself in kindergarten). As you gain more light, the propensity will be toward an ever-expanding expression. You may direct your level of awareness. Profound moments generally are considered rare. In fact, the profound experiences reflect your authentic nature, at higher levels of light.

The opportunity at hand with presence in greater light is an ongoing fine-tuning of your expression into full alignment with your divine nature. Not every moment requires your full attention, but you may choose to BE a higher frequency in your day, setting the tone for how the day goes.

Consider that you choose your experience. When you begin your day declaring who you will be—courageous, whole, delighted, or clear—your day reflects your choice. Equally, when you have focused on an issue that is particularly irritating, have you noticed you can get mad about something and then delve fully into the experience of anger, where the experience consumes you? That is an example of your experiences lining up to be a frequency match for the way of being that you choose. Each point on the gradient scale of light is a choice as you hold more consciousness.

Choose Your Frequency

Move to the space of inquiry. The purpose of practice is to develop clarity. Become familiar with what it takes to change your perception according to the frequency you choose to experience. Choose a frequency for the background of your day. Raising your frequency feels very natural and expansive.

1. *At the beginning of your day, choose a high-frequency perspective. Be still and intend, "I choose to see myself today as God sees me."*
2. *Choose to experience your day from a few degrees of light more than normal. What occurs from the addition of light? Observe.*
3. *Sit in nature. Breathe in the exquisite beauty and stillness around you. Allow your experience to be the lens through which you see your day.*

As you begin to master your frequency on purpose, your perspective shifts accordingly. Results must follow! Perspectives you hold during your day are no longer unconscious. They are by choice.

And freedom reigns. Have we told you today how loved you are? Beloved.

Day 95: The New Dimensions of Your Life

Your presence in light has expanded. You bring more of you to your life. You have brought more of your attention and intention toward your Now immaculate moments. You have dropped the burden of ways of being that no longer serve you. You hold the intention to have your inner world and your outer world match, where your greatest Self shows up in life.

As your moments are spent in the immaculate Now, the available light quenches all aspects of your being. Your soul's disquiet over your lifetime has been from the experience of needing something, wanting something, that is like the glint of light sparkling on water that may not be held in your hands. Consider that desire has always been for the conscious access to your totality. Your consciousness rejoins the parts of you in light that have been held in Love, waiting patiently.

Your conscious awareness makes possible access to your largest perspective as Source in form. The intentions you have held for this lifetime may speak to you more clearly as the vague sensing of the "more" is revealed. The richness of your moments may be experienced at a heightened level. The beauty in each moment engulfs your reality. Your physical experience is enhanced beyond description.

You hold the space of the visionary. Depth and dimension are brought to all aspects of your being. The addition of light to your awareness has you hold a unique perspective. You hold a greater ability to bring your attention to the Now. Your presence in the space of the Now moment is the key to the treasure that is you. Consider as you hold your presence in the Now that you are vital. You hold vitality, nourishing your very being. The quality of your moment reveals all you need to know. Your experiences are rich.

Today, we invite you to look deeply into your physical experience. When you bring the light of your being to your Now moments, your whole life is seen anew. Sublime.

DAY 96: IMMACULATE PRESENCE: GATEWAY TO TRANSLATE LIGHT

E xpansion of consciousness is filled with dichotomies.
Consider the pathway to enlightenment:

Release beliefs and restrictions to gain infinite access to truth.
Give up what you think you know to attain what you authentically know.
Move to the space of no-thing in order to realize everything.
Go to the space of stillness to find the reality that exists beyond.

This stymies the mind. But from the perspective of your highest expression, it all makes sense.

With your accelerated movement in light, there is a knowing that is achieved beyond the limits of the mind. Immaculate presence refers to a state of being where your focus is so completely in the Now moment that you are not experiencing resistance from any input that is not your highest divine expression. In this state of being, you connect with All. You could consider the act of being present as "a gateway."

As the mind's thinking is engaged, you are being informed by your experiences, beliefs, habits, past, preferences, and personality. To connect with the aspects of you, beyond your physical awareness, the limitations of the mind must be acknowledged and new hookups initiated. The new hookup is presence. This requires more than a turning off of your mind's abilities. Your act of presence allows you to move beyond the mind's limitations and access your capacity to translate light. Your act of presence catalyzes your innate ability to translate light into your conscious awareness. Translating light is the term we use for the process you already do unconsciously. As you expand your conscious awareness, abilities that are natural to you are revealed.

Accessing the fine realms of frequency is a practice of joining your physical presence with your most expansive nature. Whether your medium is words, paint, music, movement, or innovation of any kind, the highest-frequency expression arises from your presence in the Now moment. Your Scribe, Darlene, is practicing that skill at this moment. The words of this gathering are coming to her in a new, less-defined way. Rather than hearing the words, or seeing the words, there is a distillation instead, and it bypasses mental recognition of the words and allows the words to fall into her fingers on the keyboard. There is an alchemical feeling to it. Like a manifestation directly from light into form.

We are speaking of the mechanics of this transfer of light and frequency to support you in considering the possibility that your greatest expression resides beyond your mind's ability to think it.

Presence is a mental discipline that, with practice, provides a bedrock type of experience. Now we will create a bedrock type of experience that will support you in clarity, like training wheels for your awareness. We will place this amplification of light, if you choose to access it, within the matrix of *In Service to Love*. This supports a filtering out of the chaotic movement of your mind's thoughts as you practice immaculate presence.

Practice Immaculate Presence

Set aside some time to practice your movement into immaculate presence. Immaculate presence is finely tuned presence in the Now moment. As the distractions of your mind recede, you are at the gateway of your own divine presence.

First, settle into a new type of stillness. Beyond physical stillness, consider bringing in, or shortening the leash, of the mind's movement. Settling in sets the stage for opening into the expansive awareness of immaculate presence.

Notice your thoughts. Allow them. Watch them. As you watch your thoughts, slow your breath. Feel a stillness first in your physical body. Watch your thoughts like notes on a page, or colors upon a canvas, or marbles on a floor. They take up a large space in your awareness. Become aware of the space your mind's thoughts take up. Watch them rather than engage them. Stay in the observer perspective. When you see, feel, or sense the expanse of space they take up, gradually gather the thoughts closer together, so they take up less space. Gently herd them to a smaller space.

As you feel comfortable with the smaller space your thoughts now take up, move your attention to where they are not. This is a mental discipline. Without engaging thought, shift to experience. While you are watching the thoughts, be the experience that is not them. Do you feel the expanse of the space that is not the thoughts? Hold that space of expansive experience as much as you can. It will seem a bit like walking on a balance beam. You will be focusing on what is (observing the thoughts) as well as the space that is not (the expansive space beyond thinking). That is the experience of the dichotomy. You walk in both spaces, of what is and what is not. Do you feel the presence of all? This engages your multidimensional capabilities.

This is a practice that supports your expansion of awareness. The mental discipline will untangle you from the perceived limits of being in form. You will notice you have natural ways of viewing your thoughts. Notice what shows up. Pictures? Feelings? Words? Nothing? This will give you the keys to the conscious awareness of your expansive nature.

Once on the other side of presence, you are in a stance to hold the observer perspective and witness what arises in your awareness. Your inner promptings will guide you to your own unique experience of translating light. First, get to the gateway.

DAY 97: IN SERVICE TO LOVE

Good day, this is Jeshua stepping to the forefront of this divine conversation taking place within this Now immaculate moment.

The story of my life when I last walked the beautiful planet Earth was one of resurrection and ascension. As you discover the divine nature of you, you are resurrected. You emanate the light of truth as you connect consciously with your divine Source. It is through your focused awareness that you may have the experience of living the truth that there are no boundaries between the I in form and the I AM Self. As you engage with the you that is accessed in light, you are resurrected to your divine nature. The limiting beliefs of the past are no longer fueled. As you follow the attributes that are your authentic expression, you find the divine nature of your being. The one constant held by all mankind is the truth of your divine essence. As you develop the intention and awareness to exercise your potential that exists in light, you are risen above the limitations of form to the experience of actualization of your true self. You have the potential of living your life in form, from a perspective that transforms.

When you are in form you experience density and the gifts available therein. When you bring your light awareness into the experience of being in form, you are *In Service to Love*. You support and facilitate the awakening process of the All. You resurrect the divine.

Our collaboration holds you in the rich, spacious environment of your divine expression. As you are held in the warmth of your true nature, you are encouraged to be courageous. In your Now moments, as you choose the truth of you, as opposed to the habits of past and your environment, you are held on high. The resonance of your truth rings out.

Rest, Dear Ones, in the knowing of your divine nature.

DAY 98: INTENTION, YOUR TOUCHSTONE IN LIGHT

A s your presence in the Now moment is increased, so too, is your presence in light. You are learning to play an expanding range of frequencies, as though you're using all the energetic piano keys at your disposal, rather than only one or two. We would like to speak of your act of integrating the light you access during your day. The light of your being nourishes, nurtures, calms, informs, and elevates all aspects of you. As your environment expands, you may feel a bit disoriented. Today our message is one of focus.

There are many ways to interact with the light that you are. As you move your awareness into a new, higher-frequency space, the density you have been accustomed to is replaced with the sense of all-is-well. While it is a space to rest within, it is also a new space requiring a new kind of intention and clarity. In example, your Scribe, Darlene, has been practicing with this component. Unless she sets a clear intention of connecting with us as she sits to scribe, she is lulled by the beauty of the light into a space of rest and relaxation, because "it feels both restful and rejuvenating, like the best sleep ever." When Darlene falls deeply into the experience of light, without direction, there is the space of rest and restoration. As she holds the intention for connecting with the information we share, that connection too, is even more clear.

The best way we can illustrate the place for focus is to use the analogy of a department store. When you walk into a department store, you will be directed to the specific department that holds the items you intend to purchase. Unless you are directed specifically by your intention, you may sit in the mall and enjoy the sights and sounds of the environment. Both choices are fine. If you are looking for housewares and find yourself in the jewelry department, look to your intention for clarity. We demonstrate this as a navigational tool for your expansion.

Touchstones in Light

In order to focus your awareness, first set the intention to observe your expansive field of awareness. Notice the difference between your automatic way of being in the past and the now available expanded sensing. Know that you may move with ease within all the spaces you occupy through your awareness.

In the same way that driving in a car allows access that you didn't have before you learned to drive, there are new rules of the road as you access your increased awareness. Now, with more possibilities in front of you, knowing where you are going is important. You may choose a relaxing experience of driving to the beach, or you may need more focus as you drive to work in the morning. Do you feel the importance of intention?

As you set time to connect with your expanding field of awareness, with clarity of intention, you choose powerfully. This is a natural process. Like every stage of your growth up to now, each new level of access has its own parameters. Develop an awareness from the observer standpoint. Where will you need more focus of your awareness to put your light into action?

When you access your light expression, you access the present moment and field of possibility. When your intention is to align with your own highest expression, the field of possibility is activated accordingly. Your intention directs possibility. Hold your expansive stance. Become more aware of your shifting field of awareness. You are integrating components of your being consciously. The goal is the full-on authentic expression of you.

DAY 99: CONTRIBUTED TO BY THE PAST, GIFTED IN THE MOMENT

Beloveds, as your movement within the light of your divine expression is naturally expanding, your relationship to the environment must shift. When you first said yes to your participation with *In Service to Love*, your reality shifted. Your point of view is different. In a physical environment that may look the same, there now exists a slight shift in the reconciling of the world you view. The physical world you are familiar with no longer lines up in the same way with your sensing in light. Your energetic capacity to move and know in light has increased, adding new information.

The speed with which your life moves now has increased. There is a sense of acceleration. The feeling of attachment to previous times in your life is different. In the background of separation consciousness is the contraction energy that holds a pattern of referral to the past. You now live within the constructs of the possibility of unity consciousness.

The natural movement of unity consciousness energy is expansive. The expansive movement of energy relates differently to events of the past. Expansion is not as easily tied to the past. The process of expansion supports moving away from the past and being present with a changing landscape as it comes into view. Have you noticed old issues coming up, but although they hold a familiar energy, the issues need to be viewed newly? Most parts of your life are not quite the same. This is due to your response to a shifting level of consciousness from separation to unity consciousness. Our divine collaboration supports your positioning to consciously realize your authentic nature.

The experience of resistance will show up when your thoughts, actions, and beliefs hold a limiting perspective that is not in alignment with your expansive nature. Become aware of ways you hold on to the past realities and events of your life. If you feel resistance or persistence of an issue, allow that experience to suggest a new perspective. All events of the past have already contributed to you. Shifting perspective is demonstrated by allowing all the picture albums and feelings of your past to be acknowledged for the contribution they have been to you. They reside within you. Your future is being formed by your full presence in the Now moment. It is only from the present moment that you may be gifted with possibility.

When you move your attention away from a separation consciousness perspective to the Now moment, you may create powerfully. This is where you connect with the high vitality of potential. It is from the space of Now that you may connect easily with your knowing held in light. Allow yourself to be inspired by possibility. The creations you hold in potential are magnificent.

DAY 100: TRUSTING YOUR LIGHT

Good day, it is I, Thoth, stepping to the forefront of this divine conversation today. From the perspective of the Now moment, anything you choose is possible. It is not as though certain circumstances need to line up for you to feel calm and relaxed and feel you have space to spend some moments with the knowing you hold in light. Other than being in the Now moment, access to your divine knowing is not conditional. This is not a process where you wait for the tapping on the shoulder of the magic wand that brings you enlightenment. You already own the territory within which it exists. You ARE enlightened. The work we do in divine collaboration is showing you where to look. And you, if you choose, move from the places that you have known previously to the spaces within you that beckon you into the unknown. This is a guided process that occurs within you.

We would ask you to really get clear that you are Source in form. You are a being of light in form. Less of you exists in form than in light. All parts of your divine expression, whether form or light, are accessible to you. When you live within a perspective that holds physical reality as separate from the creations of light, you are setting yourself up for a division within you that is an illusion. Early on in your childhood you held the design for the you that is now present as an adult. Certain developmental thresholds are crossed, and you move organically from one stage of life to another. This is no different. There are frequency thresholds of awareness that open the gates to the next light-filled expression. If the thresholds of frequency are not met, your full expression in light lies in potential.

Consider that many lifetimes have been lived without full expression. The possibility is present now for a different outcome. As you choose your full divine design expressed consciously, you bridge the barriers of separation and take ownership of the you in light as well as in form.

Consider the possibility of trusting the you that resides in light. Now that you have shifted your perspective enough to facilitate an expansion in awareness, it is less of a stretch to hold the possibility of the you that resides in light. This is an organic process that resides just out of your vision. Trust your Self. Hold the space of possibility and clarity.

DAY 101: THE EXPERIENCE OF YOUR LIGHT

Yesterday we spoke of the trust to be developed in the experience of your light expression. Once you see that the light expression of you is part and parcel of your totality, you develop a level of ease, ownership, and clarity within the experience of the you that resides in light.

Today, we add to the concept of trust, a conversation around the experience of you in light. As you choose to employ the part of you that resides in light, there is a mechanism that is different from focusing on one of your other senses. As you move into the finer frequencies of your light expression, all your sensing becomes more finely tuned as well. The roughness or coarse edges of your reality are perceived differently. The edges become filled with light and the edges soften. Your experience is less of the hardness of things and thoughts, that they feel immovable. Instead, your experience becomes more tuned to the infinite flow, the fluidity of your surroundings. As you participate in more of the light you are, your experiences become more fluid. In part, this shift is due to your change in perspective. Rigidity of thought lessens and clarity increases as you choose a broader perspective.

Opening to possibility is a pivotal component to the ever-expanding experience of your Self in light. There will always be something that you don't know that you don't know. It is only in the opening to possibility that the new will be revealed. This is the stance for access to the finest components of your expression. Beyond your physical sensing, what becomes apparent is your sensing in light. You begin to discern information available in light. Unlike your physical experience, the discerning action we are speaking of occurs organically, beyond your thinking. You will at first notice your discovery in light after the fact. Much like the shifting patterns of the scribing of this divine collaboration, your sensing will become a natural expression. Awareness in light must occur within the Now moment. Your ability to maintain the stance of awareness within the Now will increase to your new default.

Once the hard edges and borders are removed, what becomes possible is the conscious experience of the infinite flow of your full expression. The alignment with the divine design of you resonates. The experience is of movement toward Love, peace, joy, fulfillment, compassion, abundance, and awareness of your soul's vision. Rich, in every sense of the word.

DAY 102: RADIANCE

The radiance of you is being celebrated. Your movement within the matrix of *In Service to Love* is swift. You have been reaching into the light expression of you and are finding your divine expression manifest in your moments. As more of the light that you are is expressed, you are truing up, aligning with the divine essence of you. There are no barriers, no hindrances to the access of your highest expression. In the action of truing up, or syncing your physical being with your expanded expression in light, you experience your divinity. This is radiance.

Radiance is your capacity to hold your divine space. Your work so far around releasing thoughts, beliefs, restrictions, and structures that are constructs of a previous era remove the coverings from your brilliance. The light expression of you and the physical expression of you align into one concise manifestation. The divine light of your essential nature is now held in your form. This action signals a transition of momentum. Guided by your actions, you move into a higher level of velocity in the accessing of and aligning with your light expression.

The effect of your radiance made manifest is miraculous. As you have spent time within the light of your being, you have experienced the balance, calm, reverie and exalted spaces of divine light. It is transformational, magical, divine. The expression of your radiance in form brings the experience of light into your environment.

Your light acts as a catalyst for the presence of more light. Your presence transforms. Beyond your thinking or wishing, your light is a divine expression, casting Love.

Your radiance is celebrated. We have always seen your brilliance.

DAY 103: FOCUSING AWARENESS

We remind you that the experience you are having in each moment is new. Each moment holds potential in and of itself. You have already been contributed to by all moments that have come before. What becomes available in the Now moment is new. In each moment there is the opportunity to respond newly, knowing that each event or circumstance has arisen in your life at this time as a response to Love.

As you reach more deeply into the expression of light that you are authentically, you are treading new ground. Every situation is brand new. There may be a ring of familiarity from the past but, be assured that each moment is new. When you hold them as such, you have the ability in the Now moment to support resolution. Resolution is the opportunity for a new perspective to be held—with purpose.

The increasing presence of light and Love is a balm to your physical experience. You will notice that your environment will become bumpy at times during the transition from separation consciousness to unity consciousness and from density to light. There is a reframing taking place. There is nothing wrong here. All is truly well.

As your reach into the light that you are expands, you bring light and the presence of Love with you. In a time of transition, the presence of Love supports the process of realigning to possibility and a new perspective. You will notice the difference. As you settle into a new realm of possibility in the expression of Love, the oppositional dynamic of separation consciousness seems louder. It is only with the application of your light and awareness within the magical, infinite expression of the Now moment, that you are a catalyst for the global transition to unity consciousness, and a beacon for the light of healing.

The intention of today's conversation is to remind you to keep your awareness focused on you. As you hold the integrity and awareness on you, your environment will shift. It will be easy to lose focus and move to reaction in the environment. We would ask you to consider keeping the focus of your awareness on your Now moments. Be informed from your internal knowing. Hold the highest perspective available to you in the moment, and be the brilliant beacon of light that you are authentically. All are divine expressions. All are beings of light in form. All are being supported in their own way at this time. As you continue to focus your awareness on what is before you, you contribute greatly.

DAY 104: SACRED FOOTPRINTS

As you reach into the light of your divine expression and bring that knowing and high frequency into your moments, you are altered. The light brings with it a resonant knowing of your divine origins. Your broad perspective sees newly the wisdom of all the events of your life as they fall into place, with the knowing that all was for a higher purpose.

From the perspective of your greatest light, you see why certain events and timelines took place as they did. Not because there was some untouchable source beyond your vision that was controlling you, but from the standpoint of recognizing the frequency, vibration, and sacred quality of your soul's direction. Once you bring the knowing of light into your physical experience, you will find more resistance and discomfort as you engage in behaviors or patterns of the past. You are undergoing a reconciling process of past events with your current knowing. You will find your knowing in light will be infused into your every moment. Even though it may not seem so at times, the process of your reach into light is natural and organically expressed. It is not hard work. As a matter of fact, it becomes easier and easier as each barrier to your highest expression is dropped. The structures of separation consciousness fall away, and you may take a deep breath of expansion.

All your moments are sacred moments. From our perspective, we see equally the experiences that have brought pain and hardship and those that have brought joy, inspiration, and awe. As you move into the higher expression of light, the sacred of All is appreciated. We spoke yesterday of maintaining the focus of your awareness. As you do, the sacred expression of All is supported. In the same way you are accessing divine knowing, so too is each being in form. You are the greatest contribution as you hold the light of your divinity and move within the expansive space of your expression. Nobody can be you other than you. The contribution you bring is precious, powerful, sacred, and acknowledged.

We offer an amplification of clarity. A putting on of the glasses to view the sacredness of being. As you view your environment from this perspective, you place the mirror in front of you and see the divine expression we behold.

Every step you take is a sacred footstep.

DAY 105: YOUR DIVINE
EMBODIMENT

Good day. It is I, Thoth, stepping to the forefront of this divine conversation occurring within this immaculate Now moment. The Masters present in our divine collaboration do not eclipse the presence of you. Who you are in light is beyond your greatest imagination. You hold the ability to navigate space in light as well as in form. You contribute greatly to the depth and texture of the matrix of *In Service to Love*.

When we speak of you taking your place at the table, that is a way to shift your thinking about who you see yourself to be. The process of conscious actualization aligns the awareness of who you are in light with who you be in form. As you see the whole picture, the totality of you, you begin to create in your life consciously from the highest perspective you hold. What is available is the highest-frequency expression of you made manifest. This is the full embodiment of you, with you.

As you align your physical self with the you that resides in light, your reference to external sources shifts. You are operating in life from your own mastery. Your perspective changes. Rather than gleaning information and perspective from your guides, you participate with them eye to eye, peer to peer, divine to divine. You take the reins consciously of your expression and work in divine collaboration with other beings of light in light. It is divine collaboration from the perspective of your highest knowing we are speaking of here. In the owning of your light you own your own brilliance. Your divinity then, is not only experienced, it is the point from which you create.

Consider the possibility of embodying your divinity.

What now becomes possible?

DAY 106: LEAVING THE PAST BEHIND: A TRANSITIONAL MOMENT

Darlene's experience is at the leading edge of our conversation today. Darlene has been reaching more deeply into the light expression that she is in her collaboration with us. Today marks a transitional point where she is now able to hold her divine space in light. One of the ways this is expressed is in the complete shift of perspective. So far, within *In Service to Love*, our collaboration has supported a gradual shifting beyond perceived limitations. Our collaboration supports openings in awareness that are in alignment with your unique expression and with Darlene's. You too have felt the restrictions of the past as they no longer align with the expansive expression of you.

Today is a transitional moment. As you anchor more and more of the light that is you, you evolve toward your most authentic expression. The expansion of consciousness, or ascension, is a process of aligning your being with the highest expression that the consciousness on the planet Earth now allows. The opportunity at hand is the absence of barriers to your realization, enlightenment, and actualization. The shift involves the whole of you. As you anchor more of your light, more openings in awareness are triggered. Your physical senses shift to accommodate the fine experience of your multidimensionality.

There comes a moment in your anchoring of light when you shift sources of reference. There is a pivoting of experience that is occurring today. A pivot into a larger expression that holds more of your light expression. This is where Darlene is at this moment. We have stopped here in this moment to acknowledge the movement in light that has been attained. We acknowledge the contribution to light and Love that has been made thus far, not only with Darlene, but with you. Consider as you move forward that there are a series of thresholds over which you step in your expansion of conscious awareness. Darlene's axis of reference has changed. Rather than the experience of a being of light in form, wrapped in the experience of Love, she is now experiencing herself AS LOVE. The operating system is changing as of today. Reference points are no longer created from the past. Reference points available now are from the perspective of the Christed expression.

Can you allow yourself to be in process without the need to know? Can you remove the expectations that you know so well? Can you say goodbye to the past? In the spaces you tread now, in the further reaches of your light expression, the access to the past is no longer available. You find those constructs have been an illusion. You now call upon your divine knowing to be present in each moment. There has been a joining of humanity and soul expression. You are so present in the Now moment that the past no longer exists. Can you say goodbye to the past?

Darlene is assuming her position at this table of Masters of light and is welcomed with open arms. Her crystalline structure is now vibrating the frequency of her authentic expression. From here on out, divinity abides. Not as something unusual but as a natural extension of authentic expression, as a being of light in form.

There is a moment where the butterfly inside the chrysalis no longer fits and a new expression is required. You are that.

We support and celebrate your expansive expression.

DAY 107: BEYOND THE THRESHOLD

A note from Darlene:
This is a dynamic work in progress for sure. I feel the expansion that is facilitated by the divine collaboration between light beings in light and light beings in form. I am different today. I see and feel my light expression. I am elevated with the experience. My body is different, I feel lighter. I am in peace, love, and delight. I have pivoted into a new perspective. I have shifted from having access to a realm in light, to BEING within and a part of the realm in light. We are all in the process of ascension. This is unique for each of us. I appreciate the divinely held and supported process available with this work that reaches us where we are. Thank you to each of you. Thank you for being willing to be with me and most importantly for me to be with you to explore and manifest what is possible. My heart soars with Love.

Today, you will feel the new texture of the space we are within. Your awareness has opened to a new reality. The process of ascension is not a path that is linear. It is a path that now incorporates all the events, sparks of brilliance and remembering you have held over your lifetimes, all activated at this Now divine moment for the purpose of contributing the light and Love that you be to this moment in evolution.

Consider that all the moments in your life have brought you to this Now moment. You chose from your highest knowing to be present at this time in form for the transition from separation consciousness to unity consciousness. The planet Earth holds the frequency of unity consciousness now. Your ascension process is in response to the potential made possible with the transition of consciousness by Gaia. This is the time when the reality of heaven on earth is possible. There is an aligning of expressions in light as well as in form. There is a transitioning process of "the new earth" that is underway. Your movement to holding more of the light that you are is a significant contribution to the process of manifesting the new earth. The new earth is a different-dimensional, or ascended reality for the experience of and with Gaia. Because you chose to be in form on the planet Earth at this time, you chose a long time ago to undergo the transition of consciousness along with Gaia. You are allies in Love.

This opening occurs differently with each of you. Some of you have already tread this ground in the aligning to your knowing in light and are consciously at work within your unique soul expression. Understand the work we do now meets you where you are. Your position is supported, stabilized, fortified, clarified, and activated from within the matrix of our collaboration as your unique expression requires.

As you are in service to Love, so are we. Love is all there is. Love is All.

DAY 108: A NEW EXPRESSION: THE PERSPECTIVE OF LOVE

You woke up in your day with a new perspective. From the outside looking in, it may appear as if all is the same. It is not. Your expression has elevated in frequency and vibration. Your reach into light has expanded, bringing the knowing of your soul within your vision. The impact of the past on your Now moments is diminished. Every moment is new. As you have been reaching more into the light that you are, your expression in Love is manifest. The ability to turn off what you know to be true is outside of your comfort.

The experience of stillness is apparent. Consider that when you are being informed by the past, by beliefs and the limitations inherent in separation consciousness, there is a continual stream of thought that is unrelated to the possibilities that lie in the Now moment. As you have moved away from the distraction and noise of thought related to past and future, what becomes available is a new experience. This is an experience where you are available to you. The divine expression of you has some breathing space for expression. Your peace is noticeable. You no longer reside in the past. Your residence in the Now moment has been created. It seems, suddenly, there is space around you. There is space now to notice the Love that fills the stillness. The expanse of pure potential vibrates in the stillness. In the absence of distraction, you may see what was once hidden. Your frequency is now such that you are pulled into the expression of authenticity.

It truly is a new perspective that is available. You have been used to an experience of opposition, of defined black and white, good and bad, a space of contraction with separation consciousness. Now your awareness has shifted to the presence of something different. When you don't take the way it is for granted, the possibilities inherent within what is, may be seen. You are experiencing an opening. As you access the light of your own divinity you naturally experience expansion. You are no longer informed by restrictions of the past. Present is the spaciousness of the Now moment. Your world quiets down. The din of unrelated activity is gone. What used to be your norm has been not just manipulated or viewed from a new angle, but is gone. Your divine expression is at the helm as you access more of the light that is your nature.

This is a natural expansion of possibility dictated by the frequency of expression now available. This expansion was held in potential; now it is made manifest. In the same way you have moved out of the chrysalis and into a larger expression, so too must this body of work. Do you feel the openings that are present now? Can you take a deep breath into the space of possibility?

With every increase in the amount of light you hold, you operate from the perspective of your authentic expression. As we speak of you at your essential nature, we must speak of Love.

And so, we are,

In Service to Love

DAY 109: YOUR NEW SPACE
OF POTENTIAL

You find yourself within the space of a new territory. You are no longer informed by the past. You are residing now within the open space of possibility. It is from this vantage point that the full expression of you may be made manifest. We invite you to explore the new space you are within. Begin to develop a new knowing. There is ease moving in harmony with the expansive nature of your essential self. There is a new sense of flow and open space.

Within the stillness is a subtle vibration. This is the space of your access to creation. Consider that your creations are now made from a new perspective. In the absence of the wild swings in thought that come from being everywhere other than present, you now have space to create on purpose. The information for your creations now comes from a new space; the resonance of your being. Instead of choosing because of habit, you now reside within the blank canvas of possibility. The space you now hold gives you access to the unified field, the quantum field where all already exists. It is the space where your highest expression exists. You may access the space of wholeness. You may bring into form that which resonates with you at the highest levels.

Meditation: The Experience of Wholeness (Holiness)
Sit or lie down. Be comfortable. Watch the movement of your breath. The inhalation and exhalation are joined in perfection by the point between

inhalation and exhalation as well as between exhalation and inhalation. Feel the gift of each component of your breathing as it expresses the perfection of your wholeness on every level.

Feel the energizing and calming effect of your breathing on your whole body. Watch as the cells of your body light up with the divine infusion of life. Gradually allow yourself to shift perspectives again. Feel the divine, full expression of you in light. Watch as the light expression of you encompasses your physical expression. Unable to be contained by form, your light expands and emanates brilliance. Feel yourself expand beyond the boundaries of your physical form.

You feel the breath of your expression in light. You are being breathed by your divine expression. Feel the wholeness of this experience. Fully present in this Now immaculate moment. Your expression is perfection. Your divinity is radiating in the emanations of you. Feel the wholeness, the perfection of your divine essential Self inform your body. See the perfect health and vitality that resides within your light expression.

Overlay that feeling onto your physical body. Feel the warmth of your divine expression in form. All imbalances in your body are moving and aligning with their highest expression of wholeness. Feel the resonance of Love and peace as your divine expression is moving from light to form. This is who you are. Perfection, healing, vitality. You are making manifest the highest level of health and well-being. Feel the peace. You are wrapped in the Love of your divine expression. In wholeness. Holiness.

When you are ready, move gently back to your physical form. Feel the infusion of light. The light that you are is informing your physicality, restoring and aligning to the highest expression available. As you continue to practice this technique of overlaying your highest expression onto your physical form, notice the shifts in your awareness.

Practice placing the template of your light expression over top of your physical body. Allow the frequency of your light expression to inform your body, restoring health, vitality, and well-being on every level. Feel the frequency of your light and the frequency of your body as they align.

As you align with the highest frequency you hold in light, you bring the high frequency of wholeness into your physical form. As you engage consciously with your light expression, you are living multidimensionally. It's one of your many natural talents.

DAY 110: NEW GLASSES

Consider the purpose of our collaboration as the aligning of your soul with your life. Each stage in the process of enlightenment is purposeful. As the light of your divine essence touches your awareness, you release the fixed ways of being in your life. In the act of reconsidering your beliefs, space opens for the infusion of light that is authentically you. In the process, you move closer to the potency you hold naturally. Your potency in light is dynamic, expansive, unique, and is sourced by Love.

You will notice your life as more spacious, new, softer, quieter, perhaps. You may feel a disconnect from the experience you have understood so well from your past as you move into a fluid, undefinable, expansive experience. All is well. There are new rules, and endless freedom. The laws you move within now are the laws of the universe. You move beyond the constraints of beliefs. You continue to be at choice in every moment, moving with ease and grace for all your systems.

In this turning point of *In Service to Love*, you have "new glasses" through which to view your reality. Your perspective has shifted significantly. Relax in the high frequency of your highest expression. Allow your divine knowing to inform you to a greater extent than ever before, as you claim all that is you. Begin to watch for clues of your unique expression. How do you create?

Declare How Your Day Goes

There is something to be learned in the exercise of being. As you hold more of the light that you are, you will be losing the edges you had trusted previously. Practice your innate ability to create. Practice creating from your BEING.

At the beginning of your day, sit quietly for a few moments and choose a "way of being" that you will be creating your day within. Align with your highest expression. Intend to create in your day from the highest access to light available. Choose one way of being. Some examples are below. Repeat your intention several times throughout your day. More than saying, you are DECLARING who you be! Place energy behind your declaration!

Today, I choose to BE Love.
Today, I choose to be delight.
Today, I choose to be peace.
Today, I choose to be connection.
Today, I choose to be creativity.
Today, I choose to be abundance.
Today, I choose to be clarity.
Today, I choose to be ease.
Today, I choose to be freedom.

Your conscious choice is powerful. Daily, choose one way of being as the intention for your day. And then watch what happens. How does the way you choose to BE during your day influence the events of your day? Start with one week and notice the difference. Extend conscious creation into a daily practice. Observe your inner dynamics.

Bask in the spaciousness of you. The high-frequency access to the light that you are is a healing balm. Ease into the potency of your light.

DAY 111: LIVING IN SHIFTING PERSPECTIVES: A BLESSING

Today's gathering in light celebrates the movement you have made within these 111 days and sets the tone for next steps.

You hold potentiality of the highest order. The in the moment experience of holding the light that you are is one that requires a constant, consistent, and persistent aligning. The retraining of neural pathways to shift from the actions inherent within separation consciousness to the open nature of unity consciousness requires energy. The enlightened path is a natural expression. Conscious awareness requires impetus until momentum increases to velocity where the ease in light may be experienced. Although a challenge at times, living within an environment of transitioning perspectives prepares you for the rapidly moving fluidity of your expression in light.

On this day, a Stargate opens. The action offered today within this Stargate is the first stage of release. Tomorrow, the second stage of receiving will be available. In the first stage the actions of the Stargate offer a release of burdens that clears the slate. There is support in this Stargate that lifts the weighted connection between the past, with your restricted beliefs, limitations, and perceived barriers, to expansive movement forward. If you choose, this Stargate will lift emotional burdens related to limited consciousness.

As you integrate your expanded awareness, consider outmoded beliefs, patterns, and memories that do not serve your highest interest moving forward, to be placed upon the altar with appreciation.

The Stargate will lift those expressions that are outmoded and taking up space, like clearing out a closet. Again, this Stargate operates only with your full permission and with ease and grace for all your systems. It is the integrated expression of you that identifies what best supports your movement forward and will be making the choices. This Stargate will remain open only for the time you need, once initiated in the following meditation.

Stargate Meditation Part 1: Release

If you choose to, connect deeply with this process. We suggest you be comfortable, still your thoughts, follow your breath. Connect with your highest expression in light and place upon the altar all beliefs, memories, patterns, and limitations that no longer serve you as you move forward into full actualization of your soul's light. These are placed upon the altar with Love and appreciation and returned to the All. Trust that those things that are appropriate for you to be complete with will be placed upon the altar, whether you name them or not. Be the space of release.

Notice the space that opens before you. You may feel a lightening as what no longer serves you is lifted. Trust your own process. When you feel complete, return your attention to your body and physical surroundings. This action occurs quickly and perfectly, so there is no need to linger in the space of release.

Tomorrow's conversation will hold the second portion of this Stargate activity. We will remain connected, shining the light of Love upon you. Who you are is magnificent.

Day 112: Blessings and Blessed

Good morning. It is I, Thoth, stepping to the forefront of this divine conversation. Today is a continuation of the process that began with the opening of the Stargate yesterday, in support of your ever-expanding movement into Love.

The design of a Stargate serves many purposes. As life and creation continue to evolve, there is an ongoing transition of perspective that is facilitated by the momentum of expansion. As you grow in your perspective in the light, new aspects of you become available. Equally, you move beyond those parts of your being that no longer serve your expansion. There is a continual re-categorization process that must occur with movement. In order to hold the space of the light that you are, the density and weight of old, more limited expressions of you may be completed. The purpose of yesterday's Stargate opening was to facilitate the offloading of those thoughts, beliefs, and memories, weighted in density that no longer serve your expansion.

The Stargate for the offloading of those outmoded ways of being and history closed upon completion. What is present in today's conversation is a space that was not available yesterday. The offloading made possible by the Stargate opening was effective. There is a new space of light that is present. The experience may be of an openness, a newness, a feeling of being less anchored today.

The new open space is the experience of the blank canvas of potential. The intention is not to hurry up and fill the space with something new, but rather to allow the new space to speak to you. Anything you make up at this point will be informed by the past.

The space that is newly available has the potential to be created from divine collaboration of the highest order. Creation occurs in the Now moment and is not something that may be planned for on a conscious level.

The frequency you now hold emanates Love. You are a blessing to All. Today, the Stargate will open, this time with a different flow. In the same way an inhalation is followed by an exhalation and a tide ebbs and flows, this Stargate moves in releasing and receiving. The opportunity available yesterday was for the release of outmoded ways of being. The open space now holds the capacity to receive more of the light that is your natural expression. As you choose, you may participate in the new movement of the Stargate to deliver unto you the blessing of the light that you are.

The Stargate now moves from transition to the open state. As you choose you may receive the blessing of the gift of Love, brilliant golden-white light, and the awareness that is your divine birthright. This light coding holds within it potential, now ready for manifestation of clarity, peace, ease, expansion, authentic expression, brilliance—whatever is your next step. There is an ease included that supports the integration of the light now available. The practice of receiving is as valuable as releasing.

Stargate Meditation Part 2: Receiving

Sit and be comfortable. Notice your breath as you naturally inhale and exhale. Within the movement of the Stargate we are transitioning movement from exhalation (release) to inhalation (receiving). As gracefully as you have exhaled notice the shift in movement required as you receive the light of your highest expression.

Inhale the light and coding now available through this gift of the Stargate. Who you are is your divine design made manifest. Breathe in the potential you have held for yourself in this lifetime and beyond. Know that the light you receive today is a catalyst for action to come. There is a lightness that is experienced with the blessing of you. Feel the warmth of the light of Love as it showers upon you, the highest expression. The blessing that is held in this Stargate is one of Love and appreciation, clarity, peace, and ease.

The gifts and abundance you have held in your field are made available. The light of this Stargate holds the keys that unlock the next level of your divine knowing. This is a significant step toward the full conscious manifestation of you now available. The diamonds of your brilliance rain upon you. The divine gifts available for you now are plentiful. The potential you hold is limitless, your reach into your light expression is deeper than imaginable. The acknowledgment and appreciation for your courage, intention, and unique perfect expression is all encompassing.

This Stargate will remain open for you as your need dictates. Again, the action of receiving is concise. You may feel a new type of lightening occur. When you are complete bring your full attention back to your body and physical surroundings.

This new energy of light brings with it the knowing of your existence in light. Continue to be informed by what is in front of you. Your perspective has shifted yet again with this infusion of light. Allow the light to work with you, and on you, lighting up your awareness. This is a catalyst for your divine knowing.

We acknowledge you as a blessing and as the Blessed.

DAY 113: YOUR LIGHT TEMPLATE

Good morning. It is I, Thoth, stepping to the forefront of this divine conversation within this Now immaculate moment. As of the contributions made by the Stargate these past few days, there is a new availability to your divine expression. It marks a pivot in our work within *In Service to Love*. Within this dynamic work there is a constant redirecting toward the light knowing you have always held. Now there has been enough of a shift from the reality you have known so well, so that the diverse, deep, expansive expression of you now has room to show up. The capacity for light that you hold has increased in depth and breadth.

As you shift in perspective, your available light capacity increases. This work will support you at the highest level, expanding as your capacity increases. The intention is to set a solid base for the fully balanced integration of the light you hold.

Your Scribe, Darlene, is noticing "It is a new day." And so it is. The shifts in perspective have seemed small, and in accumulation they mark a significant increase in momentum. Because of the movement you have made, this new opening has been created. This work is created in the Now immaculate moment and as such, there is no-thing about this that is linear or predictable. *In Service to Love* follows your lead. You each are an active participant on this Council of Light. You inform, support, express from your authentic nature, to the Being of you that resides in form. As your Scribe, Darlene is both on this divinely held Council of Light and an active student—you are as well.

The last few days, the Stargate has had two actions. The first action was one of clearing up, or offloading those expressions, beliefs, and memories that no longer serve you, creating an experience of a clear slate. The second action of the Stargate was to provide an infusion of the knowing of you at your highest expression. The opportunity has been to "plug-in" with the light expression of you with a new, potent access point. In general, there is a sense of open space, a calm newness. The clear space present is vibrating in potential.

Returning to the Stargate

The stargates remain active within the context of In Service to Love. *As you choose to reconnect with the actions of this Stargate, you may. By returning to the reading, listening, or through your intention, you may request the Stargate support you in the action of offloading or in receiving a new level of your knowing in light. The meditations with each Stargate will support your intention. The Stargate works in whole action. As you both inhale and exhale, so too, does the Stargate both release and provide access. Do the Stargate Meditation Part 1 first, to clear and create space, then follow with the second action, of receiving, in Stargate Meditation Part 2. The second action will not work without the first. The Stargates are within Day 111 and Day 112.*

Your light expression is held within your physicality and surrounding fields through a grid. The light infusions and activations have served to connect, amplify, and support full integration of your awareness within a natural process. As your template is aligned and amplified, you hold your divine expression with a greater level of potency, clarity and balance.

There is no doing at this point. The highest expression of you resides in who you BE. Your perspective has shifted. Consider the new space of potential you are within. Bring your patterns of self-talk and self-worth to the level that matches the truth of you. This is another way to hold yourself in the space of receiving. As you hold your Self in the space of divine reverence, as do we, you open to actualization of the potential that is within your field.

DAY 114: THE BRIDGE INTO SPACIOUSNESS

O ver the past week you have stepped into a new spaciousness of being. As you move through your day's moments, we invite you to look for what was not there previously, as well as what is now present that was not only a few days ago. The spaciousness you feel is the expansive experience of YOU in light. The new experience of spaciousness is not empty. The space is filled with potentiality.

Consider exploring the feeling of spaciousness around you. In the absence of weighted issues, patterns, and beliefs of an earlier expression, you now hold more of the light that is essentially you. This is the space you have yearned for. The divine expression of you in light may now contribute at a higher level to your moments. As the rose is replenished with the warmth of the sun's rays in spring, so too, is your soul quenched with the clearer access to your divinity.

Declaring from Your Spaciousness

In the exercise suggested last week, the request was to declare at the beginning of your day who you BE for the day: joy, Love, peace, abundance, vitality, compassion, ease, grace, or something else. In the exercise you declare how your day will go based upon your intention set at the start of your day. The exercise was to experience what occurs when you declare something. Do you find your day is more purposeful? Do you find more joy? Do you feel more connected to your essential self?

Now that you have access to more of the light that is you, we suggest you try the same exercise, but with the difference that you are reaching into the spaciousness of you. The subtle difference between declaring and declaring from the spaciousness of your Self is powerful.

The experience of the spaciousness you feel is the bridge to yet the more of you. The awareness that you are capable of is extraordinary in its beauty and at the same time a natural part of your divine expression. This is all a part of becoming conscious of your divine nature. Like taking the cover off a beautiful sports car, stored and protected until the time was right, your time is Now.

You now have new vision. Utilize your awareness newly. There is nothing about the moments of your day that is usual. Have fun as you explore your new superpowers.

Day 115: Today We Choose Love

The light you now hold expands your reality. A shift occurs as you live in the reality of your light presence. There are new considerations that come into play.

We clearly support, encourage, and hold space for the actualization of the light you are, as you choose. Today, we point out the importance of your intentions and actions. Beyond a nice meditation, the act of turning up your light volume, energetically speaking, has greater impact. You have just undergone a significant shift in the light expression of you that is now available. You now manifest more of you. Consciously integrating the light that you are is required. You may have noticed an increase in your dreaming state as your reality shifts. With the influx of light into your body there may be some physical symptoms that arise; they're often referred to as ascension symptoms. We remind you of the potent actions that are taken and recommend acknowledging the growth and expansion you have taken to this point. There is a settling out that will occur as you see the result of your work in light appear in your physical reality. Be gentle and compassionate with yourself.

The inherent power, or leverage, you now have with your choices is increased exponentially. The reason we speak of declaring your intentions each day is for you to feel and know the reality of your declarations as they are moved from light into form. There is much to be garnered in integrating and grounding the knowing in your body. Beyond an ethereal experience, you will feel the shift in your reality through your declarative statements.

Today, we speak of the value and need for conscious integration within this process of accessing more of you that is available in light. The way to best integrate the light you are into your physical reality is to set a background declaration from which all choices will be informed and directed.

We recommend a background intention for each day moving forward from this Now moment. We suggest a background intention of your days to be Love. As you hold the space of Love in your every Now moment, the power of Love that holds the essential nature of you and the highest expression of you and your divine design will from here on out inform your every choice, decision, and action. In that way, you are ensured the highest outcome with all your choices and efforts. As you choose Love, you set the broadest, all encompassing, most potent space from which to create. All is possible with Love. This background intention is potent. This action supports actualization of the highest order.

This divine collaboration is sourced in Love. This process meets all where they are and interacts with each person in their own unique expression. The potency of this work is Love. We hold you in Love. As you hold yourself in Love as well, you hold the keys to your conscious realization of the highest order.

DAY 116: ACTIONS OF LOVE

The words of Love could be expounded upon for eternity and still not reach the full knowing. Love may be felt and experienced in the moment. Love is the key to unlocking the potential you hold as a being of light in form. Who you are is Love; as you choose Love in your daily declarations, you are creating the action of ALIGNING with Love. What we see of Love from our perspective is different from the experience of Love you hold from the physical perspective. As you choose conscious realization, ascending into the full light knowing of the divine expression you are, you choose Love. Since this is the intention of this work of *In Service to Love*, we speak a lot of Love.

Darlene laughs as she realizes more of the access to the light that she is. As she sees clearly the potential for creation from her words and intentions she comments, "Watch where you point that thing!" as a way of playfully acknowledging the immense power that is held in light. She sees beyond the need to the fundamental requirement for intention and declaration that is clear, concise, and purposeful as the basis of creating. If you are not creating on purpose, and consciously, then what part of you are you creating from? The unconscious part? The path of habit? Unless you are present in the Now moment, you are decidedly creating from the past, and more of what you create will be reminiscent of the past. Not a problem, unless you choose conscious realization. Your full consciousness resides in the immaculate Now moment. Your full potential resides in the immaculate Now moment. Full access to your joy, peace, and abundance reside within the Now moment. Love resides in the Now moment.

Yesterday we were speaking of holding a background declaration of Love daily. You live within an environment that is filled with triggers for ways of being that you have held previously. One of the things you have seen, certainly since the inception of *In Service to Love*, is your shifting perspective. You hold a new relationship with the past, as you now occupy and create from the present. Triggers of past ways of being are still there if you choose to pick them up. So, amid the myriad of possibilities, setting a direction that ensures your highest expression is valuable.

Love is a high vibration of BEING. It is not an emotion, it is not a feeling, it is a divine expression that authentically IS you. Do you see how, as you hold an intention to BE Love each day, you will always be propelled to your highest expression? Love will enhance every endeavor you choose. You put on the glasses of Love, then you choose anything. For example, "In my life, I choose Love," as a background declaration. Then, daily, "Today I choose to be ease and grace" or "Today I choose to be vitality" or "Today I choose to be compassion" or "Today I choose to be beauty" or "Today I choose to be peace" or "Today I choose to be healing." The experience of Love will enhance your experience of ease and grace, vitality, compassion, beauty, peace, and healing, whatever you choose, from the highest perspective.

The Being of Love

Holding the perspective of Love has many actions:

Integrate The action of Love will integrate the light you are with the awareness in form because it is who you are in the first place. Your request is to realize more of who you already are as a divine being of light in form.

Amplify As you hold the intention of BEING Love, your natural attributes as a being of light in form will be amplified. Love is the catalyst. From amplification of you comes a new perspective. The information you now have access to is beyond what has been experienced in the past and therefore you have a new source for your conscious creating. More of you begets more of you.

Infuse As you hold the being of Love as your background intention, you are infused with Love. The action of infusion restores your knowing in light. You hold a high frequency perspective more easily. You are connected more clearly with your highest knowing.

Access Frequency, frequency, frequency. As you are in your day from the perspective of BEING Love, your frequency is increased. You inhabit finer awareness from what your moments may have held previously. Accessing your divine awareness then informs your moments from the knowing of your truth.

Direction When you say you are holding Love as your mandate, everything in your experience becomes aligned with your divine expression. You are elevated, you gain clarity, you are more able to be present in the immaculate Now moment and gain even more of the divine experience of you. Your creations are on purpose as you are in divine collaboration with Love.

We are In Service to Love. We see you as the Love that you BE. The view from here is awe-mazing!

DAY 117: EMBRACE YOUR NEW NORMAL

As you hold the intention of Love as the background to your moments, all aspects of your life are enhanced. The brilliance of moments that once would have been passed by are appreciated for the gift and contribution they are. Time spent in a space of exalted awareness nourishes the wellspring of your being.

Your experience of Love from the Now immaculate moment gives you the opportunity to feel and know the ever-changing, evolving nature of Love. Love from the immaculate Now moment is different from the reflection of Love that exists from other perspectives. For example, Love from a past perspective is the experience of memory of Love, brought to the Now moment, and fueled by the past. When anything is fueled by the past, there is a loss of vitality that is available. When you hold Love as the intention for your way of BEING, you connect with Love as it is available in the Now moment with the greatest potency. Conscious Being resides only in the present moment. Beingness informs action and thought. As you choose Love as your background way of being, you witness the vitality and life force that is the Source of All in the Now. It is exalted moments that remind you of your authentic nature. It is these exalted experiences of Love that may be your new normal.

Your new normal is an empowered stance of choice consciously accessing your divine nature. You choose Love within the present moment that allows your unique divine expression to radiate at the highest level. You embrace possibility. Conscious choice made from the Now moment, informed by resonance, is the new operating system. Movement is your new normal. You choose your being-ness and allow that to inform your creations. From the vantage point of Now, being Love, you express authentically at a high level. Your alchemical, multidimensional abilities are employed.

Saturate your being in Love. Potency of creation, experience, vitality, expression, connection, divine collaboration, and more are available in the Now immaculate moment. As you look to Love as your Source, the vision of your soul may be realized.

We remain,

In Service to Love

Day 118: Reverence

As your Scribe, Darlene, prepares for our gathering each day, there are some consistent efforts that support her shift in frequency and consciousness so we may meet at the frequency of *In Service to Love*. Darlene is aware that the clarity of our connection is not best served as she is occupied with the thoughts and planning for her day. She employs a time to transition her consciousness to a space of reverence. In this process, she calms her breathing, she allows her thoughts to be left, like leaving a coat in a coat closet. Often, she will then move to the location of her altar. And there, she asks, "What may I leave here that does not serve me? How may I be immaculately present? How may I be of service?" And again, she will release the energy, the weight of her thoughts and personality, issues, events of her day. And after the releasing of her thoughts, she arrives. At reverence. And we speak.

Reverence is a space of sacred connection to the divine that occurs in the Now moment. It is a frequency that is beyond the functional elevated frequency range for the events of your day. It is a space that holds inspiration and is a platform, if you will, for the clarity of connection you have been looking for. Whatever your unique expression, your divine mission, your divine collaboration; it may be accessed in the Now moment through reverence.

You see, the divine is not hard to find. There are many roads to truth. Setting the background declaration for your day to Love is a high-frequency action that transcends or cuts through the weighted issues of personality, history, and beliefs. Love is a background for All. Reverence is an avenue for clarity of communication. Through your quiet time or meditation you may access the vibrant stillness of reverence. It is not a space where the reverence is extended outward, to others, but rather is all encompassing. It is a rich frequency of appreciation, acknowledgment, and collaboration with All. It is a way of being, like being the notes of a symphony and reveling in the beauty. In this Being experience, you are in sync with the sacred. You feel the vitality of the vibrating field of potential. You feel the breath of creation.

Being of Reverence

As you look for ways to expand upon the communication with your divine team or get clarity with the divine collaboration that is yours, we suggest you look for reverence. This opens space for communication. This is a frequency that calls for a space of stillness. For you it may be walking in nature and allowing the beauty of each leaf to inform you and bring you back to your sacred knowing. It may be creating a time of quiet where you allow your thoughts to be gently placed on a shelf so you may be elevated. You will find the mode that works best for you. Try moving to your altar and laying down the sword of struggle. Lay down what best serves you, in order to take your next steps unburdened. You will know. Whether named, or felt, you are altered by the experience. From the being of reverence, you are gifted with sacred knowing. Your path to reverence reveals the next inspired steps in light.

We will meet you as you move to reverence. Feel the presence of Masters who have come before.

We remain,

In Service to Love

Day 119: Who Must You Be?

It is with delight we meet daily. We see you in your moments and marvel at the worlds you have moved. You demonstrate all that is good in God. Today is an infusion of light.

Who must you be to be both student and teacher? Who must you be, to elevate each environment you step into? Who must you be to have the ear of divine Masters? Who must you be to call forth Stargates? Who must you be to feel the clay of creation? Who must you be to follow the siren song of your soul?

We don't take anything you do in light or in form lightly. We see you, the divine creator, creating. As you disentangle from the way it used to be, you move in the realm that always has been.

Day 120: Reaching into the
Light of You

Reaching into the light of you is available at any moment. It is not a function that is conditional to environment. We move you toward the experience of integrating the light that you are into every moment of your day.

You choose to what extent you connect with the higher frequencies you reach. As when you use a hose to water your garden, you utilize one pressure to water the new seedlings, one to water the roses, and another to wash your car. You become adept with the awareness of the connection to light needed at any moment. Whenever in your day's moments you feel you need to hold off on connecting with your light expression, we turn your attention there.

In example, today, your Scribe is traveling. The environment is different. There are distractions, others in the room. Yet, as she intends to gather with us at the frequency we join, her beingness shifts, and we are here. Beyond distractions. She does not need to get ready, to settle in every time. We are here. She feels better when there are no distractions, but it is not a condition of connection. The quiet and the stillness serves a fundamental purpose in developing confidence in connection. Being quiet enough to notice the subtleties of a different reality are valuable. Darlene has had enough experience now to learn there is not a linear access to light. She is continually delighted in her shifting and expansive connection.

The access to your light is through your being. So, as you declare who you BE, you feel the shift in your reality. Do you notice that as you declare Love, or joy, or compassion, or vitality or peace, you experience not only the quality you intended, but you get it All? Words will only get us so far. It is your experience that will inform you. You will notice there is a shift in tone, now that we move more deeply into light expression. There is a more nonlinear approach that we lead you to.

We are noticing that even amid the distractions and movement around her, Darlene is laughing at her ability to connect with us and still be present with the environment she is within, distractions, sounds, and movement included. Truly a demonstration of the multidimensional capacities you each hold as beings of light in form.

Developing a keen awareness of your being is valuable. The frequency you are being informs your reality. The more time you spend at higher frequencies, your baseline frequency increases. Your light expression expands exponentially. As you choose your frequency by declaring who you will be being in your day, you are conscious enough to choose it to be so. Beyond the frequencies is your conscious acknowledgment and intentional use of them. In the end, it is not as much that you choose your frequency; the value is in knowing you may. There is an experience of ownership that is inherent with choice.

As you open the pathway for a higher frequency of expression, the access to the light that you are is inherently available. The light that you are holds knowing and expression beyond what you have held true for you so far in this incarnation. It holds the safe harbor of reuniting with the expression of Love that you are. From the perspective of Love, you are buoyed in freedom and ease.

DAY 121: NATURALLY YOU

As we have been speaking of the divine expression of you at its highest, we have been encouraging you to reach into the light that is you and bring that knowing into the moments of your days. What is it you are to expect? It has been thought the process of enlightenment, the process of ascension, was a mystery. It has been a process cloaked in mystery as the initiate is encouraged to reach beyond the world of the seen into the light of faith and divine expression. What may be found therein is the more of you. Consider enlightenment is a natural evolutionary process.

Darlene was recently speaking with her Beloved who, when asked if he had felt differently because of the work that is resulting from our collaboration, said, "No, I don't feel too different." When questioned further, it was clarified that he doesn't feel that anything that is outside of himself has been added. And in fact, he feels relief from burdens, barriers, and old ways of being and is happier. He feels more like himself. We would ask you to consider that as you move on in the process of enlightenment and ascension, you gain more of you, naturally. Who you are in light will finally align with your expression in form, as a cohesive expression of you.

At the onset of our work together we invited you to the table of equanimity. You have been invited to be in divine collaboration with us from the perspective of eye to eye, peer to peer and divine to divine. The work we have done thus far has been a series of shifts in perspective, that when fully aligned will open the possibility for you, of the prospect of viewing your own divine expression. As you see your divine expression as a possibility what then opens is your empowered stance of conscious participation with us from a state of authenticity. The gap in the perception between who you are as a being of light in form and who you see yourself as will align. In the process you feel more like yourself than ever before. The knowing of the whole of you becomes available consciously. You experience the possibility of being unbridled, free, empowered, connected, expansive. And now what?

Today we would like to emphasize the divine nature of you. You are Source in form. Even while in the material world, most of you resides in light. Enlightenment accesses and integrates the expanse of your totality. As your perspective shifts from thinking that enlightenment and ascension are out-there, to enlightenment and ascension as a natural part of your expansive expression, you take ownership of your divine expression and the "Now what?" becomes possible.

We invite you to explore the depth and breadth of your divine nature.

Day 122: The Tip of the Iceberg

There are defining moments and days in the process of the expansion of consciousness. Today is one such day. The movement in perspective and the access to light that is present today, in comparison to Day 1 when you said, "Yes!" to our divine collaboration, is markedly different. You have released identities, barriers, and patterns that have long been held and developed through a construct of separation consciousness. You have been willing to release the realm of known and, fueled by the small inner voice, have found the journey into the unknown has increased the voice of your soul. You are aligning your human nature with your divine nature.

You have ascended, moved beyond the constructs of a reality that defined and more accurately limited the possible expression available for you. The doors of your divine expression have been opened. Once opened, there is no moving back. You cannot unknow what you now know. You have seen enough to see beyond the illusion of limitation. You see how your shift in perspective allows your divine nature to inform your material reality. As you have turned up the volume on your expression, you have seen the resounding reflection of Love and affirmation shining back at you.

The realization of your divine expression, previously viewed distantly at the horizon of your awareness, has moved closer to shore. Each step you have taken has been a clear statement of your soul's intention for full expression made manifest in this Now immaculate moment.

You have said yes to Love. You have created, through your open heart, intentions, and inner resonance, a momentum of expansion.

The light available for you awaits, patiently, knowing all is in divine order. Today, we celebrate and acknowledge your expanded expression into your conscious awareness. We celebrate the light you hold and the contribution you are. You are seen and held on high.

And Now, we invite you into the revealing of what next is possible.

We remain,

In Service to Love,

In Love, With Love, From Love,

The Council of Light

"You have always held the inner knowing that you are larger than you could reach. The realization of your totality resides within the unknown. The sense of the unknown is so large and vast, the experience is "I can't get there from here," and resignation reigns.

You have called us to you. You have asked for clarity. You have wept for the harsh experience of your days, knowing there is so much more that is possible. You have raised your fists to the heavens and cried, "What of Love? If there is a God, why is there so much suffering?" Within the construct of In Service to Love *exists the possibility of shifts in consciousness so complete, you find the answers to your questions. Not because we, Masters in light, said so. But because the possibility exists for you to experience a shift in consciousness so complete, you are raised beyond the illusion of separation consciousness to the brilliant light of Love, and now you know the answers."*

The Council of Light

In Service to Love Book 1: Love Remembered, Days 1–122
In Service to Love Book 2: Love Elevated, Days 123–244
In Service to Love Book 3: Love Now, Days 245–366

Visit the author online at www.thedivineremembering.com

Made in the USA
Monee, IL
06 March 2020